Talk About Books

Also available from Bloomsbury

Bloomsbury Essential Guide for Reading Groups, Susan Osborne
Chick Lit, Rocío Montoro
Conversation in Context, Christoph Ruehlemann
Materializing Literacies in Communities, Kate Pahl
Reading Circles, Novels and Adult Development, Sam Duncan

Talk About Books

A Study of Reading Groups

David Peplow

Bloomsbury Academic
An imprint of Bloomsbury Publishing Plc

B L O O M S B U R Y
LONDON · OXFORD · NEW YORK · NEW DELHI · SYDNEY

Bloomsbury Academic

An imprint of Bloomsbury Publishing Plc

50 Bedford Square
London
WC1B 3DP
UK

1385 Broadway
New York
NY 10018
USA

www.bloomsbury.com

BLOOMSBURY and the Diana logo are trademarks of Bloomsbury Publishing Plc

First published 2016
Paperback edition first published 2017

British Library Cataloguing-in-Publication Data
A catalogue record for this book is available from the British Library.

ISBN: HB: 978-1-4725-7022-2
PB: 978-1-3500-4553-8
ePDF: 978-1-4725-7023-9
ePub: 978-1-4725-7024-6

Library of Congress Cataloging-in-Publication Data
A catalog record for this book is available from the Library of Congress.

Typeset by Newgen Knowledge Works (P) Ltd., Chennai, India

Contents

Transcription Key

Transcript feature	Key
(.)	brief pause – less than 0.5 seconds
(0.5)	timed pause
=	latching – no pause between speakers' turns
[yeah [yeah	simultaneous speech
Underlined talk	speaker places emphasis on word or phrase
>yes<	speaker speeds-up
<no>	speaker slows down
:::	drawn-out sound
Hhh	exhalation
xxxxxx	inaudible speech
↑	rising intonation
↓	lowering intonation
' '	quoted speech from third-party
((*laughter*))	paralinguistic feature or non-verbal communication feature
{RP voice}	shift into exaggerated voice
?	unable to distinguish speaker

Acknowledgements

I would like to thank the reading groups who kindly provided the data for this study. I would also like to thank the funders of the original project on which this book is based: the Arts and Humanities Research Council.

Most thanks goes to my family and friends, who have supported me throughout the researching and writing of this book.

1

Introduction

A reading group describes a collective who meet regularly to discuss a book that all members (should) have read. Reading groups can be as varied as the books they read and discuss, and can appeal to a diverse range of readers. Someone looking to join a reading group is spoilt for choice in most areas of the United Kingdom, so that the question is not if this reader can join a group, but rather what type of group to join: all-male, all-female or mixed groups; fiction or non-fiction groups; crime, romance or contemporary literary fiction groups. Some reading groups have open entry to new readers, while other groups are closed, either because these are based within institutions such as workplaces or because the members are a close-knit group of friends. Reading groups meet in numerous settings and for a variety of reasons. In the majority of cases, these groups are voluntarily attended by readers who share a love for reading and a desire to discuss their reading with others. These groups may meet in public libraries, members' kitchens, restaurants, workplaces and so on. Other reading groups meet for specific reasons, often to draw on the perceived benefit that shared reading offers to individuals. Book groups in prisons, community centres and doctor's surgeries, for instance, may meet so that the members can engage in some degree of bibliotherapy (Morrison, 2008).

The definition of 'reading group' just offered highlights the task-based nature of reading groups and the fact that each group is often regularly attended by the same individuals. Given these basic qualities, a reading group can be seen as a particular type of social grouping: a community of practice, and one of the intentions of this study is to investigate how the communities of practice (henceforth CofP) model can illuminate the social practice of particular reading groups. Although the definition of reading group offered above is generally accurate, it actually hides a lot of other work that is performed in these groups, and one aspect of this study is to consider how relational, interpersonal work between the readers in such groups is manifest in the readings that are offered. The act of discussing a book in a public space means that reading in such groups is very different from the private activity we typically associate with reading. Reading becomes a highly social activity in the reading group context, with members of groups deriving pleasure from sharing responses to texts, collaborating to produce collective interpretations, and hearing about other members' experiences in relation to books.

To illustrate some of these points it is worth considering an extract of reading group talk at this early stage. This passage is from a discussion of *The Windsor Faction* by D. J. Taylor (2013), a counterfactual account of Edward VIII's abdication. The reading group is split over the quality of the novel, with one reader (Hannah) reporting that she enjoyed the novel and the other readers claiming to have hated it. At the start of the extract, Robert is offering a negative assessment of the novel:

Extract 1.1 `What am I missing then?'

           [27: 30] Wanderers, *The Windsor Faction*

1	R	I think if you write a comedy it should be funny (1.0) if you write alternative history (0.5) different things should happen
2	J	=mmm
3	R	that is (.) you know it's kind of
4	Ma	[mmm
5	H	[well I think it was rather nice that nothing did (.) I mean
6	Ma	oh
7	Mi	=oh [gosh
8	J	[oh
9	Mo	[we wasted our lives reading it
10	Mi	yes but did you not feel it fell into the (.) erm (1.0) LTS erm (0.5) category of of
11	H	LTS
12	Mi	literature
13	H	what is LTS
14	Mi	it is my own personal category (1.0) life is too short
		((general laughter))
15	J	I was trying to think The Times Literary Supplement not that's too
16	R	you've got it the wrong way round [hahaha

17   H   [because I
like Anthony Powell to me those bits I enjoyed
it (0.5) I was reading it more literary rather
than a good read

18   Mi   I know you are very good (0.5) you know you
have got such an advantage over me there Hannah

19   J   do [you mean oh sorry

20   Mi   [can I just read you what the

21   J   I just want to talk about the language he used
but the writing but you carry on follow the
theme

22   Mi   no that's true (0.5) when I first (1.0) when I
started it the first twenty pages I was quite
into it and I thought oh you know the use of
language and everything quite drew you in but
then somehow I felt it just (.) there were
patches of writing as you went on but they got
fewer and further between or I got

23   J   you got bored

24   Mi   more and more annoyed

25   H   you were allowed to get bored

26   Mi   I got more and more (1.0) well I don't think I
was bored exactly

27   H   well you know [yes

28   Mi   [more like losing the will to
live (0.5) really than bored

29   J   I thought he was just using words as you say
for his own pleasure

30   R   it was [written for his own entertainment

31   J   [and writing to show how clever he was

32   R   =yeah [I agree

33   J   [as a sort of

34   Ma   [yeah

35   H   it wasn't as bad as Will Self (2.0)

36   Mi   no
         ((general laughter))

37   Mi   that's damning with faint praise there

38   J   but you know what you are getting with him
don't you really

39   H   what Will Self

40   J   =yes [yes

41   R   [he has got quite devil

42   J   but erm (1.0) I mean you know (.) oh a
description of the carpet that had a shadow on
it

43	Ma	=hahaha
		=oh I thought oh for goodness sake I am losing the will to live here
44	Ma	=hahaha
45	J	you know the dark afternoon shadow went to cast its gloom on the carpet (0.5) and I thought do I need to know that (.) because it didn't (.) I think the thing was I mean I was surprised because Hilary Mantel has rated it and I just love Wolf Hall and Bring out the Bodies and I could read those for hours and hours
46	R	I didn't like either of those but I am quite looking forward to the Assassination of Margaret Thatcher but [for entirely different reasons
47	J	[no no I really absolutely thought they were brilliant I thought oh I am onto a role here
48	Mi	=yes talking about alternative history
49	J	but did you think he wrote well
50	H	yes (1.0)
51	J	well what am I missing then Hannah

R = Robert; J = Jenny; Ma = Max; Mi = Miriam; Mo = Molly; H = Hannah

This extract will not be analysed in detail, but it does illustrate some key points about the nature of reading in this reading group setting.

1. Reading group talk is competitive and argumentative. The judgements of individual readers are questioned, especially Hannah's positive view of the novel. This is seen in Molly's blunt comment that the group 'wasted' their lives reading the novel (Turn 9) and in Jenny's seemingly sarcastic question to Hannah, 'what am I missing?' at Turn 51.

2. At the same time, most readers are highly attuned to the face needs of others, packaging their comments to conform to politeness norms and allowing others to talk: see the negotiation of speaking rights between Miriam and Jenny across Turns 18 and 22.

3. This talk contains a lot of co-construction between readers, with collaborative floor generally the norm. Readers will latch onto what others say, sometimes completing their utterances to show affiliation (e.g.

between Turns 22 and 26, where the readers discuss Miriam's boredom and annoyance while reading).

4. Issues of taste are foregrounded in these discussions, which is not surprising given that the fundamental purpose of the groups is to discuss and debate readings and interpretations of a shared object. Taste is omnipresent in Extract 1.1, but Hannah's defence of her enjoyment of the novel in terms of her 'literary' reading as opposed to the other members' reading for pleasure (Turn 17) is a particularly rich example of reading tastes in action.

5. Related to taste, individual readers' identities are never far away from the discussions. In Extract 1.1 these identities are mainly related to reading, with Hannah orienting to a literary critical reading identity (explicitly in Turn 17, and more implicitly with her comparisons to literary writers, past and present: Anthony Powell and Will Self). By contrast, the others in the group orient to everyday reading identities that are underpinned by common sense: for example Robert's statement at Turn 1, Miriam's sense of boredom and annoyance at the novel (Turn 22 through to Turn 28), and Jenny's scorn at the florid writing in the novel (Turns 42 and 45). These identities may be constructed by the readers themselves or may be imposed on individual readers by others.

This is not an exhaustive list, and in the chapters that follow more features of reading group talk will be identified and analysed. What ties all these features together, however, is the socially situated nature of reading group talk. The readings that are offered and the assessments that are made by these readers are bound to context, meaning that what we find in reading group discourse is not a series of disembodied, private readings but rather an interconnected web of readings, responsive both to the immediate interactional context and to the shared history of the particular reading group.

1.1 The data

This study is an in-depth account of four reading groups based in the United Kingdom. These reading groups are referred to as the Contemporary Group, the Orchards Group, the Forest Group and the Wanderers Group, and each group is described in more detail later in this chapter. The study focuses on the talk produced by these readers and, specifically, how this talk contributes to the construction of community in these reading groups. When asked about the benefits of belonging to a reading group, one of the readers remarked on the communal feel of her group:

```
Lu  it is nice to share the (1.5) sometimes you have a
    book and you want to talk to somebody about it and
    if nobody else has read it you just can't do that
    (2.0) it is nice to share that (.) it is (1.0) yes
    (.) it is just a group dynamic feeling things
```

Lucia cites the ability to share reading as an important function of the reading group. This act of sharing a reading experience and discussing this experience with others is, for Lucia, a part of the emergent 'group dynamic'. This desire to share reading is clearly felt by all happy members of reading groups, and the overarching aim of this study is to account for how this shared reading and 'group dynamic feeling' is achieved across the four reading groups.

This research is based on two longitudinal studies of reading groups: the first conducted between 2010 and 2011, and the second between 2013 and 2014.[1] Each group was audio-recorded, and in some cases observed, across at least six meetings. These meetings lasted between 30 and 90 minutes, with a total of 24 hours of reading group meeting data obtained. In addition, group interviews were conducted with three of the groups (Contemporary, Forest and Orchards), and one-on-one reader interviews were conducted with members of the Wanderers Group and the Contemporary Group. Ethical consent was gained from all readers, with readers' names and reading group names changed to protect anonymity. Where groups requested it, the researcher returned to the groups after data collection to feedback the major findings.

These groups met in various locations: the Forest Group was run through and based in a public library; the Wanderers Group used to be based in a public library but has run independently since the closure of the local branch; and the remaining two groups (the Orchards Group and the Contemporary Group) were organized entirely by the readers. These groups have all existed for a number of years, with the Contemporary Group being the longest-running at fifteen years. All four groups tend to read contemporary novels, although the Orchards Group also read collections of short stories while taking part in this study.

1.2 Communities of readers

As mentioned, the reading groups are theorized as CofPs. A community of practice can be defined as 'an aggregate of people who come together around mutual engagement in some common endeavour' (Eckert and McConnell-Ginet, 1992b: 95). At its simplest, this kind of group regularly meets to engage in some task or activity. Taking part in this regular activity (such as discussing a book) might produce mutual ways of seeing the world or lead to particular shared language features to develop. CofPs may be based within institutions, such as workplaces – as in Wenger's account of Alinsu, an insurance claims company (Wenger, 1998), or they may describe more voluntary groupings, such as sports teams (Clark, 2013). Three elements define a community of practice, and it is possession of these elements that differentiate a community of practice from other, similar types of social group, such as speech communities (Labov, 1972), social networks (Milroy and Milroy, 1993) and nexus of practice (Scollon, 2001). These three elements are:

- mutual engagement
- a joint enterprise
- and a shared repertoire

(Wenger, 1998: 73)

These will be discussed in greater length in Chapter 2 and in later chapters, but a quick gloss of each element is offered here. A community of practice comes into existence because the members are mutually engaged in 'actions whose meaning they negotiate with one another' (Wenger, 1998: 73). Mutual engagement is, therefore, the basis for the establishment of relationships that make a CofP possible. It usually involves regular interaction (Holmes and Meyerhoff, 1999: 175), whether this takes the form of habitual posts on an online discussion forum or frequent chats in the staff kitchen. Joint enterprise refers to the shared objective of a group. This objective may be a material task bestowed upon a group (e.g. employees collectively writing a report) or this may be less material and more volitional on the part of the group (e.g. a group of students performing gender). Whether joint enterprise is institutionally imposed or not, it must be negotiated at ground-level by the participants and in this sense 'belongs' to the people who constitute the community of practice (Wenger, 1998: 77). Lastly, shared repertoire refers to the practices that, over time, have become habitual in a community of practice, offering shortcuts for members of the group when they communicate. Very often, this shared repertoire takes the form of language, but it can appear in pictures or gestures, and other non-linguistic resources. Linguistic instantiations of shared repertoire include specialized jargon, abbreviated expressions, and certain preferred ways of talking about an issue – 'shared discourses' (Benwell, 2009: 301).

The community of practice model was first applied to educational environments as a model of learning, both institutionalized classroom learning and vocational apprenticeship learning (Lave and Wenger, 1991). In later work, the model was used to show the shortcomings of teacher-led classroom education and to stress the importance of learning in more democratic and interactive environments (Wenger, 1998: 8). The notion of 'practice', therefore, is tied to education, whether this act of learning refers to acquiring some material knowledge that is transferable and portable across contexts (e.g. learning how to perform an oil change on a car) or learning that is less material and much more tied in with membership of a specific group (e.g. learning how to talk appropriately in a workplace meeting, and therefore becoming a more central member of the group). Reading groups are a learning environment in both senses (Peplow, 2016), a context in which members engage in literacy practices (Barton and Hamilton, 2000) and, over time, learn how to become more central members of the group. Bringing together the notions of learning and practice, Wenger states that the two are mutually dependent in a community of practice:

> Practice is a shared history of learning that requires some catching-up for joining . . . That members interact, do things together, negotiate new meanings, and learn from each other is already evident in practice – that is how practices evolve.

(Wenger, 1998: 102)

New practices, or ways of doing things, develop through members participating in activities and negotiating new meanings. Taking a sociolinguistic perspective on the reading groups means seeing practice mainly as a linguistic phenomenon so that practice is informed and changed by the language features that develop across meetings.

This study is interested in looking at some of the dominant practices used across the four reading groups. Combining a community of practice approach with a detailed discursive analysis allows for the possibility of seeing how acts of reading get co-produced by readers on a turn-by-turn basis. The reading that is performed in this setting is highly social and situated, and the interpretations and assessments that are offered by readers exist within the 'historical and social context' (Wenger, 1998: 47) of the particular reading group; that is, the background and history of a group combined with the social relations within that group create certain types of reading.

1.3 Overview of the book

Before going on to describe the groups and the data collection methods, an overview of this book is provided. Chapter 2 surveys previous research into reading and reading groups, situating the present study in relation to this. The community of practice model is considered in more detail, with previous sociolinguistic research using the model described. Also in Chapter 2 the particular discursive approach taken is outlined. In Chapter 3, the CofP concept of joint enterprise is picked up and the reading groups' sense of their purpose is discussed, specifically the groups' varied use of external, often institutionally sanctioned resources for structuring their meetings. These resources include sets of questions and professional and non-professional reviews of the book under discussion. This chapter also considers the internally imposed organizational features used in one of the reading groups, and how resistance is offered to this practice that has developed over time. In Chapter 4 attention is turned to the use of reported discourse in the groups' talk about books and the ways in which this is an element of shared repertoire found across the reading groups. The use of direct reported speech and thought serves to support readers' assessments of texts, creates dynamic and highly 'involving' (Tannen, 2007) sequences of talk, while also allowing readers to simulate the minds of fictional characters. Building on this, Chapter 6 considers another component of the groups' shared repertoire: mimetic reading. This appears to be a preferred way of discussing literary texts across all the reading groups (and perhaps in non-academic reading more generally), involving the readers talking about literature 'as though it were real life'. As well as documenting examples of mimetic reading, the chapter also considers how this preferred way of reading is realized discursively in the groups' meetings through category entitlements.

1.4 Ethnography and the reading groups

The remainder of this chapter is concerned with introducing the four reading groups and providing information about the data used in this study. When discussing Extract 1.1 above it was noted that the talk produced was situated; that is, the talk was highly responsive to the social and interpersonal context of the group. Ethnography is one approach that is attentive to the situated nature of phenomena, and a linguistic ethnographic approach was taken in conducting this study. Originating in sociology, ethnography was developed from the Chicago School (e.g. Whyte, 1943; Hughes, 1970), and is defined by Leeds-Hurwitz as 'a method used to describe everyday human behavior, relying heavily on participant observation in natural settings' (2005: 327). Although the Observer's Paradox may always be present to some extent, ethnography aims to document behaviour that people would be engaging in 'whether or not the researcher was present' (Leeds-Hurwitz, 2005: 327).

The ultimate aim of ethnography is for the researcher to discern 'insider meanings and interpretations' of participants (Swann and Maybin, 2008: 24) and to 'uncover and record the unspoken common sense of the group they are studying' (Johnstone, 2000: 82). While sociological studies adopting an ethnographic approach may consider a wide variety of objects and behaviours to constitute data (e.g. dress, dance, ways of walking), linguistic ethnography is more focused on language. Through combining ethnography and linguistics, this specific approach explores 'the mutually constitutive relationship between language and the social world' (Swann and Maybin, 2008: 25). Sociolinguists tend to adopt an 'ethnographic perspective' (Green and Bloome, 1995), rather than engaging in the sort of wholesale approach adopted by classic ethnography. Another difference between the two traditions is that sociologists often immerse themselves in the daily lives of the participants, whereas sociolinguists tend to be interested in a specific part of their participants' lives: for example their time at work (e.g. Holmes and Stubbe, 2003; McRae, 2009; Mullany, 2007; Richards, 2006) or their time at school (e.g. Eckert, 1989, 2000; Moore, 2006).

In its focus on the production of meaning in social context, community of practice research is necessarily 'an ethnographic enterprise' (Eckert and McConnell-Ginet, 2007: 32). As such, I attended and audio-recorded at least six consecutive meetings held by each of the four reading groups. Although I did not 'participate in the behavior' of the groups (Leeds-Hurwitz, 2005: 327) by becoming a member of the reading groups, my presence at the meetings enabled me to develop a detailed understanding of how these reading groups operated. Indeed, Duranti argues that complete participation in a group can be 'extremely distracting' for the researcher (1997: 101), rendering accurate analysis of the interaction almost impossible – both in terms of participant observation and in the analysis of transcripts afterwards. While my presence at the groups' meetings very likely affected the interactions to some degree, I felt that becoming a temporary member of the groups would have totally changed the dynamic of the interaction within the groups and, crucially, would have altered the participant roles within each community of practice – with me adopting the role of peripheral member. In addition, the salient aspects of my identity in this setting (researcher, English 'specialist', male) distinguished me from the readers in the groups, who, in the main, were female and lovers of fiction rather than institutionally sanctioned specialists. Another reason for not participating in the groups' discussions was the effect this would have on my ability to observe the groups' behaviour.

For practical reasons and because of my specific research interests, the approach taken is more closely aligned to the sociolinguistic rendering of the 'ethnographic perspective' (Green and Bloome, 1995) than to the strict anthropological concept of ethnography. Data was collected from four principle sources: audio-recordings, documents used by the groups, interviews with the groups and individual readers, and (in the case of two of the four groups) non-participant observation. The four reading groups are now described and my relationship with them discussed.

1.4.1 Orchards group

This group is based in the South Midlands area of England and was accessed through family connections. The group was audio-recorded on seven occasions and a group interview was conducted. At the time of recording,[2] the group had eight members: Sue, Connie, Carol, Alex, Roger, Jackie, Julia and Peter; and all of the readers were aged between 55 and 65, were White British nationals and lived in affluent rural locations. All eight readers had been members of the group since it started. Before the group was established, Sue was the only member of the group who knew each of the other members. Although all members knew at least one other member before the establishment of the group, only Sue knew all of the other members. The readers reported that being part of the group had forged friendships, and this was seen as one of the most positive outcomes of belonging to the reading group. On the issue of the strength of pre-existing connections within this group, it is worth noting that there were two married couples in the group: Roger and Julia had been married for thirty-five years, while Connie and Peter had been married for thirty years.

Orchards Group met in members' homes to discuss a set book roughly once every six weeks. The hosting member changed with each meeting, although it was not necessarily the host's responsibility to select the book to be discussed.

The group's taste could best be described as omnivorous, ranging from modernist short stories (*Dubliners* by James Joyce) to popular contemporary fiction (*The Book Thief* by Markus Zusak). As the following extract demonstrates, the members shared an ideal that the book group should be a site of education, with 'challenging' books welcomed:

Extract 1.2 Challenging reading

        [22:26] Orchards, *Dubliners*

```
1   Ja    so I mean are they (0.5) because I mean I must
          admit I've learnt quite a lot this evening haha
          almost feel like reading it again
2   S     =[exactly
3   A     =[exactly
4   Ca    =[exactly
5   Ja    but I mean are they designed (0.5) is it part of
          you know his er wanting to do it in this way er
          I mean they are quite good for discussion really
          aren't they
6   A     =mmm very challenging

          Ja = Jackie; S = Sue; A = Alex; Ca = Carol
```

Here Jackie praises *Dubliners* (Joyce, 2006) for being 'good for discussion' (Turn 5) because reading the stories has provided a positive learning experience (Turn 1). This desire for challenge and learning possibly results from three of the eight members of Orchards Group being retired teachers. This group, therefore, defined itself as quite serious in its aims to learn and self-improve. Within the meetings the Orchards Group did not organize the talk in any specific ways, although the group often worked through sets of questions (see Chapter 3 for a full discussion of this).

The dates and times of the Orchard Group's meetings were organized in order to maximize attendance, rather than being fixed to a particular date each month. This was different from other groups in this study, which (with the exception of the Wanderers Group) meet every month on a fixed day: for example, the second Tuesday or the last Friday of the month. The reason for this difference may be down to the fact that the Orchards Group was comprised of people who, over time, became friends or acquaintances outside of meetings, and so meetings could be arranged in a more ad hoc manner. This flexibility meant that most of the group's meetings were well attended, with an average of seven members at each meeting.

New members to Orchards Group seemed to be welcomed, but only on the basis of personal recommendation from one of the members. Unlike some other groups in this study, the Orchards Group did not advertise their group openly, on the internet or elsewhere. During the group interview, the members stated that there were no plans to invite anyone else to join at present, with members reporting that eight regulars was a healthy number for the group.

1.4.2 Wanderers group

This group had been meeting once a month for ten years and, at the time of recording, had seven active members: Hannah, Miriam, Molly, Laura, Robert, Jenny and Max. It started as a library book group, and was set up by Hannah as librarian, but since the closure of the library branch members have been rotating hosting responsibilities. All members live in relatively affluent residential areas in or near to a Midlands city in England. Five members of the group were retired, with one member having previously worked as a librarian and another previously working as a professional writer. One reader fell in the 31–35 age range, another was over 80 years old, and two others fell in the 66–70 age range.[3] All are White British nationals, and all identified as avid readers – each reporting that they read several books a month. Six consecutive meetings of this group were audio-recorded between 2013 and 2014.

Although this group's meetings were previously organized for specific dates when the group was tied to the library, at the time of data collection the meetings were coordinated in a more flexible manner, determined by when the majority of members were available to meet. Although she was not in receipt of pay from the library at the time of recording, Hannah still organized the group's meetings. She coordinated hosting responsibilities and took the lead in suggesting and sourcing the books read by the group. At interview Hannah described the process of selecting books for the Wanderers Group:

Extract 1.3 Book selection procedures

```
        [10:08] Wanderers, Hannah interview

1   H   they suggest things to me and I see if I can get
        them (1.0) erm and also if I have read a good book
        with another group (.) and I know it worked well
        as a group read I will use that erm (.) so it is
        (0.5) it we have things that are not quite new
        because we are not allowed to reserve them when
        they are brand new (.) because other people are
        paying erm (0.5) and we get them free so (.) erm
        (1.0) when they have sort of gone off the boil a
        bit (0.5) we can request them (2.0) which is why
        we had the latest erm (.) Robert Harris (0.5) erm
        (1.0) and that sort of thing (0.5) erm and also
        (.) Wanderers I try and get them to read some of
        the more literary things if I can get them
```

Although Hannah was ultimately responsible for obtaining the copies of books from the library, other members of the group did 'suggest things'. The Wanderers Group was somewhat constrained in what it reads, as the books must be available in plentiful supply from the library and not so recently published that the members needed to pay. At the end of this extract Hannah alludes to an aspect of the group's taste in books, stating that she tries to get 'more literary things' if she can – although this may just reflect her personal desire, see Extract 1.1. As well as sourcing the books and coordinating the venue and time of meetings, Hannah occasionally acted as an informal chair during meetings and sometimes brought along sets of questions and critical reviews for the group to discuss (see Chapter 3 for a discussion of this).

The Wanderers Group may have started as a library group comprised of strangers, but interviews with the participants of the group show that the members came to see themselves as a group of good acquaintances and, in some cases, friends. Hannah reported to me at interview that the group belongs to its 'own genre' of reading group: it is 'not quite a library group, it is not quite a non-library group'. The history of the group has perhaps created this sense of hybridity, and this has implications for recruiting new members. At interview, Miriam reported that it was easy for new members to join the group when it was based in the library, whereas now it is more difficult:

Extract 1.4 Difficulties in recruiting
      [55:45] Wanderers, *Miriam interview*

```
1   D    so can new people join your book group
2   Mi   yes (.) yes but that has been (1.0)
3   D    how would they go about joining
4   Mi   well I don't know now because when it was in
         the library of course erm (0.5) there was a
         notice permanently up about it (.) erm (1.0) and
         anybody could come along on that third Thursday
         and just walk through the door (.) erm (1.0)
         so (.) it has become more and more difficult and
         where would you (.) you see now where would you
         advertise it
         ((30 seconds of transcript omitted))
```

```
yes so the only way would be if people brought
a friend or a colleague who were interested and
then you would probably have to know them quite
well wouldn't you for them to say to you oh
you know you are always talking about the book
group I quite fancy (1.0) so (.) so the original
point of the book group which was that it was
open to anybody and everybody (0.5) has (1.0)
has unfortunately due to the loss of the library
has been a casualty of that (.) a real casualty
of that for me (2.0) because nobody can do what
I did which is just walk into the library one
afternoon and think oh there is a book group (.)
great

D = David (interviewer); Mi = Miriam
```

In the past the group could attract new members because it was based in the public space of a local library so 'anybody could come along' (Turn 4). Since the closure of the library branch and the movement of the group to readers' houses, access became more difficult for potential new members because meetings moved out of public spaces: Miriam asks 'where would you advertise it?' (Turn 4). She speculates that the only way new members could join is by way of existing members' social networks, and even then the current members 'would probably have to know them quite well' (Turn 4). Miriam laments the lack of new members as a 'casualty' due to the 'loss of the library', expressing regret that others do not have such easy access to the group that she had.

When asked about the benefits of belonging to a reading group, the readers variously reported enjoying the 'sociable' nature of the Wanderers Group. This is not to say that all readers were equally happy with the organization of the meetings, however. The Wanderers Group had no rules concerning how the talk is organized, although at interview Hannah joked that one of her jobs as informal chair was to get particular members of the group to 'shut up'. Molly also alluded to this problem of equal access to the conversation, stating during our interview that she wished that meetings were more formally organized on this front. She compared her experience of the Wanderers Group with a more positive experience of her other reading group. This other group has certain rules over rights to the conversational floor:

Extract 1.5 Different procedures in another group
        [14:05] Wanderers, *Molly interview*

1   Mo   I find the biggest difference (0.5) and I think it
         is a lot better is (.) the person who has chosen
         the book (.) at the meeting talks about the book
         without any interruption (1.0) then passes the
         book to the next person (.) who then talks it is
         a bit like the (1.5) you are not allowed to talk
         when somebody else has got the book til everybody
         has had their say and then it is open for more
         discussion (1.0) and it does mean then that one
         single person doesn't ever dominate (1.0) you
         know it means everybody (0.5) you don't have to
         speak if you don't want to (.) but (.) everybody
         always does because I think the point of having
         gone and read it is that you want to talk about
         it really you know
         ((30 seconds of transcript omitted))
         everybody gets their total say however much or
         however little they want (0.5) I mean I think
         if you went on too long people would stop you
         ((laughs)) but that doesn't really happen and
         then everybody chips in and picks up on points
         and talks about it yes
2   D   so do you prefer that other way of running the
         meetings
3   Mo   personally yes (1.0) I do (.) really (1.0) yes
         yes
4   D   because everyone sort of gets to have their sort
         of uninterrupted say at the start
5   Mo   yes (.) you do feel that everybody can get their
         point in (.) without being sort of shouted down
         (2.0) which is not to say you get shouted down at
         the other one (0.5) but not everybody can quite
         break in (.) and contribute quite so much (1.0)
         yes yes

         Mo = Molly; D = David (interviewer)

While Molly's other reading group has rules over who has access to talk to the
floor at the start of meetings, with the book ceremonially passed around like the
conch in *Lord of the Flies*, talk in the Wanderers Group is more of a free-for-all.
Molly reports enjoying her other reading group because of this management
of talk; in the other group 'everybody can get their point in', whereas in the
Wanderers Group 'not everybody can break in and contribute quite so much'
(Turn 5). As a related point, Molly also reported that the Wanderers Group is not

as focused on the book as she would hope, and she suggested that introducing this one-at-a-time rule on the talk at the start of the meeting would help to keep the group from tangential discussion:

Extract 1.6 `More talk on the book`

`        [16:43] Wanderers, ` *`Molly interview`*

```
1   D    is there anything you would change about the
         Wanderers Group
2   Mo   I would (.) I would slightly limit erm (2.0)
         how can I put it (0.5) I would want to talk
         a bit more about the book (1.0) it is not a
         particularly long meeting and they don't talk a
         huge amount about the book (0.5) you know people
         do go off at tangents which is ok (.) you know
         but I mean it is quite a short meeting (2.0) I
         think it would be nice if everybody did have a
         little say about the book (0.5) everybody who
         wanted to and then sort of throw it open a bit
```

Molly evidently feels that the Wanderers Group does not make the best use of its 'short' meetings, and that too often the talk moves away onto discussion of off-book topics. Her 'multimembership' (Wenger, 1998) of two reading groups provides her with access to alternative ways of organizing the Wanderers Group. Molly's dissatisfaction with the group's organization was not evident in the meeting data, thus demonstrating that these groups can appear to be harmonious but are difficult to run to the satisfaction of everyone.

1.4.3 Forest group

Of the four reading groups considered in this study, the Forest Group was the only one to be based in a library. This particular branch of the library was located in a deprived area of a Midlands city. This area has a high student population, and is infamous for having a high crime rate. This group was observed and audio-recorded on six occasions between 2010 and 2011 and a group interview was conducted. Compared with other library groups that were considered as part of a wider study (Peplow, 2012), the Forest Group was quite unusual because it was comprised of readers who mostly knew each before joining the group. The group consisted of six members: Frank, Joan, Daniel, Jess, Samuel and Lucy. All of the members of the reading group lived close to the library, with the exception of Samuel, who travelled from a few miles away to attend meetings. Lucy worked as a librarian at the time of recording and, similar to Hannah in the Wanderers Group, was responsible for coordinating the group, sourcing the books, and acting as an informal chair during meetings. As with the Orchards Group, there were two married couples in the Forest Group (Frank and Joan, and Daniel and Jess), with both couples having been married for over thirty years. Furthermore, the married couples also knew each other before joining the group.

At the time of recording the Forest Group had been running for four years, with all six readers joining the group when it was first established. The strong prior connections between four of the members were crucial in motivating them to join the reading group. In the interview conducted with the group, Joan and Jess cited that they joined the group because of Frank, something that Frank denied:

Extract 1.7 Motivation for joining the group

```
        [03:52] Forest, group interview
1    D     so this is target at you more as individuals
           (0.5) what motivated you to join the group (1.5)
2    Jo    Frank
3    Je    Frank [hahahaha
4    Jo          [hahahaha
5    F            [oh that's nonsense
6    Jo    =yes you did you said it you said there's going
           to be a book group and I said I'd like to go
7    F     =well that applies to you but it doesn't [apply
           to anybody else
8    Jo                                             [no I'm
           saying you Frank just in my case
9    F     oh I see yeah
10   Jo    I don't know about [Samuel
11   S                        [no I just like reading (.)
           y'know I just like to see what
           [xxxxxxxxxxxxxxxxxxxxx
12   Je    [yeah Frank coerced us into it haha
13   Jo    I think Frank did ask you [though didn't he yes
14   Je                              [yeah yeah
15   Jo    yes (0.5) see ha (1.0)
16   Je    by word of mouth mostly haha

           D = David (interviewer); Jo = Joan; Je = Jess;
           F - Frank; S = Samuel
```

Shared stories and jokes are an important part of shared repertoire (Wenger, 1998) and in this extract it becomes an extended in-joke that Frank 'coerced' the others into joining the group (Turn 12). While this is clearly a humorous exaggeration, it appears that Frank was instrumental in the other three members joining, even if he did not actively force them. By contrast, Samuel (who did not know any of the other members before attending the group) joined entirely of his own accord, citing the common-sense reason that 'I just like reading' (Turn 11).

Lucy was working in the library when the reading group was established and, like Hannah in the Wanderers Group, was instrumental in setting up the group. Like Hannah, Lucy took part in the meetings, participating as a member of the Forest Group; however, as Lucy worked for the library service at the time of recording, her position within the group was somewhat specialized and her role notably different from that of the other members. The group met in an annex off the main room of the library and Lucy was responsible for ensuring that this meeting room is booked and that other groups vacated the room in time for the Forest Group's meetings to start punctually. Lucy brought along particular documents that the group use in the meetings: Amazon.co.uk book reviews and sets of questions – discussed in Chapter 3. She also managed the talk in the group to an extent; for instance, if there was a lull in the groups' discussion, she would ask general questions to keep the group on task. In the following brief extract from the group's discussion of *Somewhere Towards an End* (Athill, 2008) Lucy asks a question to the group after a short lull in conversation:

Extract 1.8 Lucy as facilitator
```
      [20:39] Forest, Somewhere Towards an End
1     (5.0) so what did people think about her life
      then (.) because we talked about the death aspect
      [ain't we
2     [yeah erm (.) I like the frankness about her
      sexual experiences y'know

      L = Lucy; F = Frank
```

As librarian, Lucy also played an important role in the book-selection process, compiling a shortlist of titles from which the group can choose. These titles typically came under the umbrella of 'contemporary fiction', with books that have been nominated for major fiction prizes featuring frequently. Similar to the Wanderers Group, the Forest Group was a free service to its users and book selection was generally restricted to titles already held by local library authority in sufficient number. Having said this, the Forest Group ran a system whereby members suggested books and Lucy attempted to source these where possible. In sum, Lucy clearly occupied an institutional role in the Forest Group, but one that she attempted to play down through active participation in the group's discussions. Although she occasionally acted as chair in the group, asking questions and getting the group 'back on track', she reported that she was more interested in being another member of the group, on an equal footing with the other members (personal communication).

As mentioned, the Forest Group had a core membership of six members, all of whom have been regular attendees of the group since it began. A strong sense of shared history existed within the group, as demonstrated in Extract 1.9, taken from the group interview.

Extract 1.9 Contested history of the group
            [00:18] Forest, *group interview*

```
1    D    so::: how long has this group been going
2    F    th[ree years
3    S      [two years
4    F    three years would it be
5    Je   yeah possibly three years (.)
          [it would be two or three
6    L    [I think it's more than that
7    F    more (0.5) really
8    L    because [it was
9    Je           [it's quite a while
10   L    it was (.) pretty soon after I started as a
          librarian
11   F    oh
12   L    =and I started in two-thousand-and-six (2.0) it
          ca-
13   Jo   no it can't [be before
14   L                [it must
15   S    it's not as long [as that
16   Jo                    [that'd be nearly five no it
          hasn't been going that long
17   S    certainly not as long as that
18   Je   no
19   L    =rea::lly

          [D = David (interviewer); F = Frank; S = Samuel;
          Je = Jess; L = Lucy; Jo = Joan
```

This lively discussion over when the group was established was just the start of a debate that lasted a further two minutes. In the end, the group compromised that they had (probably) been running between three and four years. Regardless, the group enjoyed invoking their shared history and also their shared sense of identity. One aspect of this group identity was the group's sense that they are 'unique' and 'individual':

Extract 1.10 Group as 'unique'

```
      [07:38] Forest, group interview
1  Jo  we're quite (1.0) an individual group I think
       Lucy would agree (0.5) ha[ha
2  L                            [unique
3  Jo  quite un[ique hahaha
4  Je          [unique haha

      Jo = Joan; L = Lucy; Je = Jess
```

The group's sense that they are 'unique' is endorsed by Lucy, who facilitates other library reading groups and so can judge from wider experience. Part of this group identity was formed in opposition to other library groups, and seemed to be linked to the group's location in a deprived urban area. In the following extract Samuel relates his negative experience of attending another library reading group prior to joining the Forest Group:

Extract 1.11 Welcoming and unwelcoming groups

```
       [07:59] Forest, group interview
1   Je  cos you found one group quite unwelcoming
        [didn't you one
2   Jo  [oh you did
3   Je  =one (.) one group you went to (.) book group
        did[n't you find them very unwel-
4   S      [yeah the cent- central li- er central
        library they were (.) terrible like y'know
        (1.0) they looked as if I was (0.5) something
        the cat dragged in (0.5) it was really I felt
        uncomfortable
5   Je  =yes
6   Jo  =well that's horrible
7   Je  =yeah
8   S   and (0.5) I wasn't the first that said that
9   Je  =mm[m
10  S      [cos the lady when I told her that like y'know
        (.) cos she started this one [here
```

```
11   L                               [mmm
12   S    and I told her that
13   Je   mmm
14   S    and she said well other people have said that
15   Jo   what a sh[ame
16   S               [which is peculiar to the central (0.5)
          I mean completely different here er y'know

          Je = Jess; Jo = Joan; S = Samuel; L = Lucy
```

In this extract Jess nominates Samuel as having a story to tell about another reading group that provides a contrast to the Forest Group (Turns 1 and 3). Samuel takes up this nomination and relates the story about the 'unwelcoming' group he tried to join at the 'central library' (Turn 4). The existing members in this other group looked at Samuel as if he was 'something the cat dragged in', making him feel 'uncomfortable'. At the end of the extract he remarks that the situation is 'completely different here' in the Forest Group (Turn 16). After this passage of talk, Samuel went on to describe the readers in this other group as 'very snooty and snobbish', unlike the members in the Forest Group, who Joan jokingly refers to as 'plain commoners' by contrast.'

Another important aspect of their group identity was the Forest Group members' love for debate and argumentation. The members frequently discussed their predisposition to disagree with one another over books. In the following example, the group is discussing *The Shack* (Young, 2007), an evangelical Christian novel that all members of the group reported hating. As the group did not often agree on texts, this rare agreement was something to be remarked upon:

Extract 1.12 Agreement as rare
```
          [01:13] Forest, The Shack

1    Je   but I think [one thing that we
2    F                 [they must be utter simpletons y'know
          (0.5)
3    Je   could all agree on (.) this must be the first time
          (.) that (.) [we've all agreed on a book
4    Jo                [all agreed
5    D                 [all agreed
6    S                   [on a book
7    L                        [hahaha
8    Je   because usually >we're sort of I hated it (.)
          some say I lov[ed it and<
9    L                  [yeah yeah
10   Jo   =yeah

          Je = Jess; F = Frank; Jo = Joan; S = Samuel; D =
          Daniel; L = Lucy
```

Across Turns 1 and 3 Jess remarks that a negative assessment of *The Shack* is 'one thing we could all agree on'. She directly invokes an aspect of the shared history of the group, saying that 'this must be the first time that we've all agreed on a book' (Turn 3). As mentioned, it was part of the Forest Group's identity and folklore that the members do not agree on books – they actively sought disagreement, and this propensity is animated in Jess's use of direct reported speech at Turn 8 as she demonstrates the group's typical behaviour: 'usually we're sort of I hated it, some say I loved it'. The fact that all members agreed on their assessment of *The Shack* confounded this predisposition and therefore strengthened the group sense that the novel was objectively bad. Jess's comments at the start of this extract reflect the Forest Group's collective identity and strengthen their joint resistance to the novel. Even more interesting is the way that four others in the group go about agreeing with her across Turns 4–6, offering affiliative overlap and collectively finishing her sentence: 'all agreed on a book'. This co-construction of shared meaning between the readers shows shared opinions and thought in the form of the talk as well as in the content. As a rare example of agreement between members, Extract 1.12 ironically demonstrates the Forest Group's propensity for disagreement and resistance. For a longer discussion of this particular group and this meeting, see Peplow (2014).

1.4.4 Contemporary group

The Contemporary Group met once a month in the café of an urban arts venue. For most months the group met on the second Wednesday, but exceptions were made if a few members were unable to attend. This group was observed and audio-recorded between 2010 and 2011 on several occasions, and then audio-recorded on a further six occasions between 2013 and 2014. A group interview was conducted after the first data collection, and one-on-one interviews were conducted following the second data collection. In 2013–2014, the group consisted of seven members: Richard, Lizzie, Colin, Mark, Lucia, Debbie and Ben. In 2014, the group had been running for around 15 years, with a couple of the readers (Debbie and Richard) having belonged to the group since it started. Colin joined the group more recently, while data was being collected from the group between 2013 and 2014.

Compared to the other reading groups in this study, the origins of the Contemporary Group are quite complicated. Originally the group was run by the local branch of a large book-store chain, with meetings held once a month in the store. After a few meetings it became apparent that the group was too large for the shop to facilitate, so some members were asked if they wanted to split off and establish their own group elsewhere. The Contemporary Group was the product of that split from the book-store. These slightly troubled beginnings became part of the folklore of this group. During our interview Richard explained the group's beginnings as a book-store reading group, describing in glowing terms the facilitator who used to lead the meetings:

Extract 1.13 History of the group

     [18:14] Contemporary, *Richard interview*

R   yes it started in [name of book shop] and they
       used to hold it in [name of book shop] and we
       had an absolute (0.5) we had somebody from [the
       book shop] who led the group (1.0) and he was
       brilliant (.) every book that he enjoyed was in
       his top ten (0.5) and it was like an accordion
       (1.0) it was his expanding top 10 (1.0) he
       was so enthusiastic (0.5) he was absolutely I
       think his name was Joe (.) he was absolutely
       delightful (0.5) marvellous person (1.0) I
       really, really miss him (.) it was (0.5) he
       would have been a fantastic teacher as well I
       think because with that enthusiasm but then he
       left (1.0) I think he went to the [place name
       omitted] branch so I presume it was [place name
       omitted] actually (.) and then a woman took
       over and I have never seen such a complete
       opposite character (1.0) I mean she was sour is
       the only word I can use to describe her (1.0)
       nothing seemed to amuse or and nothing seemed
       to make her enjoy it (1.0) and if I had been
       less serious a person I might have tried to
       make her laugh

Since becoming independent of the book shop the Contemporary Group no longer has a facilitator. This was something that Richard seemed to lament in our interview and is apparent in his desire for reading group 'rules' (for a full discussion of this, see Section 3.4).

Richard reported that one particular benefit of having a facilitator was that the responsibility for book selection was moved out of the group and onto this third party. Since the group lost its facilitators book selection has been difficult. The Contemporary Group has attempted various methods for selecting books to read for meetings. In the group interview Debbie stated that 'originally people would just say something we think is interesting', but the group reported that this lead to 'bad books' being selected. The next method was for members to each suggest a book, then for one of these suggestions to be pulled out of a hat. However, this system did not work because someone would 'inevitably' refuse to read the selected book. At the time of data collection, the group operated a system of recommendation, with a member suggesting a title that they had previously read, although not all members liked this system because it meant that at least one person does not get to read a new book each meeting (see Section 3.4 for more on book selection protocol in this group).

Lizzie acted as administrator for the group. This involved sending out emails to the members, reminding them of upcoming meetings and managing the group's online presence on a book group website. This website lists book groups by geographical area, providing prospective members with the contact details of book group administrators.[4] New members usually accessed the group through this website, although current members have brought along friends in the past. However, this system of friend recommendation has not been wholly successful, with Debbie citing 'work commitments' and lack of enjoyment as reasons why these friends do not stay:

Extract 1.14 New members

```
        [20:33] Contemporary, group interview

   D    well in the beginning people used to (.) like
        we'd (.) like you'd bring a friend (0.5) but
        a lot of those people have sorta dropped away
        as well (.) erm (1.5) I mean I've brought a
        couple (0.5) one (2.0) who's not coming because
        of work commitments (.) but then she also just
        said well (0.5) actually I don't like most of
        the books that we've read
```

Although the Contemporary Group had a core set of members that have been attending for some years, during the group interview Lizzie aired her concern over the high turnover of members:

Extract 1.15 Difficulty of retaining new members

```
        [21:07] Contemporary, group interview

1  L    I can't help but feel that we're not very
        likeable cos a lot of people turn up
2  N    =and never come back
```

```
3    L    =for a few times and haha never come back (0.5)
          but I think that's partly just a
4    N    if they stayed you'd just have a massive group
5    L    =ye:::ah and and it's (2.5) obviously people
          are going to try it and then maybe try several
          different groups [to find
6    N                      [yeah
7    L    =one that suited them

          L = Lizzie; N = Natalie
```

Lizzie initially concludes that the high turnover of members must mean that their group is not 'very likeable' (Turn 1). At Turn 4, Natalie offers a conciliatory response and Lizzie then agrees that the group's high turnover is probably normal for reading groups and is not down to their disagreeable nature. Ironically, Natalie left the group and was not a member during the second phase of data collection (2013–2014); the reasons for Natalie leaving are not apparent. A minute later, Debbie offers another reason for the high turnover – the group's frankness:

Extract 1.16 Massacring a book
```
          [21:30] Contemporary, group interview
1    D    yeah (0.5) I mean I remember (2.0) we massacred
          the book (.) we had this one woman who came
2    L    =oh yes
3    D    and she >it was like< the second time and she
          rec- she rec- first time she recommended a book
4    L    =I can't think who was it who did that (.) I
          can't even remember what they looked like or
          anything [now
5    D             [no it was a Rose Tremain book
6    L    =yeah
7    D    uh and (0.5) everybody hated it and she lo::ved
          it (0.5) and so that was sorta the end of her

          D = Debbie; L = Lizzie
```

The Contemporary Group 'massacred' a Rose Tremain novel that was recommended by a new member of the group, and this was the 'end of her'. As this extract suggests, the candidness of the Contemporary Group may explain why there was a high turnover of readers in the group. Related to this, many of the members of the Contemporary Group are self-confessed 'book snobs', and in the following extract (also taken from the interview), members of the group are discussing their resistance to reading typical 'book club books'; a resistance that originated from their once-facilitator, Joe:

Extract 1.17 'Book snobs'

```
            [08:47] Contemporary, group interview
1    L      I think we're book snobs actually haha
2    D      I think we are
3    L      ye[ah you can't really not be
4    D        [hahahahahahahahahahaha
5    N                    [hahahahahahaha
6    L      =can you
7    D      I mean this particular group I think >I mean
            when I talk< to other friends about books (.)
            and they're just like (.) boy (0.5) I mean I'm
            opinionated anyway (.) but so (.) so it's made
            me even MORE strongly opinionated about books
            than I used to be (0.5) to the point where
            it's sorta like I have to be careful when I
            talk to xxxxxxxxxxxx cos I think we are pre-
            (.) probably book snobs (.) I mean (1.0) you
            weren't in the book group yet (.) before when
            it was xxxxxxxxxxx I can't think of his name
            now (.) the guy that worked at [name of book
            store] before Sarah did it (1.0) and
            [he was sorta
8    L      [no no no
9    D      he was very much (.) it's not a book group (.)
            book group (0.5) so it was xxxxxxxxxxxx an idea
            that there are book group books
10   DP     yeah
11   D      like the oprah [book group
12   DP                    [yeah
13   D      or like the erm (.) y'know richard and judy (.)
            and we as a reading group we don't read book
            group books (.) we read (1.0) literature (.)
            [something with a
14   L      [hahahahahahahaha
15   N                    [hahahahaha
16   D                        [so yeah I think I agree (.)
            yeah I I would think that we're a snobby book
            [group
17   DP     [yeah
```

```
18   D    I don't know what you think (.) compared to
          your other book groups but (.) yeah
19   L    I've certainly noticed if you go on amazon
          (2.0) I wouldn't ever suggested that we pick a
          book that's got less (0.5) than (3.0) four (.)
          four five stars on amazon (.) if it's got like
          three and a half (0.5) that that's a distinctly
          bad book hahahahaha

          L = Lizzie; D = Debbie; N = Natalie; DP = David
          (interviewer)
```

The Contemporary Group's 'book snob' identity is celebrated in this extract. Lizzie and Debbie are unapologetic about their group's desire to define themselves in opposition to perceived typical reading groups. Lizzie accounts for this by stating that all reading groups are necessarily snobbish in some way (Turns 3 and 6), while Debbie reports that being a member of the group has made her even 'MORE strongly opinionated' about the quality of books (Turn 7). Similar to the Forest Group, the Contemporary readers enjoyed constructing a group identity that differentiated them from other book clubs. While for the Forest Group this identity was constructed in opposition to the perceived snobbishness of other book groups however, for the Contemporary Group their collective identity was defined against mainstream TV book clubs: 'Oprah' (Turn 11) and 'Richard and Judy' (Turn 13). The Contemporary Group read 'literature' as opposed to 'book group books' (Turn 13), and would not read books that have less than 'four' stars on Amazon (Turn 19). The organizational practices of this specific group is considered in more detail in Chapter 3, where the group's resistance to critical reviews and their particular ways of structuring talk in their meetings is discussed.

1.5 Conclusion

This overview of the four reading groups has presented details of the specific organizational practices inherent in each community of practice. In-jokes, invocation of shared histories and the sense of a collective identity are evident in the short snippets of data presented so far, demonstrating that these groups operate as CofPs. In the next chapter the community of practice model is discussed in greater detail, with reference to previous sociolinguistic studies that have adopted this approach. This study combines the CofP approach with the detailed analysis of transcripts of group talk, and so Chapter 2 also provides an overview of conversation analysis, the interactional method used alongside CofP in the analysis. Before considering these approaches, however, an overview of previous research into reading groups is offered, with the present study situated within this.

2

Communities of Readers

This chapter offers a review of the main influences on the approach adopted in this study. Having introduced the four reading groups in Chapter 1, the CofP model is discussed in more detail in this chapter and its usefulness in accounting for the groups' behaviour is further demonstrated. It is proposed that the reading groups constitute archetypal CofPs, as these collectives all possess the three key characteristics of CofP outlined in Wenger (1998): mutual engagement, joint enterprise and shared repertoire. The reading groups meet regularly (usually once a month), so the members can be said to be mutually engaged in activity together; these groups are focused on a particular activity (discussing and debating the merits and meanings of fiction texts), which is the members' joint enterprise; and each reading group has specific ways of talking about texts that have become habitual over time, which is the members' shared repertoire. This study is focused on the social practice of the four reading groups, considering this in terms of the interaction used in the groups. The reading groups are theorized as CofP, and this approach explains, at a macro-level, what a book group is and what the readers do when they meet. In subsequent chapters this CofP approach is underpinned by the detailed consideration of transcripts from the groups' meetings, and elements of conversation analysis are drawn on in order to do this. In the latter part of this chapter conversation analysis is described and previous research in these areas is discussed.

Before considering CofP and conversation analysis, the first part of this chapter focuses on previous research into reading groups, starting with general sociological approaches and moving towards sociolinguistic accounts of reading groups that are more akin to the present study. This chapter is divided into three sections:

- A summary of previous research into reading groups (Section 2.1).
- A definition of community of practice and a selective account of research drawing on the approach (Section 2.2).

- An overview of conversation analysis, with reference to some key features of the reading group discourse (Section 2.3).

First, recent research into reading groups is considered, with the present study situated within this field.

2.1 Reading and reading groups

In the last seventy years of literary criticism there has been a professed movement *away* from conceiving of literary meaning as residing in the author or in the structural features of the text and a movement *towards* considering readers as meaning-makers. This shift began in the work of Wimsatt and Beardsley (1946), was extended by Barthes (1977), and in more recent years has led to the establishment and growth of 'reader-response' criticism within literary departments, most famously associated with Culler (2002), Fish (1980) and Iser (1978). However, the conception of the reader in this reader-response criticism tends to be highly idealized. Reader-response scholars frequently emphasize the incongruity between their 'readers' and flesh-and-blood readers: Culler warned against taking 'too seriously the actual and doubtless idiosyncratic performance of individual readers' (2002: 300); Iser was interested in a highly theoretical 'implied' reader that 'in no way should be identified with any real reader' (1978: 34); and Fish did not actually apply his concept of 'interpretive communities' – groups of like-minded readers 'who share interpretive strategies' (1980: 171) – in his own literary criticism (Mailloux, 1982; Pratt, 1982) and the model was left as a theoretical model for those in empirical literary study to test and expand (e.g. Dorfman, 1996). One of the central aims of this study is to challenge 'the armchair sophistry of reader-response' (Nightingale, 1996: 64) outlined above by building on recent research into 'real' readers from stylistics, sociolinguistics and sociology, conceiving of readers as flesh-and-blood agents who generate readings of texts based on a range of factors not covered by idealized models of reading.

Research has typically focused on reading as an individual and solitary act, and often this is the approach taken by scholars who are interested in reading as a cognitive phenomenon. The last sixty years has seen a 'cognitive turn' across a number of academic disciplines (Steen, 1994), and a large body of research has developed focusing on the mind/brain processes underlying reading. The cognitive approach to reading is based across three areas: the psychology of reading (e.g. Graesser, Kassler, Kreuz, and McLain-Allen, 1998; Graesser, Millis, and Zwaan, 1997; Morrow, Bower, and Greenspan, 1989; Zwaan, 1994, 2004), the empirical study of literature (e.g. Miall and Kuiken, 1994, 2001, 2002; van Peer, 1986; Sotirova, 2006) and cognitive poetics (e.g. Gavins, 2007; Stockwell, 2002, 2009; Semino and Culpeper, 2002). The former, psychology of reading approach has tended to focus on how people in quasi-laboratory conditions process very small chunks of narrative. This research draws heavily on cognitive psychology, theoretically and methodologically. Methodologically, these researchers closely follow experimental paradigms used within cognitive science, carrying out reading tests with participants in laboratory conditions. In devising these experiments, the researchers strive to eliminate all extraneous variables so that, as much as it can be, the cognitive processes of reading can be isolated and studied as independently as possible.

Research within the second, empirical study of literature field tends to use the same experimental methods as the psychology of reading, providing participants with short sections of text in quasi-laboratory conditions. Broadly speaking, what distinguishes the empirical study of literature from psychology of reading research is its more expansive focus. While the psychology of reading has generally looked at basic-level reader comprehension, the empirical study of literature tends to focus on testing or establishing reading concepts within the field of stylistics. For example, Fialho (2007), Miall and Kuiken (1994, 2001, 2002) and van Peer (1986) have all tested the stylistic concept of foregrounding using readers, while Sotirova (2006) has considered readers' spontaneous responses to passages of free indirect discourse in modernist fiction.

Although this empirical research has been crucial in testing out assumptions often made in traditional literary criticism (see Sotirova [2006] and Martindale and Dailey [1995]), there are some problems with this approach. These studies are mostly well-designed and make a contribution to our understanding of a particular type of reading, but there are questions regarding the 'ecological validity' of this empirical, experimental research, with this approach criticized for existing in a 'frustratingly parallel universe', failing to inform scholars on the 'phenomenon it purports to tell the researcher and the readers of that research about' (Hall, 2008: 31). The quasi-laboratory methods adopted in much of this research serves to decontextualize the reading process, often failing to replicate sufficiently the ways in which literary texts are naturally read (Hall, 2008). Allington and Swann (2009) further suggest that experimental approaches to reading mainly assess the subjects' ability to perform appropriately in the particular test rather than showing us how 'reading "normally" proceeds' (2009:

224). Instead, these critics advocate that research on reading should use more ethnographic methods, and in recent years the naturalistic study of reading field (NSR) has developed as an alternative approach. Although some of this research has focused on individual readers (e.g. Collinson, 2009), in the section that follows the NSR field is discussed in terms of reading group research as this is the area most closely aligned to the current study (for a more extensive discussion of experimental versus naturalistic methods, see Peplow and Carter, 2014).

2.1.1 Reading groups: An overview

The focus of this study is on one particular site of naturalistic reading: the reading group. This constitutes a natural setting because reading group members voluntarily come together to discuss books. Discussing individual, private reading practices Collinson notes that books 'provide a site of common ground, a territory which provides a location for discussion' (2009: 78). Collinson's point is that all reading has a social component and creates a potential for discussion, but it is in the reading group that these qualities are most in evidence. As natural sites of reading that exist prior to and beyond academic research, reading groups can show us how reading is done outside the academy, while also demonstrating the necessarily social aspects of reading.

People have been talking about books in groups for many centuries, although it is only since the eighteenth-century that these groups have been comprised of non-professional, lay readers, existing outside the universities. Since the 'library revolution' in eighteenth-century Britain during which time 'early public libraries' and 'reading clubs' emerged (Pearson, 1999: 160), reading groups have been an important part of Western reading practice. It has been predicted that there are around 50,000 face-to-face reading groups in the United Kingdom, around 500,000 in the United States (Hartley, 2001: vii), and approximately 40,750 such groups in Canada (Rehberg Sedo, 2002: 13) although this number is likely to have risen in the fifteen years since these surveys were conducted. The rise in popularity of reading groups over the last thirty years has been helped in no small part by the amount of media attention shared reading now receives. In the United States, *Oprah's Book Club* has engaged many thousands of readers, while in the United Kingdom, the *Richard & Judy Book Club* has run since 2004 and, similar to *Oprah's Book Club*, encourages the public discussion of literary texts. *The TV Book Club* on Channel 4 and BBC Radio 4's *Bookclub* have also proved incredibly popular in UK broadcast media; while in UK print media, many of the broadsheet newspapers run highly successful book clubs. This wealth of media attention that book groups receive in the United States and the United Kingdom may not explain the underlying popularity of these groups, but it does reflect a sense shared by many that literary reading naturally leads to discussion, and that books (good and bad) are worth talking about.

As defined in Chapter 1, a reading group describes a collective who meet regularly to discuss a book that all members (should) have read. Typically, face-to-face groups meet once a month, so that members have time in between meetings to read the book and formulate their views on it. These meetings can be seen as a literacy event, an activity 'where literacy has a role' (Barton and Hamilton, 2000: 8) and which involves some talk around texts. Seeing reading groups as events in this way 'stresses the situated nature of literacy', emphasizing the importance of 'social context' (Barton and Hamilton, 2000: 8). Groups can be organized across a range of different social contexts, all of which will make for different literacy events. Institutions as diverse as libraries, schools, prisons and workplaces are increasingly running and hosting reading groups, 'book circles' (Daniels, 2002; Duncan, 2012), and 'shared reading' sessions with a bibliotherapy focus (e.g. Dowrick et al., 2012; Hodge, Robinson and Davis, 2007). For private or 'closed' groups that have grown out of friendship networks, members may take turns at hosting or may meet in a pub, bar or restaurant. In Chapter 1 some of these differences were acknowledged when the reading groups used in the current study were described.

As the four reading groups in this study show, different book selection procedures are used across various groups. Again, there is variation between groups run through institutions and those run privately. Often, the readers in more institutional groups have little or no choice over deciding which books they read. Certainly the library (and ex-library) groups in my study have a relatively restricted choice compared to the private groups. Some libraries have a system whereby a long-list of texts is drawn up for the year and groups select books from that list. These library groups can opt to read a text that is not on the list but this may require members to buy their own copies of the text. As public libraries are becoming increasingly impoverished, practical and logistical factors play an important role in this free service offered to readers, and consequently the list of books is typically comprised of texts that local libraries hold in plentiful supply. Often, these are texts that local reading officers have decided will prove popular with groups.

Compared to library groups, privately run groups tend to have more choice over the books they read and greater freedom over the process for selecting texts.

Hartley (2001: 47–8) lists some of the most common ways for these groups to select books. Some groups choose books by nominating a 'leader' who selects the books; some groups follow the book selections from popular media sources (e.g. *Richard & Judy Book Club* or *The Guardian's* Book Club). The benefit of this latter method is that no one member is responsible for book selection, which diminishes the potential risk of the book selector being offended if readers in the group report disliking the book and/or the book leads to an unsatisfactory meeting. Another popular way for books to be selected is for groups to have certain 'themes' for a fixed amount of time. For instance, a group may decide to read African writers for six months, or epic poems for a year. Hartley (2001: 45) reports that the most common method is for members to take it in turns to select titles, as this is the most democratic method. Some of the specific organizational practices of the groups in my study are discussed in Chapter 3. In the next section of this chapter, sociological, sociolinguistic and stylistic research into reading groups will be discussed, with the current study will be positioned in relation to this previous research.

2.1.2 Reading group research

Although the proportion of people reading fiction for pleasure seems to be in decline (Knulst and van der Broek, 2003), reading groups are becoming increasingly popular (Hartley, 2001). The growing importance of book groups to contemporary reading practices in the United Kingdom and the United States has led to an increased academic interest in the phenomenon. Reading groups, in their current manifestation, originated in the United States and remain more popular there than in any other country (Rehberg Sedo, 2002). It is unsurprising therefore that American scholars have led the way in research into reading groups. Radway (1987, 1997) and Long (1992, 2003, 2004) have considered the sociological significance of the book club and the relation between today's conception of the book group and its manifestations throughout history. Long's work is of particular relevance to this study, as she conceives of reading as a collective activity rather than a purely private enterprise. She also considers reading groups to be gendered, and in her extensive study of historical and contemporary reading groups in Texas, she argued that these spaces were 'predominantly women's groups' (Long, 2003: 31) and that by focusing on such groups we can show the influence that this marginalized section of society has had in influencing the past and shaping the present (Long, 2003: 34). Elsewhere, Long analysed the way that readers in groups gravitate towards discussing aspects of character (1992: 199), often resisting avant-garde forms of literature that do not easily facilitate this kind of reading (1992: 203; 2003: 151). Long found resistance to literary academic discourse and academic reading practices to be endemic and spread across multiple reading groups. The groups in her study also contested the notion of literary 'classics' and the literary canon venerated by the academy. Owing to this culture of resistance within her reading groups, Long argued that their meetings tended to be more egalitarian than comparable contexts within academia (2003: 147). For Long, reading groups exist primarily to give the members a space to understand aspects of themselves and others, so that the book under discussion is often a pretext 'for the conversation through which members engage not only with the authorial "other" but with each other as well' (Long, 1992: 194).

In recent years sociological and sociolinguistic research within the United Kingdom has focused on the reading group in three principal ways: as a significant cultural phenomenon (Hartley, 2001), as a site of social practice (Allington and Swann, 2009; Benwell, 2009; Procter and Benwell, 2014; Swann and Allington, 2009), and as a site of social reading and interpretation (Peplow et al., 2015; Whiteley, 2011). For the remainder of this section the latter two areas will be described and research surveyed: reading groups as a site of social practice, and reading group data as evidence of social reading and literary interpretations.

The Discourse of Reading Groups project (Allington and Swann, 2009; O'Halloran, 2011; Swann and Allington, 2009) investigated the significance of book groups to modern Britain, focusing in particular on the content of the interpretations generated by book groups and on the ways in which argumentation is performed in this setting. This project considered the language used in sixteen face-to-face reading groups based in a variety of settings (e.g. prisons, private homes, workplaces), and two online reading groups. The aims of the project were twofold: 'to understand reading groups as a contemporary cultural phenomenon' (Swann and Allington, 2009: 247), and to offer a 'naturalistic' approach to readers and reading that moved away from the 'experimental' methods discussed in Section 2.1 (2009: 247–8). Swann and Allington define the experimental approach to literary reading as that which 'seeks to isolate specific types of interpretation, or interpretational activity' according to the 'pre-specified' interests of the researcher (2009: 248). Like Hall (2008), they argue that this high level of control in 'experimental' studies leads to 'rather artificial reading behaviour being investigated' (2009: 248). In contrast to experimental methods, Swann and Allington (2009) advocate a naturalistic approach to reading practices that is informed by ethnographic techniques.

This approach focuses on 'interpretations that emerge in habitual processes of reading' (2009: 248), allowing researchers to consider non-academic reading practices on the readers' own terms, rather than probing particular aspects of non-academic reading and potentially changing the reading experience altogether for the participants. Research in the naturalistic tradition should be conducted in a 'bottom-up' fashion, which may mean that researchers find themselves considering elements of the qualitative data that are highly salient for the readers, but were not necessarily of interest to the researcher(s) from the outset. One limitation of this approach, therefore, is that researchers cannot control their data in the way that they might like, and as a result, researchers may have to 'let go' of certain interests if the readers do not attend to this in their talk (Swann and Allington, 2009: 249). In general, *The Discourse of Reading Groups* study approached the recorded and observed data using qualitative methods of analysis, although O'Halloran's (2011) account of argumentation strategies combined quantitative and qualitative approaches.

Swann and Allington (2009) describe how the reading group recordings were divided into episodes manually and then codified thematically using qualitative software. These codes were established on the basis of the type of talk that frequently recurred in the meetings and were related to the content of the talk. Three of the most important codes were 'On book' (discussion on the specific book), 'Act of reading' (discussion of interaction with the text outside the meeting), and 'Interpretation' (evaluative judgements of the text). The principal findings from *The Discourse of Reading Groups* study focused on the fundamentally social aspect of the talk conducted in reading groups, where the readers' 'interpretational activity is contingent upon aspects of the contexts in which they read and is closely embedded within the sets of social and interpersonal relations' (Swann and Allington, 2009: 250). In the book group context, interpretations of texts 'are collaboratively developed rather than being the property of individual speakers' (Swann and Allington, 2009: 262). This propensity for co-construction within the reading groups reflects the importance of face-work for members, meaning that the act of discussing books 'constitutes an interactional resource through which interpersonal relations are managed' (2009: 262). Talk in a reading group need not be 'merely' talk about a book, therefore, but more generally an act of social engagement between readers.

Reading groups have also been considered as a transnational social practice (Benwell, 2009; Procter and Benwell, 2014). Like Swann and Allington (2009), this research employed an ethnographic methodology, combining this approach with insights from literary theories of reading and interactional sociolinguistics.

Naturally occurring data was collected from various reading groups' meetings over a six-month period. These groups were located in a number of different countries, many of which have post-colonial ties to the United Kingdom. Although for the most part the reading groups were recorded discussing texts that they would have been reading anyway, the dataset in this project also consisted of multiple reading groups' discussions of novels with a post-colonial focus: for example *Small Island* (Levy, 2004) and *White Teeth* (Smith, 2000). With a particular focus on discussions of race, Benwell argued that the reading group data allowed for the consideration of the 'shared discourses on particular texts, the place occupied by literary culture in everyday life, and cultural regimes of value informing the interpretations that are collaboratively arrived at' (2009: 301). The reading group data also demonstrated the ways in which readers attended to 'commonsense anti-racism' when they offered interpretations of the post-colonial fiction. The readers often positioned themselves as anti-racist when analysing characters who were perceived to be racist (Benwell, 2009), while also pitting themselves against other voices in society (sometimes real people and sometimes cultural types) who were seen as holding overtly racist views (Benwell, 2012; Procter and Benwell, 2014). For the readers, therefore, '"commonsense anti-racism" is discursively achieved by a process of "othering" – the construction of an overtly racist group against which the speaker's values are implicitly contrasted' (Benwell, 2009: 309).

As in Peplow (2011) and similar to the current study, Procter and Benwell (2014) sees reading groups as CofP, and the application of this model illuminates the discussion of how groups manage discourses of multiculturalism in order to achieve social ends. The reading groups draw on wider media discourses of multiculturalism in order to 'achieve the social business . . . of a reading group community: establishing solidarity, negotiating meaning, disagreeing, "being" or "not being" a certain kind of person . . . and so on' (Procter and Benwell, 2014: 179). Benwell and Procter's work (Benwell, 2009, 2012; Procter and Benwell, 2014) therefore sees the discursive practices that occur in the reading group as moving beyond mere discussion of the literary, with the CofP approach in particular demonstrating the situated nature of reading as a collaborative activity (Benwell, 2009: 309).

Building on the idea that reading is a social practice, other research into reading groups has attempted to bring together the notion of reading as a social practice with insights from cognitive stylistics in order to consider the 'conceptual and social activity' that is performed in reading group discourse (Peplow et al., 2015: 277). Drawing on a pooled corpus of reading group data, comprising interviews, group meetings, ethnographic observations, Peplow et al. (2015) looked at the interplay between literary text, reader talk and social context in face-to-face and online reading groups. Instead of seeing reading as purely social or as purely individualized and private, Peplow et al. (2015) broadened the remit of discourse analytical and cognitive stylistic approaches by discussing reading group discourse as the product of social cognition and 'inter-thinking' (Littleton and Mercer, 2013).

As discussed in Chapter 1, the present study takes a linguistic ethnographic approach and so builds on some of the insights from previous such studies of reading groups (Benwell, 2009; Long, 2003; Swann and Allington, 2009). For the most part, the focus is on discursive, interpersonal and rhetorical aspects of reading group talk as opposed to cognitive or conceptual elements of this talk, which are also considered in Peplow et al. (2015). Having said this, at certain times in this study the reading practices discussed are conceptual as well as discursive phenomena; for example, the concept of mimetic reading (Chapter 5) and the idea of character simulation through reported discourse (Chapter 4), and in discussing these aspects it is difficult (and undesirable) to prize apart the cognitive and the discursive. The two specific analytical approaches employed in this study are similar in both stressing the situated nature of social life and the centrality of discourse to this; while CofP (originating from ethnography) is interested in the ways in which meaning is situated in practice, conversation analysis (originating from ethnomethodology) is concerned with how meaning for participants is established through the structure of their talk. In the next section of this chapter the CofP approach is further described, with reference to research in this area. Following this, conversation analysis is outlined in Section 2.3.

2.2 Communities of practice

Communities of practice (CofP) is an approach to social life that aims to account for our actions by seeing them as rooted in practices and tasks. According to CofP, our social actions are not explained merely by our apparent belonging to 'objective' sociological categories (e.g. gender, age, sexuality) but can be analysed in terms of the mutual endeavours in which we are engaged, in the communities to which we belong. CofP was originally theorized as an approach to education (Lave and Wenger, 1991) but has since been co-opted by academics and practitioners across a number of disciplines: for example, pedagogy (Wesley and Buysse, 2001), business studies (Ardichvili, Page and Wentling, 2003) and economic geography

(Gertler, 2001). As a result, a number of diverse groups have been conceived of as CofP: family GPs (Endsley, Kirkegaard and Linares, 2005), internet discussion forums (Pratt and Back, 2009), sexual education classrooms (King, 2014), sewing cooperatives (Vickers et al., 2012) and the family (Hazen, 2002).

CofP has been used extensively within sociolinguistics since the early 1990s, receiving perhaps its most extensive application in Eckert's (2000) work on a variety of practices in an American high school. The CofP model has also been utilized by scholars of language and gender (Eckert and McConnell-Ginet, 1992a, 1992b, 1999; Holmes and Meyerhoff, 1999; Ostermann, 2003) and those interested in workplace interaction (Holmes and Schnuur, 2010; Holmes and Stubbe, 2003; Holmes, Stubbe and Vine, 1999; Mullany, 2007).

One of the reasons CofP has been used extensively by gender researchers is that the approach offers a credible alternative to considering gender in terms of the 'domination' model that typified early language and gender research (e.g. Lakoff, 1975; West and Zimmerman, 1977) and the 'difference model' exemplified in the work of Tannen (1987, 1991). In an early application of CofP to gender studies, Eckert and McConnell-Ginet (1992b) issue a call-to-arms, arguing that the domination and difference models encourage language and gender researchers to indulge in 'too much abstraction' and over-generalization:

> Abstracting gender and language from the social practices that produce their particular forms in given communities often obscures and sometimes distorts the ways they connect and how those connections are implicated in power relations, in social conflict, in the production and reproduction of values and plans.
>
> (Eckert and McConnell-Ginet, 1992b: 89)

Seeing certain groups of people as CofPs removes the temptation for researchers to see individuals' actions as merely a product of assumed essential categories (e.g. gender, age, sexuality). For CofP researchers, social actions should be seen as a product of a specific community, and a community must be studied in detail so that these social actions can be understood. However, the CofP approach is more nuanced than this description suggests. These researchers do not argue that social action is entirely a product of social environment, with the member of a community necessarily forced into a particular identity by virtue of being part of a CofP. Rather, each CofP is unique and is constantly being negotiated and defined by its members so that the relationship between the individual actor, seemingly objective aspects of their personal identity (e.g. gender), and social context is always symbiotic and dynamic – a point made clearly in Freed (1996).

An important aspect of any CofP is participation in practice. Members of a group will occupy different positions, and these positions are likely to change over time. A child entering a new school will need to integrate by adopting the customs and practices (linguistic and otherwise) of the particular social group(s) to which she wants to belong. In CofP terms, this child will start as a marginal member of the community, and then assume a peripheral position when she is initially accepted by this group. If the child wants, she can engage more in the group's practices, moving from the periphery to the core and towards 'more complex and fully engaged participation' (Holmes and Woodhams, 2013: 276). A member's social identity is linked to their position within a group, making the CofP approach highly compatible with constructivist methods, which stress the 'discursive', 'emergent' and 'positional' nature of identity (Bucholtz and Hall, 2005). This idea of a trajectory from periphery to core, from ignorance to 'competence and experience' (Wenger, 1998: 138) is somewhat idealized in the original accounts of CofP (Lave and Wenger, 1991; Wenger, 1998), and Davies (2005) successfully shows how this movement might be unwanted by some members of a CofP, and impossible for others.

In Chapter 1 the three defining characteristics of any CofP were introduced: mutual engagement, joint enterprise and shared repertoire. These are described in more detail here, as joint enterprise and shared repertoire in particular are drawn on extensively across Chapters 3, 4 and 5.

Mutual engagement is the most basic requirement of a CofP and is necessary for the inclusion of members. For Wenger, mutual engagement involves participants frequently engaging in 'actions whose meaning they negotiate with one another' (Wenger, 1998: 73), while Meyerhoff argues that this entails members getting 'together in order to engage in their shared practices' (Meyerhoff, 2005: 527). Mutual engagement can include interaction that, although not fundamental to the basic functioning of a group, helps to foster a sense of cohesion in a community. Wenger (1998: 75) cites one member of a claims processing team he studied who regularly brought in snacks for her fellow workers. While her kindness may have had little direct effect on the team's productivity, it did facilitate a sense of community cohesion that went beyond the strictures of the group's task at hand. Although regular interaction on an online forum could well fulfil the criterion of mutual engagement, it is more likely to be fulfilled with regular face-to-face interaction and this has been the typical focus (Davies, 2005: 561). Wenger argues that 'given the right context, talking on the phone, exchanging electronic mail, or being connected by radio can be part of what makes mutual engagement possible' (Wenger, 1998: 74). As shown in Chapter 1, the reading groups in this study meet once a month typically, with some members meeting each other outside of these sessions socially and others seeing each other everyday by virtue of being married! All of these groups are long-standing and all have developed shared practices as a result of this mutual engagement. These groups meet regularly to negotiate meaning together, both in terms of debating what books mean (negotiating literary meaning) and in the more abstract sense of negotiating what it means to be part of the reading group.

In CofP terms, the task or goal of a group is referred to as joint enterprise. Analysing a group's joint enterprise is crucial for a CofP analysis in two ways: one empirical and one methodological. Empirically, analysing a reading group's joint enterprise helps us to account for what that group is doing when they meet. Methodologically, defining joint enterprise helps researchers to consider whether reading groups are prototypical CofPs. Joint enterprise forms the basis of McConnell-Ginet's famous definition of a CofP as 'a group of people brought together by some mutual endeavour, some common enterprise in which they are engaged' (McConnell-Ginet, 2003: 71). Joint enterprise is often the most obvious of the three components to distinguish in a CofP, even if this can be difficult to define precisely in all cases. A team of fire-fighters has the joint enterprise of responding to emergency calls made to it and ensuring that people are safe where there are fires. In this way, joint enterprise can be relatively straightforward to distinguish in groups where the task is clearly marked out, externally imposed upon participants, and where these participants are held accountable (e.g. in many institutional and workplace groups). However, King (2014) warns that it is dangerous to see a group as a CofP just by virtue of the members 'participating in an activity together' (2014: 62). Indeed, it may be the case that a group that shares a very obvious purpose or task is not a good example of a CofP because this task may be strictly imposed on the group from outside, leaving little room for the participants to negotiate meaning 'with one another' locally (Wenger, 1998: 73). In this way, institutional groups, such as those in some workplaces, may not be the best examples of CofPs (King, 2014: 63) because the participants may not have much say over how they are going to respond to 'their conditions, and therefore to *their* enterprise' (Wenger, 1998: 79 – emphasis in original). This local negotiation of joint enterprise is even more necessary in 'self-constituted' groups (Davies, 2005) where there are fewer guidelines directing joint enterprise, such as reading groups.

If the reading group is a literacy event (Barton and Hamilton, 2000) then it is also easy to see that the work readers do with texts is socially situated and task-oriented. Barton and Hamilton (2000: 12) argue that 'typically literacy is a means to some other end', so seeing the talk produced in reading groups as part of a joint enterprise should be a fruitful way of considering what literacy means in this context. At the most general level, a group's joint enterprise is to discuss texts that the attending members (should) have read. Hartley offers a similar minimal definition of book groups, drawing on the task the group performs: a reading group is 'a group of people who meet on a regular basis to discuss books' (2001: 20). Although useful as a starting point, these definitions risk over-simplifying what reading groups are and why they meet. Long similarly finds problems with this basic definition, arguing that 'any formulation of . . . [reading groups'] central cultural practice as simply reporting what each thought about a book almost entirely misses the point of why the participants are there at all' (Long, 2003: 144). As well as discussing books, participants in reading groups are engaged in forging, maintaining and, perhaps in rare cases, damaging interpersonal relations with others in the group. Acknowledging the importance of relational work in reading groups is vital to any understanding of the evaluations and interpretations that participants offer. As Swann and Allington argue, 'readers' interpretational activity is contingent upon aspects of the contexts in which they read, and . . . is closely embedded within sets of social and interpersonal relations' (Swann and Allington, 2009: 250). In addition to discussing and debating textual meaning, this kind of interpersonal relational work must also be seen as a vital component of reading groups' joint enterprise. Joint enterprise will be discussed in relation to the specific groups and extracts of talk in Chapter 3.

The third defining feature of a CofP is shared repertoire. This feature is probably of most interest to linguists, as it concerns the ways in which groups make meaningful statements about the world (Wenger, 1998: 83). Important to these meaningful statements are 'words' and 'discourse', but a whole lot of other features too:

> The repertoire of a community of practice includes routines, words, tools, ways of doing things, stories, gestures, symbols, genres, actions, or concepts that the community has produced or adopted in the course of its existence, and which have becomes part of its practice . . . the discourse by which members create meaningful statements about the world, as well as the styles by which they express their forms of membership and their identities as members.
>
> (Wenger, 1998: 83)

Elsewhere, Wenger (1998: 125–6) argues that, among other things, the following two linguistic features characterize a CofP:

- Jargon and shortcuts to communication
- A shared discourse that reflects a certain perspective on the world.

Over time groups develop these communicative 'shortcuts' and 'shared discourse', and these form important manifestations of a CofP's shared repertoire.

Sociolinguistic research using CofP has tended to focus on shared repertoire precisely because of Wenger's emphasis on language (1998: 83, 125–6). Some of these studies have focused on other features of shared repertoire such as clothing style (e.g. Eckert, 2000; Mendoza-Denton, 1997), group pastimes and hobbies (e.g. Moore, 2006; Vickers et al., 2012), but the emphasis in linguistic research is on 'repertoire' as language, and 'shared repertoire' as a shared language within a group. Meyerhoff (2002: 528) describes shared repertoire as 'resources (linguistic or otherwise) [that] are the cumulative result of internal negotiations'. These 'internal negotiations' seem to refer to the joint enterprise of a group, so that shared repertoire is both a product and a constituent feature of a group's joint enterprise. In other words, the language used in a CofP creates and reflects the members' joint task.

Eckert's (2000) research into social practice among adolescents at a Detroit high school focused on phonological practices as shared repertoire across three social groups. Eckert distinguished student groups on the basis of how far members conformed to the institution of the high school. The 'jocks' strongly upheld the values of the high school (playing sport, pursuing academic success, wearing high school clothing), the 'burnouts' strongly rebelled from the institution (truanting from school, taking drugs, 'cruising' in cars), while the 'in-betweens' participated in some of the activities encouraged by the school and some of the 'burnout' practices outside school. Eckert's research is situated within the variationist tradition of sociolinguistics, and her study mainly focuses on shared repertoire as a phonological phenomenon. She links the different social groups' pronunciation of particular vowel sounds to the groups' respective adherence to, or rebellion from, the institution of the high school. While the 'jocks' conformed to standard norms of vowel pronunciation, the 'burnouts' deviated away from this, adopting the more innovative (albeit less generally prestigious) pronunciation changes that were occurring across Northern US cities at the time. In a similar study, Mendoza-Denton (1997) analysed shared repertoire at a phonological level, finding that vowel pronunciation among Californian adolescents reflected individuals' participation in different groups and gangs. Within the groups in these two studies there was coherence between various manifestations of shared repertoire (e.g. dress, pronunciation) and joint enterprise (i.e. conforming to/ rebelling from a high school, engaging in gang life).

Although much of the work on shared repertoire has focused on phonological variation between different groups (e.g. Eckert, 2000; Finnis, 2014; Fought, 1999;

Mendoza-Denton, 1997) other research has also considered shared repertoire more generally as the 'speech patterns' or 'communicative styles' specific to a CofP (Freed, 1996: 67). Some of these studies that focus on shared repertoire as a product of interaction have considered particular 'gendered' styles of communication to constitute a shared language. For instance, Ostermann's (2003) study into how reports of domestic abuse were dealt with by two all-female institutional groups in Brazil found a supportive speech style adopted by volunteers in a women's refuge group, which contrasted with the unsupportive and dismissive speech that was the norm in an all-female group of police officers. In a similar vein, Ehrlich (1999) used the CofP model to consider the communicative practices of members of a university tribunal panel who were hearing a sexual assault case. Ehrlich found that the three members of the tribunal panel constituted a CofP through being mutually engaged 'on a regular basis in university disciplinary tribunals' and through adopting a particular interrogative style (or shared repertoire) when questioning the two female plaintiffs (Ehrlich, 1999: 251). The tribunal members' shared repertoire 'jointly construct[s] an interpretive "frame" that minimizes the complainants' resistance, and ultimately functions to (re)construct the events as consensual sex' (Ehrlich, 1999: 251). Finally, research on language in the workplace (e.g. Holmes and Stubbe, 2003; Holmes, Stubbe and Vine, 1999; Mullany, 2007) has used the concept of shared repertoire to account for localized gendered practices, taking a more expansive view of shared repertoire than a focus on phonological dialectal patterns alone would allow.

In Chapters 4 and 5 shared repertoire is discussed in relation to dominant reading practices that emerge from the groups' talk; in particular, the use of specific forms of reported discourse (Chapter 4) and category entitlements (Chapter 5) constitute shared repertoire across the reading groups. These form particular 'speech patterns' and 'communicative styles' (Freed, 1996: 67) in, and across, the reading groups.

2.3 Conversation analysis

In order to look systematically at how the reading groups in this study negotiated textual meaning, it is necessary to apply a linguistic model of interaction. Developed as a model of learning (Lave and Wenger, 1991), and then workplace management (Wenger, 1998), CofP alone is not equipped to account for discursive phenomena in a group. This lack of focus on language in CofP has been criticized (Contu and Willmott, 2003; Myers, 2006) and, as a result, in the subsequent analyses of the reading groups the CofP model is combined with a form of conversation analysis (henceforth CA).

CA is the study of naturally occurring conversation. It mostly focuses on 'everyday interaction' (Atkinson and Heritage, 1984: 2) or 'mundane social action' (Psathas, 1995: 1). At its inception, CA researchers such as Harvey Sacks broke new ground merely by considering casual conversation as worthy of study. In the late 1960s when Sacks delivered his seminal series of lectures (collected in Sacks, 1992), much of the research conducted in linguistics and the sociology of language was highly influenced by Chomskyan transformational grammar, which stressed the need for language to be studied in the abstract if linguistics was to 'be a serious discipline' (Chomsky, 1965: 4). Sacks believed that conversation was worth studying, precisely because in talk there is 'order at all points' (Sacks, 1984: 22). Everyday interaction is generally the focus of CA because such talk is seen as extraordinarily complex, even though most conversations are conducted in an orderly fashion. Talk is seen as a series of 'practical actions' (Psathas, 1995: 3) through which people act upon the world but also through which they make sense of it. CA is rooted in the ethnomethodological approach of sociologists such as Garfinkel (1967) and so is concerned with meaning as defined by participants rather than the researcher's interpretation of that meaning; thus, according to Schegloff, CA should be concerned with 'what was going on in it [the conversation] *for the participants*' (Schegloff, 1997: 174 – emphasis in original). In practice, it is difficult to prize apart participant meaning from researcher interpretation when conducting research (see criticisms of CA on these grounds from Blommaert [2005] and Hammersley [2003]), but a primary focus on the words in the transcript (Peräkylä, 2004) and an acknowledgement that talk is social action and a series of practical accomplishments (i.e. it gets stuff done for participants) should maintain the ethnomethodological focus.

The focus of CA tends to be on the structure of conversation rather than on the content of what is actually said. At its most basic, conversation is comprised of turns at talk and in order for a conversation to function it is 'fundamental . . . that one speaker take a turn and is followed by another speaker' (Drew, 2005: 80). In addition, turns at talk are dependent on or 'conditionally relevant' (Schegloff, 1968) to what has gone before. This is demonstrated by the prevalence of adjacency pairs, in which the first part of a sequence dictates that a second part should normally follow: for example question/answer, greeting/greeting. The existence of these normative patterns establishes certain preferences in conversation, so that it is expected that a greeting will follow a greeting, for instance. In certain adjacency pairs typical preferences determine how turns may be designed, and if there is some deviation from normative adjacency pair rules in the second part then this would have to be flagged-up. For instance, an invitation to dinner will have the preferred response of acceptance, and if the speaker in the second position (i.e. the one being invited) wished to refuse then she will very likely package her response to reflect the fact that it is dispreferred – this is discussed in more detail in relation to assessment sequences in Section 2.3.1.

Certain rules or expectations also govern how multiple, consecutive turns are organized. Turn-taking had been acknowledged before (e.g. Goffman, 1955), but the first systematic treatment of how turns are structured across a conversation is found in CA. In an influential paper, Sacks, Schegloff and Jefferson (1974) argued that a rule of 'one speaker speaks at a time' governs most conversation but that 'instances of more than one speaker talking at a time are common, but brief' (1974: 700–1). Change of speaker tends to occur at the end of a turn, and people are generally competent at predicting when this is likely to be (Jefferson, 1986). How much overlapping talk there is in a conversation is likely to be determined by context, with overlaps and even interruptions acceptable in talk between friends but unacceptable in a law court. Transition relevance places (TRPs) are points in turns when it is acceptable to change speakers, and often these will occur around a pause. Whether or not a particular transition is admissible will be shown in the resulting passage of talk. Generally speaking, a turn transition that is deemed to be unacceptable, occurring away from a TRP, is referred to as an interruption, whereas one that occurs at a TRP is an overlap and is more likely to seen as an acceptable conversational move (Jefferson, 1986; for a different view on the admissibility of interruptions and overlaps, see Goldberg, [1990], Cameron [2001], Lerner [2002] and Kitzinger [2008]). This discussion of overlapping talk is continued below in relation to the notion of conversational 'floor' in Section 2.3.1.

Before moving on to discuss some aspects of CA that are particularly relevant to the reading group data, it is necessary to stress that there are different forms of CA, some of which allow for discussions of wider social context and others that remain tightly focused on the transcript (for discussions of this debate, see Hutchby and Wooffitt [2008], ten Have [1999] and Peplow [2011]). In this study the former, 'applied CA' approach is favoured because the focus is on studying talk in a particular context (reading groups) rather than on the study of talk in itself. In this sense, the application of CA is more akin to that of Richards (2006), Benwell (2005), Benwell and Stokoe (2006) and Myers (2004), who all offer 'detailed analysis of particular episodes' of talk, but go 'further than most conversation analysts would feel comfortable with' (Richards, 2006: 18). Hammersley (2003) argues that CA should be 'combined with other . . . approaches' in order to offer 'more effective scientific study of social life' (2003: 772) and this is what the present study attempts to do in bringing together CA with CofP.

2.3.1 Assessments and floor

In the following section some aspects of CA research that are most relevant to the reading group data are considered. First, as reading groups are spaces in which readers give and respond to opinions on books, Pomerantz's (1984a) work on assessments and preference organization is discussed. Secondly, the concept of conversational floor is introduced, with particular reference to the work of Coates (1996) and Edelsky (1981).

For reading groups the professed business of their meetings is talking about and interpreting literary texts. Assessments are seen to be central to social life (Goodwin and Goodwin, 1992), and the importance of assessments is particularly evident in the reading group data. Much of the time the groups' talk takes the form of evaluations, with assessments dominating the discussions. Assessments often occur in sequences, spanning 'multiple utterances' involving 'different speakers' (Goodwin and Goodwin, 1992: 159). In these assessment sequences it is often permissible for more than one speaker to talk at any one time, as 'norms' of sequential organization are 'relaxed for assessments' (1992: 164). This may lead to the development of collaborative floor, as discussed below.

When assessments occur in sequences, there are particular preferences that govern how speakers design their turns, specifically a preference for agreement (Pomerantz, 1984a, 1984b). The management of epistemic rights between speakers is often demonstrated in the sequential organization of assessments, and research has considered how speakers go about offering 'second assessments'; that is, assessments that follows initial assessments. For example:

```
James:  That meal was disgusting
Barry:  Yeah it was pretty bad
```

Pomerantz (1984a) argues that the second assessment in a sequence like this is constrained by the first assessment, forming an adjacency pair. It is expected that an initial assessment will prompt other speakers to also assess the same referent, assuming that the other speakers have access to this. In the above example, once James has given his assessment of the meal, Barry is expected to offer his own review. Alternatively, Barry could deny giving an assessment of the meal if he lacked knowledge or experience of it. In either case, Barry's turn is constrained by James's initial assessment.

A further constraint when offering second assessments is the 'preference for agreement' (Pomerantz, 1984a). Assessment sequences are full of agreements and/or disagreements because in these passages of talk 'participants negotiate and display to each other a congruent view of the events' (Goodwin and Goodwin, 1992: 182). While second position agreements are generally designed to highlight the agreement, second position disagreements are often structured so as to minimize the impact of the disagreement (Pomerantz, 1984a). In practice, this means that agreements tend to follow on contiguously from the first assessment (Sacks, 1987), are often prefaced by an explicit agreeing token (e.g. 'yes', 'definitely'), and agreement generally occupies the whole turn (Pomerantz, 1984a). By contrast, when people offer disagreement in the second assessment position this tends to display 'dispreferred' features (Pomerantz, 1984a). The onset of these turns will often be delayed, containing false starts and hesitation. Disagreements may omit a disagreeing token such as 'no' or 'I disagree', and are frequently prefaced by an agreement token (e.g. 'yes').

As discussed, normative turn-taking procedures can be 'relaxed' in assessment sequences (Goodwin and Goodwin, 1992: 164), potentially leading to collaborative floor: highly dynamic interaction with frequent turn transitions and overlapping talk. The term collaborative floor was devised by Edelsky (1981) in her study of workplace meetings. She defines 'floor' as *the acknowledged what's-going-on* within an interaction (1981: 405 – emphasis in the original), aligning floor closely with the topic or function of a current section of talk. In her workplace meeting data, Edelsky found that much of the interaction was governed not by orderly one-person-speaks-at-a-time; rather, the talk was much more of a 'free-for-all' (Edelsky, 1981: 391), with speakers engaging in simultaneous talk, overlapping, and sharing the conversational floor in a collaborative fashion. When collaborative floor is used, participants can demonstrate that they are 'on the same wave length', jointly constructing utterances (Edelsky, 1981: 391).

In her analyses of 'women talk' (Coates, 1996) argued that the predominant form of talk in her data was best described using the concept of collaborative floor. Coates found that in much of her all-female data the participants 'DON'T FUNCTION AS INDIVIDUAL SPEAKERS' (Coates, 1997: 117 – emphasis in original), and more recently, Coates and Sutton-Spence (2001) extended this discussion of floor, arguing that deaf signers also tend to orient towards the collaborative floor model. Coates found that the all-female talk in her study typically displayed the following features: incomplete utterances (allowing other speakers to fill in the gaps), collaborative searches for the right word, jointly constructed utterances, joint construction involving simultaneous speech and overlapping speech (Coates, 1996: 117–51). The latter three of these features are now discussed, as these were highly prevalent in the reading group data.

In jointly constructed utterances speakers 'work together so that their voices combine to produce a single utterance or utterances' (Coates, 1996: 118). Two manifestations of joint construction can be distinguished: first, when a speaker tags a word (or words) onto the end of another's utterance, thus completing the prior speaker's turn (Coates, 1996: 118–20), and secondly when a speaker attempts to project the end of the prior speaker's turn with simultaneous speech (Coates, 1996: 121–2). Extract 2.1 is an example of a jointly constructed utterance, while Extract 2.2 is an instance of joint construction with simultaneous speech:

Extract 2.1 Joint construction

    [09:09] Orchards, *So Many Ways to Begin*

P   somebody would discover and
Co =take the baby away

    P = Peter; Co = Connie

Extract 2.2 Joint construction with simultaneous speech

    [15:43] Orchards, *Dubliners*

A   so the implication was that he might have done
    [something that would've prevented him
Ca [something that would've prevented him

    A = Alex; Ca = Carol

Extract 2.2 is particularly interesting, not just because Alex and Carol make exactly the same point, with Carol successfully predicting the completion of Alex's turn, but because what is said in the simultaneous speech spans an entire clausal element – a phenomenon Coates also found in her data (1996: 119). These examples of jointly constructed utterances show speakers paying 'extremely close attention to each other, at all linguistic levels' (Coates, 1996: 119) and displaying 'understanding, affiliation, and agreement' with one another (Lerner, 2002: 250).

More extended examples of overlapping talk are also found in the reading group data. As in Coates's examples, the speakers in Extract 2.3 are pursuing 'a theme simultaneously, saying different, but related things' (1996: 131). At points in the extract there are examples of overlapping echoing between speakers (e.g. 'the good stuff'):

Extract 2.3 Compassionate character[1]

```
       [06:27] Orchards, Book Thief
   R     because he's a compassionate (.) [entity
   Ca                                      [yes and he's
         having to pick up all [BAD stuff that's going
   R                            [having to pick up all the
         bad
   Ca    =ro[und
   R       [and the good stu[ff
   Ca                       [an and the good
         st[uff as well
   R       [and the good stuff (.) but (.) all the bad
         stuff

         Ca = Carol; Co = Connie; R = Roger; S = Sue; Ja =
         Jackie; A = Alex
```

Floor type is related to topic, and the establishment of a collaborative floor depends largely on whether the various speakers have access to the current topic of conversation, so when more speakers have access to the topic of conversation, there is a greater likelihood of a collaborative floor opening up (Erickson, 1982). The prevalence of collaborative floor in the reading groups may result from the fact that the groups are focused on a joint activity (see Section 2.2 and Chapter 3), where all readers have access to the topic under discussion.

2.4 Conclusion

In this chapter the research background to the study has been established, with the main theoretical influences described. The present study has been discussed in relation to previous research into reading and, more specifically, existing studies of reading groups. Following some of these previous studies of reading groups (Benwell, 2009; Long, 2003; Swann and Allington, 2009), the present study adopts an ethnographic approach to the groups, both in terms of data collection and analysis. As part of this ethnographic approach, the reading groups are seen as CofPs, and this chapter provided a detailed overview of existing CofP research and definitions of some of the important CofP terminology used across this study. The specific focus of this study is on how the talk used in the groups indexes certain shared practices and produces community, and so an applied form of CA is combined with CofP in order to produce rich analyses of data. Being rooted within ethnomethodology, CA shares some of the same principles as CofP, in particular a focus on meaning as situated in use and context (Peplow, 2011). In the final part of this chapter CA was introduced and specifically relevant research within this paradigm was discussed: assessments and collaborative floor.

In the next chapter the CofP concept of joint enterprise is discussed in relation to data from the reading groups. The focus is on organizational practices within the four groups, and how these practices are created, maintained and occasionally resisted by the participants.

3

Reading Group Organization

A poster seen in a bookshop reads: 'What I like about reading groups is that it's the only place in life where you get amicable disagreement.'[1] This quotation, presumably from a member of a reading group, succinctly captures one of the key attractions of reading groups and also some of the features of the talk found in this context. According to this reader, reading groups are a place like no other and can facilitate a form of talk ('amicable disagreement') that is not found elsewhere, either in everyday or institutional contexts. Contemporary reading groups challenge any simple distinction between formal and informal contexts because these groups are usually highly organized spaces, focused on a joint enterprise, in which informality and friendliness is also highly valued. The discourse produced by reading groups displays some of the features of institutional language, in particular through being goal-oriented (Peplow et al., 2015), but yet the talk in this setting is not reducible to this and, as discussed in this chapter, problems can arise in groups when meetings are seen as being conducted in a too rigid and formalized way.

Compared with other public reading contexts, such as classrooms and seminar rooms, the organization of reading group meetings tends to be informal. Any express aims or rules belonging to a group tend to be created by the group members rather than externally imposed. The joint enterprise of most reading groups, therefore, tends to be 'defined by the participants in the very process of pursuing it' (Wenger, 1998: 77). Exceptions to this are reading groups that exist within institutional constraints and for the intended benefit of the members in some way: for example reading groups in prisons, reading circles in schools, bibliotherapy groups. By contrast, the reading groups considered in this study may not be classically institutional settings but do exist within particular constraints and expectations about how assessments of texts ought to be articulated and how the talk should be organized. Since their growth in popularity reading groups have become more commodified, with publishers and booksellers developing ways of encouraging their books to be used as reading group material. TV and other forms of media also have particular notions of what reading groups are, both in the groups that are run through this media (e.g. *Richard & Judy Book Club*, Radio 4's *Book Club*) and in fictional depictions of reading groups (e.g. Channel 4's comedy series *The Book Group*).

While external forces such as publishers, booksellers and the media may exert some influence, however, the reading groups in this study ultimately create their own procedures and negotiate their own practices and, like other CofPs, each reading group responds to 'institutional conditions with an inventiveness that is all theirs' (Wenger, 1998: 79). This chapter considers some of the specific organizational practices of these reading groups and how these practices orient the groups towards their joint enterprise. In some cases external resources are used, such as publisher-produced sets of questions, while in other groups specific, and fairly unique, organizational practices have been devised by the members themselves. We will consider instances when readers in groups are complicit with particular organizational practices and other occasions when members of groups are resistant to such 'rules'.

3.1 Reading group resources and joint enterprise

Reading groups can be organized in a variety of ways, and this organization will affect the members' experience of the group and ways in which texts are discussed. In order for a reading group to be successful and operational, its members must share an over-arching aim to meet and discuss books. In CofP terms the aims of a group are conceptualized as joint enterprise, a term that captures not just the express purpose of a community but also creates a sense of belonging and 'mutual accountability' within that group (Wenger, 1998: 77–8). Commitment to this joint enterprise may vary from one meeting to the next, if say a group feels indifferent towards the text or if some of the members have not finished reading the book (Benwell, Procter and Robinson, 2011), but without this basic-level joint enterprise it is difficult to see how a reading group could exist as a 'reading group'. Assuming that this over-arching joint enterprise exists within a group, its members can negotiate the finer points of their purpose: how 'serious' should discussions be, how meetings are to be organized, what sorts of books should be read, and so on.

Some reading groups considered in this study structured their meetings in quite formalized ways, whether drawing on structuring resources produced by publishers or the groups devising their own methods of organization. Even reading groups that create their own ways of structuring meetings must exist within a wider context of being a reading group because practice always 'looks outward' and 'involves a relation to the world' (Eckert and McConnell-Ginet, 2007: 28). For some of the reading groups this looking 'outward' means engaging with other voices that are offering opinions on texts from outside the group. The act of offering assessments of books is often responsive to the wider institution of literary reading, whether that is professional or amateur, and members of reading groups are often keenly aware of the hierarchies of taste (Bourdieu, 1984) that govern their own responses and those of others.

All four reading groups that form this study used some kind of external resource in order to guide their meetings, and other studies suggest that this is a popular reading group practice (Procter and Benwell, 2014: 22). The resources used by the groups take the form of various documents: reading group guides, notes on books, sets of questions and reviews of the books – both critical and non-academic. These documents serve important functions in guiding the talk and can determine the types of textual interpretations offered. Drawing on data from the groups' meetings and on the interviews conducted with the groups, this chapter looks at how the groups utilize the wide range of resources and reading group aids that have materialized since the increased popularity of reading groups. The use of some of these documents has become 'reified' (Wenger, 1998: 58–9), in the sense that the process of drawing on these physical objects (e.g. sets of questions) and/or voices (e.g. critical opinions on the text) have become focusing practices that are 'congealed into fixed forms', attended to at particular times in meetings (Wenger, 1998: 60).

Reading group questions are considered in the next section of this chapter (Section 3.2), with a particular focus on how three of the four groups use this resource. These sets of questions are a powerful structuring force in the groups and may produce certain kinds of responses from the readers; however, the groups are resistant when they feel that the questions negatively affect their discussion, either through being biased or being overly formal. In Section 3.3 the presence of other, absent readers is considered. Reading group members are rarely just in dialogue with the other members of their group when they debate texts; instead, they are in negotiation with absent 'voices' of others: critics, other readers and judgements of literary taste. Two forms of voice are considered: amateur readers and professional readers. The invocation of these other readers' voices allows members of the groups to situate their own readings within a wider context of taste and the institution of literary reading. Section 3.4 focuses on the Contemporary Group and how particular 'rules' have been developed over time within this specific group. The status of these rules is constantly under negotiation, with members of the group holding different opinions on the usefulness of these rules to the group's joint enterprise.

3.2 Sets of questions

There are a number of resources available today for reading groups to use in structuring their meetings and their literary responses. The publishing industry has been quick to capitalize on the reading group phenomenon, and an extensive range of guides and advice books is available to anyone uncertain as to how best to run their group (e.g. Laskin and Hughes, 1995; Loevy, 2006; O'Hare and Storey, 2004; Shriver, 2008; Slezak, 2000). Other guides can be found on websites: blogs managed by reading group enthusiasts (e.g. ReadingGroupGuides.com, 2015), and others run by publishers (e.g. Penguin, 2015). This plethora of guides available to reading groups reflects the way that such groups have become institutionally sanctioned as a custom or practice that is regarded as important within society. The prevalence of these resources not only reflects the perceived importance of reading groups in the United Kingdom, but also creates and solidifies norms for reading groups to follow, if they choose.

The sets of reading group questions that are produced for specific books by publishers and media outlets (e.g. newspapers) are a particularly important resource for reading groups. The groups in Hartley's extensive survey offered a range of opinions on the value of these questions, with some groups describing the benefits of using this resource, citing the 'structure' that it provides to the discussion (2001: 147; see also Devlin-Glass, 2001), while other groups reported that following these reading guides can lead to rather static discussions (Hartley, 2001: 99). At worse, these guides and sets of questions can make readers feel as if they are back in institutional education: 'the teachers among us say that it is like being back at school' (Hartley, 2001: 99). Similarly, Devlin-Glass found that some groups actively rejected these notes and questions, arguing that they 'kill enjoyment' and can be poorly written (2001: 578–9).

Three of the four reading groups in this study used questions in their meetings, with only the Contemporary Group choosing not to use this resource. Commitment towards and enthusiasm for sets of questions varied between groups and within groups, and from one meeting to the next. Of the three groups that used questions, the Orchards Group used this resource with the greatest regularity and appeared to treat the questions with the most seriousness. The importance and value of the questions is demonstrated in Extract 3.1, which comes from the start of the Orchard Group's discussion of *The Road* (McCarthy, 2006). Here, Alex attends to the importance of the set of questions, discussing their usefulness in 'guiding' meetings:

Extract 3.1 They give you a 'purpose'
          [00:14] - Orchards, *The Road*

1	S	Alex (1.0) is going to is going to lead the discussion this even[ing
2	A	[hhh I'm not going to lead the discussion I've merely downloaded some questions from the internet which will make a (.) guided thing (.) it's what we do at my book club and does [actually
3	Ca	[haha
4	A	give you (1.0) a purpose
5	S	ok
6	A	=and also it tends t- you tend to find that you anticipate other issues as you talk through the questions as well
7	S	[ok
8	A	[and th- there's ten questions (.) erm and the first one was simply (0.5) <why do you think McCarthy wrote the road> (2.0)
9	Ja	I'd been wondering that much haha

          S = Sue; A = Alex; Ca = Carol; Ja = Jackie

Alex presents the questions she has brought as a resource that, independent of the group members, has the ability to structure meetings. She has downloaded these questions 'from the internet' and these will make a 'guided' discussion (Turn 2), providing the group with a 'purpose' (Turn 4). Alex invokes her multimembership status within the group (Wenger, 1998), reporting her positive experience of using sets of questions in another reading group: 'it's what we do at my book club' (Turn 2). Alex offers a further benefit of using sets of questions by reporting that 'you tend to anticipate other issues' as answers to the questions are offered (Turn 6). According to Alex, a good set of questions will not just guide a discussion but will also facilitate new ideas in the readers.

Alex's account of the sets of questions as giving 'purpose' and enabling a 'guided' discussion is fairly typical of the way the Orchards Group attends to this resource. The next example displays the group structuring their meeting according to a set of questions obtained from a publisher's website. Sue has brought along these questions to use in the group's discussion of *So Many Ways to Begin* (McGregor, 2006). She reads the first question out six minutes into the meeting:

Extract 3.2 Attending to the question #1

```
       [06:27] - Orchards, So Many ways to Begin
1   S   I've got questions here and actually the one
        where (.) the one (.) the first one is er how
        does Julia's revelation change David's life
        which I think we've just we're just discussing
        there (.) erm obviously it changes it
        completely doesn't it (.) it really shakes er
        all the foundations [er
2   Co                         [exactly it rocks his
        [foundations
3   S   [rocks his foundations to the very core doesn't
        it (.) erm (.) and why do you think Dorothy
        chose not to tell him (.) and what do you think
        of her decision (1.0)
4   Ja  well she didn't tell the father [either did she
5   Ca                                   [I know
6   Co                                       [I know
7   Ju                                       [I know
        I can't
8   Ja  =I found [that a little bit strange
9   Ca           [yeah I did to be honest
10  S                          [yeah
11  Ju  =I thought it was a bit of a flaw actually
        S = Sue; Co = Connie; Ja = Jackie; Ca = Carol;
        Ju = Julia
```

After Sue has announced that she has brought questions along and has read out the first part of the first question she offers a brief answer herself, suggesting that the revelation in the novel changes a character's life 'completely' (Turn 1). Across Turns 2–3 Connie and Sue share the metaphor of the revelation shaking/rocking a character's 'foundations', before Sue asks the two further supplementary questions. From Turn 4 onwards, and beyond the end of this extract, members of the group attempt to answer this question by imagining the effect on the character David and judging his mother's decision. A collaborative floor develops, with overlapping talk and turns shared between readers. The group is quick to respond to the question, perhaps because it directly relates to the discussion they are engaged in already: having asked the first part of the question, Sue remarks that the group was 'just discussing' that issue (Turn 1).

The Orchards Group demonstrates similar commitment and seriousness towards the set of questions later on in the same meeting. At this stage the group is discussing the 'complex' narrative ordering of *So Many Ways to Begin* (McGregor, 2006):

Extract 3.3 Attending to the question #2
```
            [12: 16] - Orchards, So Many Ways to Begin
1    R      it's quite a complex little [er er
2    Co                                  [a lot of books that
            you read [now
3    R                [yeah
4    Co     are written in this way that they [they
5    R                                         [yeah
6    Co     =they dip into the past [and go into the future
7    S                               [yes I think
8    R                               [I think that was clever
            actually
9    S      =this f- yes next question (.) the novel doesn't
            follow a traditional (.) linear (.) narrati[ve
10   R                                                  [yeah
11   S      but unfolds characters' stories using artefacts
            from their lives for a framework for each
            chapter (.) why do you think McGregor chose to
            structure in this way and how effective did you
            find it (.) erm so it's not a linear novel is it
            [it goes backwards forwards
12   Co     [no::: but recently I've read a few books that
            have been written in exactly the same way

            R = Roger; Co = Connie; S = Sue
```

As in Extract 3.2 the group has unwittingly pre-empted the question, before Sue asks it across Turns 9 and 11. Prior to the question being asked, Roger and Connie are discussing the non-chronological narrative structuring of McGregor's novel, which is described as dipping 'into the past' and then 'into the future' (Turn 6). Sue interrupts the flow of the talk in order to ask the question, making a bid for the floor at Turn 7, and securing the floor at Turn 11 by latching onto the end of Roger's turn. As the talk had naturally moved onto the topics covered by the question, it could be seen as odd that the flow of conversation should be broken so that the preset question could be asked. However, after Sue has done this the conversation picks up from the same place as before, with Connie reiterating a point she made a few turns earlier at Turns 2 and 4. The fact that the group does attend to the question (and that inserting the question into the flow of conversation is accepted as a legitimate move) demonstrates the pervasiveness and the importance of these questions, both as organizational devices for the discussion and as 'tasks' to work through. For the Orchards Group, these sets of questions seem to provide support for the legitimacy of the topics naturally covered in their talk. These two examples show the process of reification that the sets of questions have undergone and the close link that the sets of questions have to the group's joint enterprise of interpreting texts.

While the Orchards Group reports finding sets of questions useful as a structuring and focusing device for meetings, the Forest Group and the Wanderers Group generally show less enthusiasm for this resource. On occasion, the use of sets of questions in these groups leads to a formulaic and staid discussion, and at other times groups show playful resistance to the questions. In Extract 3.4, the Forest Group is discussing *Beatrice and Virgil* (Martel, 2010), with Jess asking questions obtained from the publisher's website. For various reasons, this particular discussion is rather staid:

Extract 3.4 Staid response to question

```
         [05.15] - Forest, Beatrice and Virgil
1   Je   right the next question (0.5) what did you think
         of the character Henry (0.5) what purposes do
         you think he served in the novel
2   L    which Henry
3   D    yes which Henry
4   Je   I don't know I didn't read the book so I
         ((laughs)) so I didn't read the book so I don't
         know (1.0) so those who read the book hands up
         (2.0) so no comment then

         Je = Jess; L = Lucy; D = Daniel
```

In this instance, the question is passed over due to the lack of specificity, with Lucy and Daniel asking 'which Henry?' (Turns 2 and 3). In addition, Jess seems to shut down any possible responses with her confession that she did not read the book and her consequent inability to rephrase or answer the question (Turn 4). Contrary to the findings in Benwell et al. (2011), Jess's act of not reading does not seem to make her morally accountable and in the current exchange she seems or orient more to her participant role as questioner than as reader. This kind of exchange was typical of this particular meeting in the Forest Group, with the questions read out, a short amount of time for responses, and then the 'answer' written down on the question-sheet by Jess. However, this kind of staid discussion was unusual in the Forest Group and could be the result of members of the group not having completed the novel rather than the quality of the questions.

Another example taken from the Forest Group shows the readers engaging with a set of questions in a much more dynamic way. Having said this, in this discussion of *The Shack* (Young, 2007) there is a great deal of group resistance to the wording of the questions, which are taken from a fan website:

Extract 3.5 Bias in the questions

```
        [31.29] - Forest, The Shack
1   F   do you think suffering draws people closer to god
        (0.5) churches were full at the time of the Cuba
        crisis weren't they hhhh (1.0)
2   L   mmm
3   F   [fear xxx
4   ?   [xxxxxxxx
5   S       [th- th- the the assumption the assumption of
        this si- it's it's assuming the existence of god
        all the [time y'know
6   L               [mmm yeah
7   J                   [yeah
8   F   =yeah yeah yeah
9   S   =those questions

        F = Frank; L = Lucy; S = Samuel; J = Jess
```

Although the Forest Group often used sets of question to guide their meetings, these questions were not treated uncritically. This resistance was particularly evident in the group's discussion of evangelical Christian novel *The Shack* (Young, 2007), as the readers challenged the partiality of the questions that the librarian, Lucy, had brought along to the group. This attitude towards the questions was part of the group's wider resistance to the perceived ideology of the novel and the readers' attempts to distance themselves from the target audience of the text (for a detailed discussion of this meeting, see Peplow [2014]). On the specific issue of the questions, the group felt that these presupposed that readers were also Christian. The question 'do you think suffering draws people closer to god' (Turn 1) is enunciated by Frank, a member of the group who defines himself as a Christian. At other points in the discussion Frank is keen to appear more offended by the Christian overtones of *The Shack* than any of the other readers, but in this extract he seems to accept the terms of the question and seeks to answer it after a brief pause: 'churches were full at the time of the Cuba crisis weren't they' (Turn 1). Samuel, however, rejects the terms of the question by challenging the underlying assumptions: 'it's assuming the existence of god all the time y'know' (Turn 5). Samuel's statement could equally apply to the novel, as the group had repeatedly stressed that this was one of the major problems with the text. However, in this context Samuel clarifies that he is referring to 'those questions' rather than the novel (Turn 9). This was just one instance of resistance towards the questions from this particular meeting. This opposition was intensified when the readers discovered that the questions were taken from a fan website, with the group feeling justified in adopting a highly sceptical position towards the assumed Christian bias of the questions.

In a similar fashion, the Wanderers Group was sceptical of the authorship of the questions that Hannah brought along to the group's discussion of *Flight Behaviour* (Kingsolver, 2012):

Extract 3.6 'Have we answered the question?'
          [27.30] – Wanderers, *Flight Behaviour*

1	H	right I have got some questions off a website which was American
2	Ma	oh right ((laughs))
3	R	you have got some questions to ask us
4	H	yes
5	R	oh dear
6	H	{exaggerated RP voice} why do so many Americans fear or dislike science (1.0) why do so many others fear or dislike religion (0.5) what impact do these attitudes have on the nation now and what do they portend for our future
7	L	oh gosh
		. . . (group offers answers to the question – 60 seconds of transcript omitted)
8	R	they have even tried to evangelise it into other countries (0.5) I mean there has been you know examples of where they have tried to put money into schools in other countries (1.0) even in the UK where you know they wanted to influence the teaching so it is (1.5) I think it is quite concerning (2.0) have we answered the question ((laughs))

          H = Hannah; Ma = Max; R = Robert; L = Laura

At the start of the extract Hannah announces that she has brought along some questions, taken from an 'American' website (Turn 1). Objectively, the nationality of the questions should be irrelevant but Hannah's detail is heard as a confession by the other members of the group, as demonstrated in their responses: 'oh right' (Turn 2) and 'oh dear' (Turn 5). It is impossible to know what cultural stereotypes are being invoked here but the addition of the 'American' detail appears to draw attention to the dubious provenance of the questions. Hannah's voice quality changes when she asks the question at Turn 6, shifting into an affected form of Received Pronunciation. This shift in voice functions to indicate that the question does not belong to Hannah (i.e. that she is the animator rather than the author), humorously putting some ideological distance between herself and the question and demonstrating that she is not entirely complicit with the wording and/or the content. Although readers in the Wanderers Group respond to the question in a surprised and perhaps sceptical fashion (e.g. Lucy's exclamation at Turn 7) Robert does offer an answer at Turn 8. However, he ends his turn by highlighting the potentially formulaic nature of the question/answer structure of the talk, playfully asking 'have we answered the question?' (Turn 8).

Issues over the provenance and wording of these questions are raised again a few minutes later in the same Wanderers Group meeting:

Extract 3.7 'School marm' questions
```
      [33.32] - Wanderers, Flight Behaviour
1   H   {teacher voice} what is the significance of the
        novel's title (1.0) talk about the imagery of
        flight (0.5) how is it (1.0) {normal voice}
        aren't these sort of school marm sort of
        questions
2   R   pretentious questions (2.0) yes ((laughs))
        . . . (30 seconds of transcript omitted)
3   L   it is a bit like an essay question that isn't it
4   H   [yes
5   Mo  [yes
6   L   =prove this point ((laughs))

        H = Hannah; R = Robert; L = Laura; Mo = Molly
```

Once again, Hannah animates the question in an affected RP accent glossed as 'teacher voice' in the transcript. At the end of Turn 1 she returns to her normal voice to offer an evaluation of the 'school marm' questions. Robert agrees that the questions are 'pretentious' (Turn 2) and thirty seconds later Laura jokes that the question is reminiscent of an essay question for which the student must 'prove this point' (Turns 3 and 6). Although the group is resistant to this question, it is worth noting that readers do subsequently offer answers to it, with Robert in particular suggesting a number of reasons why the novel's title was thematically appropriate.

Sets of questions can help certain groups fulfil their joint enterprise of conducting focused, on-task discussions of the books. For reading groups that use them, these questions tend to encourage certain types of reading, perhaps promoting affiliation with characters and often assuming that readers have enjoyed the book and see some merit in it. However, the readers in the groups studied are not duped into complicity by the questions; they can be, and frequently are, resistant to the ideologies masked by the questions and can see it as their joint enterprise to fashion interpretations and evaluations of the book that go beyond the sometimes narrow confines of the questions. Devlin-Glass (2001) similarly found that some reading groups treated questions and publishers' notes with disdain, but that this often served to bind a group through collective feelings of superiority. Tastes are not just positively asserted but can be justified through refusal of other tastes (Bourdieu, 1984: 49), and this would seem to be true for some of the extracts analysed in this section, where readers subtly or explicitly mark their assessments as different from, and beyond, the tastes and responses implied in some of the questions. So rather than always accepting the legitimacy of the sets of questions, the reading groups frequently enter into a dialogue with them, questioning the questions. For the groups that use them, working through these sets of questions may become a reified practice, but not a practice that is beyond critique.

3.3 Voices of other readers

The second part of this chapter focuses on another resource used in the reading groups: the voices of other readers. In discussing texts, members of face-to-face reading groups are not just in dialogue with others in their group, but are also in interaction with physically absent voices: those of professional literary critics and other 'amateur' readers. On one level this engagement with other voices is inevitable when issues of taste are at stake, whether or not readers are consciously aware of what has been said about a text before. When engaging with artistic works audiences, viewers and readers necessarily create a 'relation of distinction' (Bourdieu, 1984: 224), situating themselves in relation to other consumers. In the reading groups these relations of distinction are being played out constantly, as members compare their readings and literary judgements up against others in the group and those outside the group. In this section, reading group practices that demonstrate this engagement with absent voices are considered; specifically, the Forest Group's practice of looking through customer reviews from the Amazon website and discussions of professional reviews in the Contemporary Group and the Wanderers Group. For the Forest Group, the act of looking through and commenting on the Amazon customer reviews is an important structural element of their meetings, while for the Contemporary Group and the Wanderers Group the invocation of professional reviews is more spontaneous. Both practices, however, are important in shaping the ways in which these groups react to the literary texts under discussion.

3.3.1 Amazon reviews

This section focuses on the Forest Group's use of a particular resource: customer reviews from Amazon. It is argued that using this particular resource provides a focus for a section of the group's meetings and gives the readers the chance to validate their own evaluations and interpretations of literary texts through engagement with the voices of other (physically absent) readers. Although the Forest Group uses a number of resources during meetings in order to facilitate discussion (sets of questions – see Extract 3.4 and Extract 3.5, and newspaper reviews of the text), looking through the customer reviews from Amazon was an important part of each meeting and seemed to afford members of the group the most pleasure. The librarian Lucy brought along these Amazon customer reviews for the readers each month, typically printing off a selection of 5* reviews of the book and a selection of 1* reviews. Roughly half-way through meetings the readers in the *Forest Group* turned to these reviews, often reading them out as reported discourse (see Chapter 4 for an extensive focus on reported discourse) and comparing their own textual responses to those of the Amazon customers. In this way, the readers entered into a dialogic relationship with the Amazon reviewers (Bakhtin, 1981), distinguishing themselves against or aligning themselves with these absent voices.

The *Forest* Group drew on these Amazon reviews in all of their meetings, reporting that this practice helped to facilitate a good discussion of the book. In particular, the group's discussion of *The Shack* (Young, 2007) was enlivened by this process of going through the Amazon reviews. As mentioned earlier in the discussion of Extract 3.5, *The Shack* provoked a strong response in the group (all members loathed it) and a rare occasion when all members were in agreement: 'this must be the first time we've all agreed on a book' (see Peplow, 2014). The group spent much of the meeting attempting (and failing) to comprehend how and why so many people would find *The Shack* so compelling, and how it had become a *New York Times* bestseller (see http://www.nytimes.com/best-sellers-books/2008–06–08/overview.html). The Amazon reviews afforded the group the opportunity to react to, and have a form of dialogue with, specific reviewers' comments – both positive and negative.

As mentioned, members of the Forest Group quoted sections from these reviews. The act of reporting this discourse often served as evidence for the readers' own position. For example, Daniel from the *Forest Group* quotes a 1* customer review of *The Shack* to support his own negative view of the novel:

Extract 3.8 Affiliation with a customer review[2]

    [20:06] – Forest, *The Shack*

1   D   haha I like that (.) 'I kept reading because
          I couldn't believe it could get worse but it
          did' haha

Prefacing the reported discourse with 'I like that' and framing the quoted review with laughter demonstrates Daniel's affinity with the opinion expressed in the review. One of the functions of reported discourse is to provide seemingly objective evidence for a position (Couper-Kuhlen, 2006; Myers, 1999a), and Daniel's act of quoting serves to stress the factuality of his position on the novel. Quoting from the Amazon customers, therefore, often provided the reader with a justification and a 'basis outside their own opinions' for holding their particular view (Myers, 1999a: 387).

This passage of talk continues with Frank and Joan also picking out choice quotations from other 1* Amazon reviews of *The Shack*:

Extract 3.8a – Affiliation with a customer review #2

    [20:06] – Forest, *The Shack*

1   D   haha I like that (.) 'I kept reading because I
          couldn't believe it could get worse but it did'
          haha
          ((laughter))
2   D   very good (2.0) second page (6.0)
3   F   'americanocentric' (.) yeah yeah (.) 'trite'
          yeah I reckon (5.0)
4   J   'overly senti[mental'
5   F   [oh good it says 'whoever compared
          it to pilgrim's progress has never read that
          book' haha mmm (1.0) hohhhh

          D = Daniel, F = Frank; J = Joan

Along with Daniel, Frank and Joan find affinity with the 1* reviews of *The Shack*. Similar to Daniel's positive framing for the quotation at Turn 1, Frank follows his two quotations with agreement: 'yeah I reckon' (Turn 3). Having interrupted Joan's direct quotation as '"overly sentimental"' (Turn 4), Frank introduces a reviewer's comment with 'oh good it says . . . ' (Turn 5). The interrupting interjection 'oh good' serves as a bid to win speaking rights, demonstrating that Frank has something of note to say. Similar to Daniel's assessments 'I like that' (Turn 1) and 'very good' (Turn 2), Frank's 'oh good' displays his positioning in relation to the Amazon reviewer's comment, signalling his solidarity with it (Myers, 1999a: 389–90). The specific point made by the Amazon reviewer (that *The Shack* does not bear any relation to *The Pilgrim's Progress* by John Bunyan) was, in fact, a comment made by Frank earlier in the meeting.

In this short passage of talk the readers in the Forest Group directly quote from Amazon reviews in order to display affinity with these customer comments. In rhetorical terms, the reported discourse serves to provide an evidential basis for the group's negative view of *The Shack*. This evidential aspect of reported discourse is not the only function of the quoted reviews in the *Forest Group*, however, as the Amazon reviews also serve as a series of opinions *against* which the readers can position themselves. More often than not, the readers are not in full agreement with the view expressed in a review, or at the very least do not want to appear to be adopting exactly the same position as that put forward in the review. Rather, the readers subtly position themselves in relation to the quoted Amazon customers, using the reviews to flesh out their own views of the text. The following extracts in this section all involve readers from the Forest Group differentiating themselves from the reviews in this way.

The next example also comes from the Forest Group's discussion of *The Shack*. Predictably, the positive customer reviews of the novel were treated with disdain and, at times, disgust – for example:

Extract 3.9 Reintroducing the death penalty
[14:50] – Forest, *The Shack*

```
1    L    they're all the five (2.0) stars
2    S    hmph
3    J    five [stars
4    S         [hahahahaha
5    F    =hhh
6    J    lord oh lord
```

```
7     S      I reckon that eh the guy that wrote that in
             [xxxxxxxxxx
8     D      [yeah haha
9     F      hhhh I really want to reintroduce the death
             penalty
10    L      and [these
11    J          [they're all wonderful
12    L      they're not (.)th- those ones are all from
             people in England aren't they (3.0)
13    F      oh
14    L      =evangelical [int it
15    D                   ['so much truth in it' (.) ha
16    F      =yeah (2.0)
17    Je     evangelical (4.0)
18    J      'highly recommended to read' hhhhhhh

             L = Lucy; S = Samuel; J = Joan; F = Frank; D =
             Daniel; Je = Jess
```

At the start of this extract Lucy hands out the 5* reviews. Before reading them, members of the group articulate shock and dismay that such opinions could exist at all; most obviously, Joan's incredulous 'five stars?' (Turn 3) displays this, but the members' bemusement can be seen at extralinguistic level too with Samuel's sigh ('hmph' [Turn 2]) and Frank's drawn-out exhalation ('hhhhh' [Turn 5]). Owing to the unanimous negative assessment of *The Shack*, the readers speculate on the sort of person who would like it and who would be moved to give the novel a 5* review. Samuel suggests that the author of the novel could be responsible for the positive reviews (Turn 7), while at line 10 Frank jokes (presumably) that the death penalty should be reintroduced for reviewers that gave the novel 5*. The fact that these positive reviews are from 'England' is another source of collective dismay for the group (Turn 12 and Frank's response at Turn 13). Earlier in the meeting the group had extensively discussed the likely readership of the novel, assuming that only American readers would be inclined to like the novel (see Peplow [2014] for an extended discussion of this process of out-group creation). In the final part of this extract, members of the group quote some of the positive comments from the reviewers, reacting to these with disdain to show their distance from these opinions: for example, Joan's direct quotation followed by an exaggerated drawn-out exhalation: '"highly recommended to read" hhhhhhh' (Turn 18).

The reactions to the Amazon reviews considered so far show the *Forest Group* members positioning themselves in complete agreement or in opposition with reviewers' comments; often, however, members of the group offered more measured agreement or disagreement with the review. For example, the following extract is taken from the group's discussion of *Room* (Donoghue, 2010). Joan is displaying partial agreement with the reviewer:

Extract 3.10 Measured agreement with a reviewer

```
           [20:54] - Forest, Room

1    J    yeah you see I agree with that one xxxx 'to
          using language and understanding concepts that
          is too advanced for a child this age made this
          story unconvincing' (1.0) I mean I felt that
          what he was supposed to know and read and
          everything (.) and then the language he used
          didn't sorta tie with (0.5) what he was (.) you
          know supposed to know and how he could read
          this
2    L    =mmmm
3    J    =and he used words that you wouldn't expect a
          five year old (.) to use or er understand (4.0)
          but I wouldn't say it's 'boring'

          J = Joan; L = Lucy
```

Earlier in the meeting Joan had repeatedly expressed her view that the child-narrator of *Room* was unconvincing, at times highly precocious and at other times very naive. Initially, Joan offers strong agreement with a particular review that criticizes the novel on similar grounds, for overestimating the intelligence of the narrator: 'I agree with that one . . .' (Turn 1). This unmarked and unqualified agreement positions Joan in relation to the reviewer before she quotes the review across the rest of her turn. Having directly quoted the reviewer, however, Joan reiterates her own view, signalling the difference between her voice from that of the Amazon reviewer. She repeats the first-person pronoun to announce the start of her own opinion as distinct from that of the reviewer ('I mean I felt') and then offers her view that the language used by the narrator did not 'tie in' with his broader knowledge (Turn 1). An unmarked agreement that agrees entirely with the view of another can be interpreted by others as a weak position to assume (Heritage, 2002), and Joan seems to be keen to stress her own personal perspective. Following this, there is silence for four seconds as Joan continues to read the review. She then marks her position as obviously different from that of the reviewer, offering a downgraded version (Heritage, 2002; Pomerantz, 1984a) of the reviewer's assessment of the novel: 'but I wouldn't say it's "boring"' (Turn

3). The emphasis Joan places on the reviewer's adjective 'boring' suggests that she sees the reviewer's opinion as too extreme; instead, she carves out a position for herself that is seemingly more measured than that offered in the review.

In Extract 3.11, taken from a few minutes later in the Forest Group's discussion of *Room* (Donoghue, 2010), Joan again positions her own view of the text as similar yet slightly different from a 1* Amazon reviewer. Again, the focus of the review is on the child-narrator in the novel:

Extract 3.11 Upgraded agreement with a reviewer

```
      [24:34] - Forest, Room

1   J   'the lack of consistency used in the baby talk
        also really annoyed me(.) the child using phrases
        such as fasterer and I knowed it could also
        master grammatically challenging hi- hippopotami
        was unrealistic' (.) and well yes bloody annoying
        hahaha (2.0)
```

The direct quotation takes up most of Joan's turn and, as in Extract 3.10, she quotes the review because she largely agrees with the point made in it. In contrast with the previous example, however, Joan offers positive agreement with this review, tagging her own assessment on the end of the review: 'and well yes bloody annoying hahaha'. This time, Joan's assessment upgrades the assessment of the reviewer, offering a more extreme view of the novel than that conveyed by the review. The reviewer's assessment 'unrealistic' is upgraded by Joan to the extreme case formulation 'bloody annoying' when she gives her appraisal of the narrator's voice. As 'ultimate, or end-of-the-continuum expressions' extreme case formulations (ECFs) describe or assess objects in ways that maximize the positive or negative qualities of those things (Edwards, 2007: 33). While ECFs can be rhetorically brittle, these can also be seen to strengthen an opinion by way of displaying a particularly strong commitment to a position; additionally, ECFs can convey a sense that the view is held objectively and not contingently for the purposes of the current interaction (Pomerantz, 1986). In one way, Joan's upgrading of the reviewer's 'unrealistic' to her own 'bloody annoying' may not succeed in making her view appear more objective, as 'bloody annoying' is likely to be seen as a more, subjective opinion than 'unrealistic'; however, Joan's agreement with the reviewer displays strength in numbers, while her deviation away from the opinion of the Amazon reviewer through an upgraded ECF demonstrates that she has reached her own, independent evaluation of the novel rather than just following the view of the reviewer. Combined, these factors may serve to strengthen Joan's evaluation of *Room* in the group context.

Although the extracts discussed so far suggest homogeneity of opinion between the readers in the *Forest Group* in reference to the Amazon reviews, it is actually more common for there to be a split of opinion over the books discussed. It is common for the members of the group to assess the Amazon customer reviews differently from one another and, consequently, for the discussion of customer reviews to display and intensify disagreements between readers. The final example in this section is taken from the group's discussion of *Wolf Hall* (Mantel, 2009). Frank and Samuel both enjoyed *Wolf Hall*, while the other readers present at the meeting (Daniel, Jess, Lucy and Joan) were not impressed by the novel, finding it a difficult and unenjoyable read. This split of opinion caused a certain amount of tension within the group. This tension was evident when the group began discussing the 1* customer reviews of the novel:

Extract 3.12 One star reviews of *Wolf Hall*
        [14:17] – Forest, *Wolf Hall*

1	L	there were eighty-three one star reviews on Amazon
2	Je	hahahaha
3	D	haha[haha
4	S	[hahahaha
5	L	mo- mostly about
6	F	eighty [three
7	L	[the lang you know the way it was written and [er y'know
8	Je	[yeah yeah
9	L	=very confusing and all that
10	Je	it was written in a very confusing language so you know er er
11	L	so we're not on our own
12	Je	this is why you have this book club isn't it (.) cos you're (.) 'I gave up' ha
13	F	I think she put a lot of work into it [and she
14	Je	[that's yeah
15	F	=expects the reader to as well

        L = Lucy; Je = Jess; D = Daniel; S = Samuel; F = Frank

Lucy's introduction of eighty-three 1* reviews is met with incredulity by those who enjoyed the novel, particularly Frank: 'eighty-three?' (Turn 6) and with appreciation by those who disliked the novel. Lucy and Jess summarize these negative reviews as focusing on the 'very confusing' language in the novel (Turns 9 and 10), something that had been discussed at length earlier in the meeting by those who had not enjoyed the novel. Lucy and Jess draw on the high number of 1* reviews ('eighty-three') to validate and support their own negative opinion of the novel, using highly collaborative language to support one another's view. Laughter is vital in this pursuit of intimacy (Jefferson, Sacks and Schegloff, 1987; Coates, 2006) with Jess offering positive back-channelling to Lucy at Turn 8, and Lucy predicting and completing Jess's utterance at Turn 11. Lucy explicitly states that these Amazon reviews serve to validate the negative view of *Wolf Hall* put forward by members of the group, proving that these readers are 'not on our own' (Turn 11). Although there is only one instance of direct reported discourse in this passage ("'I gave up"' [Turn 12]), the reading group members who did not like the book find support for their views in the sheer number of Amazon reviewers who were similarly unimpressed by the book.

As a reader who enjoyed *Wolf Hall*, Frank obviously cannot draw on these 1* star reviews for support; instead, he questions the amount of effort invested by these readers, comparing this with the 'work' that the author has invested (Turns 13 and 15). This serves as a criticism of the 1* reviewers on Amazon and, by association, the readers in the group who offered negative assessments of the novel. This appeal to the authority of the writer seems to be an effective argument from Frank, albeit one that is potentially face-threatening to the readers who did not like the novel as it implies that they have read the novel in a superficial manner (and that Frank has *not* read it in this way). Frank's point is difficult to argue against because he equates not liking the novel with a lack of readerly effort, while also drawing on his perception of authorial effort, both of which are difficult to assess or quantify.

In the *Forest Group*, these Amazon customer reviews have become important documents through which the group members articulate their own evaluations of texts. Whether these reviews are used to validate a particular view or to challenge a view, these documents serve as an important focal point of the meetings, allowing the readers to share the reading experience with absent others, even if group members do not always agree with their evaluations and interpretations of texts.

3.3.2 Professional reviews

So far, this chapter has focused on various external voices that are brought into, and affect, reading group discussion. These voices, in the form of sets of questions and Amazon customer reviews, have served an explicit structuring purpose for the groups, providing them with ways of organizing their meetings. In this section the professional review is considered as another form of external voice, although the groups' invocations of these voices do not constitute a recurrent practice. Unlike the sets of questions and the Amazon reviews, the professional reviews do not serve to structure meetings as such but do provide an important sets of voices against which the readers measure their own responses to literary texts.

Through adorning book covers and inside covers with reviews, modern book publishing practices allow readers to engage with other views on the text they are reading. The express purpose of placing these positive reviews on selected parts of the paratext is to sell the text, encouraging the would-be reader to buy and read the book (Genette, 1997: 20). Even if the professional reviews do not affect a reader's decision to buy a book, these paratextual elements may come to influence the reading of the book subsequently. Readers may flick between the paratext and the text during the reading process, contextualizing their own views on the book in relation to critics' reviews. As with the use of sets of questions and Amazon customer reviews, the professional reviews considered in this section are oriented to in various ways by the readers: on some occasions the voices of critics are used as support for the readers' view, while at other times these reviews are collectively mocked by groups. Bourdieu argues that the distinction in taste between 'intellectuals and artists' and the 'general public' can appear to be absolute, with intellectuals looking 'suspiciously . . . at dazzlingly successful works and authors' (1993: 116). In a similar but different way, the members of the reading groups may reverse this logic, looking 'suspiciously' at texts that have received critical acclaim by 'intellectuals'.

As mentioned, readers often move between text and paratext when offering their opinions on the book under discussion. Readers can report moving between professional review and main text during their solitary reading of the novel or they can do this on-the-hoof during the social reading that takes place in reading groups. In the following extract Ben from the Contemporary Group reports his experience of reading a review of *The Lighthouse* (Moore, 2012) while reading the novel:

Extract 3.13 'Maybe it is not just me'

       [7:20] – Contemporary, *The Lighthouse*

1   B   and I was thinking (0.5) ooh his prose style
           reminds me of Magnus Mills

2   Lu   yeah [xxxx

3   B   [and I looked on the back and it said his
           prose style is very much ((laughs)) so I thought
           oh right so maybe it is not just me

           B = Ben; Lu = Lucia

Ben reports seeing stylistic similarities between the writing of Alison Moore (author of *The Lighthouse*) and Magnus Mills, and then having this opinion corroborated by the review 'on the back' (Turn 3). Throughout this brief passage of talk Ben uses reported discourse to relate the story of his private reading (see Section 4.2.1 for more examples of this form of reported discourse). At Turn 1 he describes his thoughts while reading using direct thought, claiming that at the time of reading he 'was thinking' of the stylistic similarities. In doing this he provides an evidential and historical basis for his opinion, demonstrating that he held the view at the time of reading. Following this, Ben reports finding a similar view being offered by a critic on the blurb of the book: 'it said his prose . . . ' (Turn 3). He then moves back into his own direct thought at the time of reading to relate his feeling of affinity with the review and his pleasure at having the validity of his view confirmed: 'it is not just me' (Turn 3). The chronological ordering of Ben's story and the use of direct thought are important, as these allow him to demonstrate that the stylistic similarities between the two writers was something he noticed independently. At the same time, invoking the professional review from the paratext provides support for this view.

In a similar fashion, three members of the Wanderers Group invoke professional reviews in order to justify their enjoyment of *An Officer and a Spy* (Harris, 2013):

Extract 3.14 Using reviews and literary award as support

       [37:00] – Wanderers, *Officer and a Spy*

1   J   I just thought it was just (1.0) and apparently
           it is very (.) very (0.5) >well according to the
           reviews< it is very very much to (.) to you know
           to the actual

2   H   =yes

3   R   =I believe so [yes

4   H   [it has won

5   J   =events yes

6   H   the Steel Dagger award

           J = Jenny; H = Hannah; R = Robert

An Officer and a Spy (Harris, 2013) is a fictional retelling of the Dreyfus Affair, and at Turn 1 Jenny praises the novel for being an accurate depiction of this political event, citing 'reviews' as the source of this opinion. Hannah and Robert agree, respectively latching on to the end of each others' utterances to show their affiliation (Turns 2 and 3). Hannah goes on to cite 'the Steel Dagger award' as another professional critical resource that demonstrates the quality of the novel (Turns 4 and 6). Like Jenny's invocation of the 'reviews', Hannah's mention of the prestigious award serves to provide external evidence for the group's positive reaction to the novel.

Not all reviews are treated in this positive fashion, however. On occasion, the reading groups treated critical acclaim with disdain, especially if readers felt that a particular text had been overhyped by critics. Two passages of talk from two different reading groups are presented below in which professional reviews are challenged by readers. In the first example newspaper reviews of *The Windsor Faction* (2013) are mocked, and in the second reviews from the paratext of *Tinkers* (Harding, 2009) are criticized. In each instance, this challenge to the professional review serves to affirm the group's collective negative view, creating an out-group of literary critics who have been duped by the text.

In Extract 3.15 the Wanderers Group is discussing newspaper reviews of *The Windsor Faction* (2013), a novel that received highly negative assessment from all but one reader in the group:

Extract 3.15 'Incremental creep' or 'nothing happens'?
        [37:05] – Wanderers, *The Windsor Faction*

```
1    Mi   the Telegraph says erm (0.5) Telegraph liked it
          erm
2    R    =it would
3    Mi   erm [the
4    H        [well a lot of papers did a lot [of them did
5    Mi                                        [the
          Independent liked it [yes
6    Ma                        [yeah
7    R                         [they would
8    Mi   =it says (.) 'in less skilful hands this sort
          of fictional game' (1.0)
9    L    yeah
10   J    =mmm
11   Mi   being on the other corner when another bus goes
          past (.) >as you say< (.) 'can produce fairly
          crude cartoons' >blah blah blah< (.) 'it is
          much harder to show historical change occurring
          through (1.0) incremental creep' (1.0)
```

```
12   L    oh
13   J    =oh (.) now that's quite
14   Mi   ='rather than sudden swerves of direction'
          (0.5) well if you want
15   R    =that's a polite way of saying [nothing happens
16   Mi                                  ['incremental
          creep'
          ((laughter))
17   R    isn't it (.) let's be honest
18   H    =oh but that lovely bit of John Betjeman
19   Mi   =yes
20   H    =and that was true
21   Mi   I have a feeling incremental creep is going to
          pass into the vocabulary
          ((laughter))

          Mi = Miriam; R = Robert; H = Hannah; Ma = Max;
          L = Laura; J = Jenny
```

Hannah was the only reader in the Wanderers Group to report enjoying *The Windsor Faction*, with the other readers offering highly negative assessments of the novel – as is evident in Extract 3.15. Here, the readers present and critique the views of British newspapers that have positively reviewed the novel. Miriam presents the views of two British broadsheets in particular, the *Daily Telegraph* and *The Independent*, offering a very general paraphrase of the *Daily Telegraph*'s review ('Telegraph liked it', Turn 1) and directly quoting from the review in *The Independent* (Turn 5). Robert is nonplussed after hearing that the *Daily Telegraph* reviewed the novel positively ('it would', Turn 2), and he is equally unsurprised to hear that the other newspapers evaluated the novel similarly ('they would', Turn 7). For Robert at least, the newspaper reviewers are predisposed to like a novel such as *The Windsor Faction*, although neither he nor the other readers goes into detail as to why this should be the case.[3] Miriam goes on to quote from the review published in *The Independent* across Turns 8, 11 and 14, with Laura, Jenny and Robert offering evaluations on the quotation as she reads: Laura and Jenny react with bemusement ('oh', 'oh now that's quite'), which may be in response to the content of the review (i.e. the fact that it is so positive) or a reaction to the tone used in the review, or perhaps a mixture of both. Robert's evaluation of the quotation from *The Independent* is less equivocal, as his paraphrase of the review criticizes both the tone and content: 'that's a polite way of saying nothing happens' (Turn 15). Although Miriam has brought the reviews and read the quotation from *The Independent*, she also displays her distance from these along with the other readers, inserting negative evaluations as she reads ('blah blah blah' – Turn 11) and placing emphasis on a particular phrase from the review: 'incremental creep'. This phrase is stressed in the first reading (Turn 11), repeated in a decontextualized fashion at Turn 16, and then returned to again at Turn 21 when Miriam humourously comments that 'incremental creep' will become part of the group's vocabulary. The 'polite' and pretentious way of discussing books associated with professional reviews is placed in oppositon to the reading group's apparently more honest reviewing, and this distinction serves to validate the readers' views, especially the views of those readers who assessed the novel negatively.

The newspaper reviews are variously criticized on three counts: having a vested interest in praising *The Windsor Faction*, giving unwarranted acclaim to the novel, and adopting a pretentious literary critical tone. However, this critical stance is not shared by all members of the group; Hannah invokes the positive reviews as evidence for the quality of the novel (Turn 4), just as readers did in Extracts 3.13 and 3.14. She is in the minority here, however, and the rest of the group find ways to critique the position and tone of the newspaper reviews, which seems to trump Hannah's argument.

In the final example of readers orienting to professional reviews, the Contemporary Group compares their textual responses to those of critics. The novel under discussion in this meeting was *Tinkers* (Harding, 2009) and the voice of the critic is quoted from the paratext – the back-cover of the novel. Debbie selected the novel to be read by the group and at the start of Extract 3.16 she is discussing why she chose the novel for the group:

Extract 3.16 Professional reviews and the 'emperor's new clothes'

       [41:09] – Contemporary, *Tinkers*

1   D   it's just such (.) it is a really (.) it was a
          really mixed bag (1.0) that got great reviews
          (0.5) and erm (1.0) and given that it was short
          asking people to read it (.) and seeing what
          other people thought (.) I didn't think would
          be too onerous (0.5) to see what other people
          thought about it because I just wasn't really
          entirely sure what to make of it
          . . . (30 seconds of transcript omitted)
          if you read Barry Unsworth who was the one (.) we
          read him for something (.) erm (2.0) 'there's a
          striking freedom of style here which allows the
          author to move without any sense of strain or
          loss of balance' (.) well I would disagree with
          any sense of strain or any loss [of balance

2	M	[hahaha mmm
3	L	[mmm yeah

4   D   'from the very ecstatic to the exquisitely
        precise' (0.5) so again they're saying that it
        <moves> without y'know (.) that it just flows

5   R   =mmm

6   D   =and if anything it doesn't flow (.) it's like
        you read something really good and then you get
        this turgid bit (.) that's y'know your word is
        good (0.5) and then you re- you get (.) you push
        yourself through that because as you say it's
        very short so (1.0) but it's the kinda thing
        where again it sorta pushes you to read it cos
        [it's

7   L   [maybe

8   D   =like because you've read all this and they say
        it's fabulous you think well (.) [wh-

9   L   [do

10 D   =wh- if I just keep reading
        [maybe it'll get there

11 R   [mmm

12 L   [ha do you think all the reviewers have done what
        we've done because I kinda skim read those bits
      · (.) admittedly quite fast thinking (.) xxx the
        main one was I noticed he was trying to describe
        a lake and I just kinda went I don't understand
        why

13 M   [no

14 D   [yeah

15 L   and just kinda skim read it and carried on (0.5)
        and do you think all the reviewers have done what
        I've done and thought (0.5) maybe there's some
        meaning in this that I can't see

16 D   =yeah

17 L   so they've reviewed it in a kinda emperor's new
        clothes kinda way because they like some bits

        D = Debbie; M = Mark; R = Richard; L = Lizzie

Tinkers provoked a mixed response from the Contemporary Group. Parts
of the novel were seen as being fantastically well-written, while other parts
were regarded as 'turgid' (Turn 6). This ambivalence was thrown into light
when praise for the novel was discussed and, although it is not mentioned

in Extract 3.16, also by the fact that *Tinkers* won the 2010 Pulitzer Prize for Fiction – an accolade advertised on the paratext. At the start of the extract Debbie justifies suggesting the book to the group in terms of her own personal reading experience, remarking that she wanted the group to read the novel because she 'wasn't really entirely sure what to make of it' (Turn 1). Debbie appeals to a form of cultural authority, citing the 'great reviews' that *Tinkers* received from critics (Turn 1), placing these reviews against her own less enthusiastic view of the novel. Given the cultural capital (Bourdieu, 1977, 1984) of literary critics as supposed reading experts, it is potentially difficult for a non-academic book group member to challenge such an authority single-handedly. However, as with the reading groups' criticism of the sets of reading group questions explored in Section 3.2, this action of dissent is not as difficult if undertaken as a group. In Extract 3.16 members of the Contemporary Group distinguish their views on the novel from that of the critics, and question the basis on which the critics came to their readings of the text.

Debbie quotes two parts from Barry Unsworth's review on the back-cover of the novel. The first part of the quotation runs as follows:

There's a striking freedom of style here which allows the author to move . . . without any sense of strain or loss of balance. (Turn 1)

Having quoted this, Debbie gives her negative evaluation of Unsworth's opinion: 'well I would disagree with any sense of strain or any loss of balance' (Turn 1). Prefacing her disagreement with a dispreferred turn marker 'well' (Pomerantz, 1984a), Debbie indicates that the act of dissent she is performing is potentially problematic. As a display of agreement and support for this potentially problematic position, three group members chime in with affiliative overlaps while Debbie is still speaking (Kitzinger, 2008; Tannen, 1984): 'yeah . . . mmm yeah . . . yeah' (Turns 2 and 3). Debbie then continues to quote from the review:

From the very ecstatic to the exquisitely precise. (Turn 4)

Debbie offers her own paraphrase of the quoted section immediately after:

So again they're saying that it moves without y'know, that it just flows. (Turn 4)

In her paraphrase, Debbie uses the plural pronoun 'they', suggesting that Unsworth's view is the one widely held by a homogeneous out-group of literary critics.

After this Debbie presents her own view in relation to Unsworth's quoted comment:

> And if anything it doesn't flow, it's like you read something really good and then you get this turgid bit, that's y'know your word is good.(Turn 6)

Perhaps because she has received positive feedback for her earlier criticism of the critic (Turns 2, 3 and 5), Debbie now seems more forthright in the presentation of her disagreement with literary critic Unsworth. This can be seen at the level of the turn design, as Debbie does not mitigate her view with any hedges, nor does she preface her disagreement with a dispreferred turn marker. When offering an evidential basis for her opinion, Debbie inserts a brief side sequence (Jefferson, 1972; Schegloff, 2007), quoting one of the other members' comments from earlier in the meeting. Richard had previously described the writing style in *Tinkers* as 'turgid' and Debbie quotes him here, acknowledging the source of the word in its present context: 'your word is good' (Turn 6). The adjective 'turgid' to describe the novel's style is directly contrasted with Unsworth's idea that the style is 'ecstatic' and 'precise' (Turn 4). So just as intragroup collaboration is seen in the feedback support that Debbie receives for her initial dismissal of Unsworth's review, this collaboration is also evident in Debbie's repetition (Tannen, 2007) of Richard's earlier word 'turgid' and in her metadiscursive address to Richard: 'your word is good'. This reciprocal show of support allows the group to accomplish the potentially difficult task of taking on the professional, expert critic.

Having differentiated themselves from what is seen as the accepted critical opinion of the novel as a masterpiece, the Contemporary Group then moves on to surmise how these literary critics might have reached their positive view of the text. Towards the end of Extract 3.16 the group present their negative view of the novel as based on more solid ground than that of the critics. Across two turns Lizzie describes her reading experience, citing her reading of a passage in the novel in which a lake is described:

> The main one was I noticed he was trying to describe a lake and I just kinda went I don't understand why . . . and just kinda skim read it and carried on, and do you think all the reviewers have done what I've done and thought, maybe there's some meaning in this that I . . . can't see. (Turns 12 and 15)

Recounting her personal reading experience, Lizzie positions herself alongside 'all the reviewers' (Turn 15), rhetorically asking if she, and the reviewers, have looked for meaning in the novel when it is not really there. Given what has been said in the group's meeting, Lizzie then distinguishes herself from the fawning reviewers:

> So they've reviewed it in a kinda emperor's new clothes kinda way because they like some bits. (Turn 17)

Like some of the other members of the group (e.g. Debbie), Lizzie seemed to arrive at the meeting uncertain as to how to assess the novel. However, through collaboration, the sharing of ideas and hearing others' opinions Lizzie came to the conclusion that *Tinkers* was as much poorly written as it was well-wrought. By contrast, in her view the reviewers have been duped by the novel, attaching meaning when it is not there and following a fad in an 'emperor's new clothes kinda way' (Turn 17). Throughout this passage, the Contemporary Group creates an 'Us vs. Them' dichotomy between themselves and the critics. Presenting the critics' perspectives as mistakenly biased ultimately serves to validate the group's sceptical view of the novel, and crucially, this difficult task is achieved as a group.

This practice of creating distinctions between the tastes of literary critics and the tastes of the reading group members is highly evident in Extracts 3.15 and 3.16, but is not restricted to these examples (see also Extracts 3.5 and 3.7, in which the sets of questions are evaluated as biased and 'pretentious', respectively). Where these distinctions of taste are made, the groups are defining their own interpretative practices up against an elite group, the literary establishment. We might expect that a non-academic reading group would defer to the cultural authority of professional critics, just as in Bourdieu's work the 'working-class aesthetic' is often 'obliged to define itself in terms of the dominant aesthetics' (1984: 41), but this is not what happens in practice. Deference may be the norm when individuals take on powerful symbols of cultural capital, but when this resistance to intellectual opinion is performed as a group there seems to be more confidence displayed in the legitimacy of this resistance to assumed cultural capital (see also Procter and Benwell, 2014: 27).

To conclude this section, the use of reading group resources is highly prevalent in the groups studied and across reading groups more widely. These resources often take the form of external voices: sets of questions and reviews ('professional' or 'customer'), and the reading groups draw on these voices in order to contribute towards the joint enterprise. Even when a reading group does not use any 'official' reading group resources it can be seen engaging in dialogue with external voices; just as the Forest Group enters into dialogue with the Amazon reviews (often to validate members' views on the text) the

Wanderers Group and the Contemporary Group both take on the views of professional critics.

These documents can give the groups that use them focus, keeping those groups that want to engage in a serious discussion 'on-task'. This function of keeping groups 'on-task' was seen as a particular benefit of the sets of questions used by some of the groups (see Extract 3.1). For the groups that use this resource, the questions can be quite strictly adhered to leading to rather odd passages of talk in which a member of the group stops the conversation in order to ask a question that has already been 'answered' by the group in the natural flow of talk (Extract 3.3). However, the reading groups that use them do not blindly accept the authority of these resources unquestioningly (see Extracts 3.5–3.7). Discussing joint enterprise, Wenger (1998: 58–9) considers the ways in which the workers rebel against the institutional systems and documents that shape their day-to-day work (e.g. targets, procedures, forms), negotiating more effective ways of carrying out their tasks. Similarly, the reading groups in this study tend to positively orient to the resources, such as sets of questions, where these are useful for producing a good discussion and challenging them when they feel, say, that particular questions are poorly expressed, biased or not in keeping with the tone of the group's discussions. For the groups in this study that disputed the legitimacy and/or appropriateness of the sets of questions or the professional critical opinions, these collective acts of resistance encouraged 'bonding' within groups (Devlin-Glass, 2001: 579). Compared to the workplace CofPs that Wenger (1998) and Lave and Wenger (1991) were concerned with, this element of rebellion from the strictures of the 'reified' documents (Wenger, 1998: 58–9) seems to be even more apparent in the reading groups.

In spite of the ways in which the reading groups' organization and discourse resemble that of workplaces (Peplow et al., 2015: Chapter 5), reading group meetings ultimately form part of members' leisure-time in which members decide for themselves how meetings are to be organized. In spite of this being leisure time, however, tensions can emerge in groups when 'official' protocol is challenged as shown in the next section.

3.4. Reader roles and rules in the Contemporary Group

In her discussion of nineteenth-century all-female book clubs, Long (2003) notes that these groups were strictly organized and usually had a 'constitution and by-laws in place after only a few meetings' (2003: 39). While contemporary reading groups do not tend to be organized in quite such a rigorous fashion, there is evidence from the present study that some groups have developed particular ways of structuring their meetings. This section focuses on the Contemporary Group and the specific organizational practices used within this group. These practices have developed over time in the group but are not liked or adhered to by all members. In the following extracts the nature of these practices is considered, as well as how resistance to these perceived 'rules' is presented. Throughout the discussion we consider what these procedures and disputes indicate about joint enterprise within this reading group.

Rather than using sets of questions or any other external, official organizing resource, the Contemporary Group has developed its own ways of structuring meetings. As demonstrated in Section 3.3.2, the readers in this group bring in professional reviews to their discussions, but these external voices are invoked in a rather ad hoc manner, with no obvious procedure evident or any specific time in the meeting dedicated to discussion of these reviews (unlike the Forest Group's use of Amazon customer reviews, for instance). The rules that the Contemporary Group has devised for its meetings seem to stand in the place of sets of questions that other groups might use, offering a form of structure to the meetings with the intended aim of keeping the group on-task. In addition, the express intention of the rules is to ensure that good books are read by the group and that no one reader dominates the discussion.

The three rules that govern the Contemporary Group's meetings concern book selection and the organization of talk within meetings; these rules are as follows:

1. The book read by the group must be recommended by one member. This member must have read the book prior to recommending.
2. At the start of each meeting there is time dedicated for each reader to have their uninterrupted say on the book.
3. During this phase of the meeting, the member who recommended the book has their say last.

Richard is the main proponent of the rules and he explained these to me during our interview, justifying why these procedures are used. He explained to me the origin of the first rule (that the recommender must have read the book before suggesting):

Extract 3.17 Book recommendation rule

        [22:01] – Contemporary, *Richard interview*

```
1    R    I recommended two books which sounded
          absolutely brilliant in the reviews I had
          read in the Guardian and turned out to be (.)
          appalling (0.5) and so we (.) that was our first
          rule that we would only recommend books that
          we had actually had (0.5) direct experience of
          rather than indirect experience
```

The first rule came into existence following Richard's own errors in which he unwittingly recommended two 'appalling' books. He then went on to explain how a similar mistake had been made recently by a new member, Colin:

Extract 3.17a Book recommendation rule

```
3    R    erm. . . (2.0) and that has <been fairly
          successful> other than I think Colin wasn't aware
          (.) of our procedure (.)

4    D    mmhm

5    R    and when (0.5) I can't remember what the book was
          (.) that we absolutely lambasted but it was quite
          embarrassing because he had recommended it

6    D    ha

7    R    and erm (.) it transpired that he had it on his
          bookshelf and had just taken it off the bookshelf
          and hadn't read it (.) but just recommended it
          because he had it (1.0) and he didn't like it
          either (0.5) and I mean to my mind I think it is
          absolutely frustrating to propose a book (.) that
          you either haven't read or when you do read it
          don't like it anyway (.) I mean what a waste of
          time

          R = Richard; D = David (interviewer)
```

A situation is described where Colin recently recommended a book that had been sitting on his bookcase but that he had not yet read. The book was subsequently 'lambasted' by the group, and by Colin. For Richard, reading a book for the group that no-one enjoyed was a 'waste of time' (Turn 7) and the express aim of this first rule is to ensure that at least one member of the group enjoys the book and can defend it, if necessary.

The second rule concerns the organization of discussion in meetings, with a single floor (Edelsky, 1981) operating, at least at the start of meetings. In our interview Richard explained this rule and the rationale for it:

Extract 3.18 One person speaks rule

```
     [24:45] - Contemporary, Richard interview

1    R    some of the people in the group weren't (1.0)
          very forthcoming in (1.0) talking (.) was that
          (1.5) it wasn't a free for all (0.5) that there
          was a sequence in which people (.) which didn't
          mean other people couldn't (.) add their bit
          during the time when somebody spoke (.)but they
          weren't dominant (0.5) if you know what I mean
```

According to Richard, the second rule ensures that there is a 'sequence' in which readers speak as opposed to a 'free for all'. This rule allows those in the group who are not 'very forthcoming' to have their chance to speak. He then went on to give Lucia as an example of a member who benefits from this rule, as she 'is very reserved'; for Richard, the group ultimately profits from Lucia's input because she 'has a lot to offer'.

The third rule brings together the previous two rules, stating that the member who recommended that the book should have his/her turn at talk last. Richard explained the reason for this rule:

Extract 3.19 Book recommender speaks last rule

       [23:35] – Contemporary, *Richard interview*

```
1   R   the person who recommends the book goes last
        . . . (30 seconds of transcript omitted)
        it is quite frustrating when somebody who has
        recommended the book goes first (0.5) because they
        go into a large amount of detail of the book that
        you have just read yourself (.) so you don't need
        that
```

As with the second rule, this third rule aims to ensure that all members have reasonably equal access to the floor at the start of the meeting. In the third rule, the focus has shifted from just enabling all readers to have access (as in rule two) and towards all readers have equal quality of access to the floor.

Although these three rules reportedly came out of discussions that the group had a few years ago when members were deciding how best to organize their meetings, Richard is the member of the group who now seems to be most committed to upholding the rules. Despite Richard's enthusiasm, other members of the Contemporary Group actively challenge the rules, and some instances of this dissent are considered later in this section. Richard has been a member of the group since it started, around 15 years ago, and has been regularly attending ever since. Owing to his long service to the group and, in particular, because of his enthusiasm for the group's rules and its special methods of organization, Richard is a core member of the CofP. Aside from upholding the rules of the group, Richard also acts as an informal moderator or facilitator in meetings, as the following extract demonstrates:

Extract 3.20 Richard as informal chair

```
        [26.52] Contemporary, The Lowland
1    R    now you've described the book (1.0) what did you
          think of it though
2    M    what did I think of it
3    R    =yes (0.5)
4    M    erm (3.0) well I would have shortened it
          ((laughs)) it was >it was very long< I thought
          (.) I always think that the most interesting
          thing of books like that <is that when people
          move> into a different culture and what it does
          to them (1.0) I think that is the real interest
          to me about the book
5    R    xxx did you like it
6    M    =oh yes
7    R    =yes
8    M    =I enjoyed particularly enjoyed reading it
          Richard like you
9    R    =oh yes
10   M    =yes
11   R    =would you (.) would you read another of her
          books
12   M    =yes (0.5) erm (1.5) but I have learnt often wi-
          with that I don't want to read a book (.) before
          this one was published
13   R    yeah I know what you mean

          R = Richard; M = Mark
```

Immediately before this extract, Mark had been offering his view of *The Lowland* (Lahiri, 2013) in a single floor fashion, according to the group's second rule. At the start of this extract, he has come to the end of his comments and Richard prompts him with a question: 'what did you think of it though' (Turn 1). Following a request for clarification from Mark and an affirmative from Richard (Turns 2 and 3), Mark answers the question by offering his assessment of the novel. Evidently Mark's response still does not answer Richard's question, and Richard rephrases again: 'did you like it' (Turn 5). Mark's responses now seem more appropriate (as far as Richard is concerned) and Richard moves on to ask a different question at Turn 11. In this passage of talk Richard offers no opinions on the novel, except for perhaps Turn 13 where he provides agreement with some elaboration; for the most part, he just prompts Mark with questions, seemingly adopting the role of an impartial group facilitator. Richard's conduct here is fairly typical of his behaviour in the group and goes towards creating his position in the Contemporary Group as a central member who enables others to talk and, further to this, encourages others to talk about the book under discussion in an orderly and focused fashion. At the same time, the privileged role that Richard has assumed as organizer and, at times, impartial facilitator puts him at a remove from the rest of the group. This is particularly evident when challenges are made to the rules, as examples below demonstrate.

The first challenge to the group's rules presented here comes from the Contemporary Group's discussion of *Americanah* (Adichie, 2013). This is new member Colin's first meeting and at the start of the meeting Richard explained the rules to him:

Extract 3.21 Explaining the rules to Colin

[2:10] - Contemporary, *Americanah*

1	R	Colin (.) you might want to go towards the end to see how everyone performs or not
2	L	=ha
3	R	=<u>ideally</u> (1.0) one person speaks (0.5) and then the next person speaks and so on (.) rather than we all chip in
4	M	but
5	R	=but normally a certain person would chip in whatever happens erm
6	M	=no I am being
7	C	=naming no names
8	M	=very controlled
9	R	=naming no [names
10	L	[there is a kind of chip in when issues are raised isn't there
11	R	=yes [yes
12	D	[yes
13	C	=ok
14	D	=it's not quite so
15	L	yes that's right
16	R	=[formal
17	D	=[prescribed at that yes (.)but it just we want to make sure everybody gets a chance (0.5) but (1.0) I I like having a conversation
18	R	absolutely
19	C	well everyone gets to make like (.) an (0.5) opening [statement

```
20   R               [yeah
21   D               [yeah
22   C      =but then there is the
23   R      it's just that some people's (.) opening
            [statements
24   D      [hahaha
25   R      =are slightly longer than other people's
            opening [statements
26   L               [hahaha
27   D      I would (.) kick him under [the table
28   R                                 [haha
29   M      =no (.) I I I I am saying nowt

            R = Richard; L = Lizzie; M = Mark; C = Colin;
            D = Debbie
```

As in Extract 3.20 Richard adopts the role of the chair, taking it upon himself to explain the rules of the group to Colin. As a new member Colin is a marginal member of the CofP, and Richard's summary of the one-at-a-time rule at the start of the extract (across Turns 1, 3 and 5) attempts to grant Colin access to the legitimate participation in the group's practices. In a CofP, 'learning involves gradually increasing participation' (Holmes and Woodhams, 2013: 276) and in this extract Richard explains the rules of the group and provides Colin with some insider knowledge about the group, telling him that 'normally a certain person would chip in whatever happens'. Richard is referring to Mark, who often unwittingly transgresses the one-person-speaks rule in his enthusiasm for conversation. Although this could be contrued as face-threatening behaviour from Richard, the talk at this stage is good-humoured, with Mark promising to be 'very controlled' on this occasion. Lizzie attempts to appease the situation by arguing for a position that upholds the rule but also Mark's transgressive past behaviour, stating that members of the group typically 'chip in when issues are raised' (Turn 10). Debbie agrees with Lizzie, arguing that the organization of the talk is not so 'prescribed' as Richard's earlier description suggested, but that the purpose of the rule is to ensure that 'everybody gets a chance' to speak (Turn 17). Following some brief hesitation, Debbie goes on to say that she likes 'having a conversation', something which she implies is not readily facilitated in the 'prescribed' rules set out in Richard's conceptions of the rules. Colin gives his understanding of the rule across Turns 19 and 22, and Richard offers mitigated agreement with this understanding, picking up on Colin's notion of 'opening statements' but stating that some members' opening statements (i.e. Mark's) are 'longer than others' (Turn 25). Again, no names are mentioned but they do not need to be in this CofP, in which it is a running in-joke that Mark talks more than other members. The rest of the group understand Mark to be the referent of Richard's light-hearted dig, and Debbie offers to kick Richard under the table on behalf of Mark (Turn 27). The passage of talk ends with Mark professing to say 'nowt'[4] on the issue or in his defence.

The tone of Extract 3.21 is light-hearted, but the act of explaining the group's procedures to newcomer Colin does give rise to some tension as members of the group offer slightly different conceptions of the one person speaks rule. Debbie's point at Turn 17 in particular implies that Richard's understanding of the rule is overly prescriptive and does not allow for free-flowing conversation. At the same time, the existing members of the group indulge in shared jokes across the extract, humorously and indirectly reflecting on the frequency with which the one-person-speaks rule is broken. Mark is the butt of this joke but he seems to take it in good humour, and it is testament to the friendly and welcoming nature of this group that Colin is allowed to join in on the joke (Turn 7) even though he is a marginal member of the group.

Before moving on to a less amicable passage of talk in which the Contemporary Group debate the legitimacy of the rules, two brief extracts are presented from meetings where Richard was not present. In both extracts Mark and Debbie discuss how the group should organize the meetings with Richard absent:

Extract 3.22 Rebelling from the rules
[17:30] - Contemporary, *Mouse and the Cossacks*

1	M	sorry you go on about the book (0.5) I am just [xxx
2	D	[no no no I am happier when we do it like this ha
3	M	=you are happier when we do it like this
4	D	=yes (.) I don't like it
5	M	=you would rather do it (.) that's fine
6	D	=and when Richard is here
7	M	he wants everything scientifically down in a line doesn't he
8	D	yes (0.5) no

M = Mark; D = Debbie

Extract 3.23 'Can we just talk?'

```
       [5:50] - Contemporary, The Unfortunates
1   M   ok is there a rule or can we just talk
2   D   we can just talk
        ((laughter))
3   M   I loved it (0.5) I thought it was fantastic
        M = Mark; D = Debbie
```

In the first example Mark apologizes for talking at length about the book (not included in the extract) and for talking over Debbie (Turn 1). Debbie dismisses his apology and they agree that they would be 'happier' doing away with the rules (Turns 2 and 3). Between Turns 6 and 7 the two members discuss Richard explicitly, jointly constructing the idea that his application of the rules is too 'scientific' and that this application presumably, stifles conversation. Similarly in Extract 3.23 Debbie and Mark jointly decide that the group can 'just talk' (Turns 1 and 2) as Richard is absent; a decision that seemed to be welcomed by the other members present at that particular meeting.

With Richard absent, therefore, members of the Contemporary Group decide to abandon the rules and 'just talk'. It is quite evident that a spilt has developed within the group over the application of the rules and this divide was most apparent during a passage of talk in the group's meeting on *Fragrant Harbour* (Lanchester, 2002). Once the group had finished discussing the novel, Richard takes the opportunity to ask for the members' views on the rules:

Extract 3.24 Extended discussion of the rules

```
       [39:20] - Contemporary, Fragrant Harbour
1   R   I would like to have your opinion because we
        have generated a kind of (1.0) ad hoc set of (.)
        inverted commas (.) rules through our experience
        (0.5) the first rule I have been talking to Colin
        about (0.5) is we don't recommend a book that we
        haven't read
2   M   yes
3   R   because reviews don't (.) reviewers don't write
        about the books they have xxxx reviews on (1.0)
        I remember myself recommending two books because
        there were glowing reviews in the Guardian and
        they were (.) appalling (0.5) so that's the first
        thing (0.5) the second thing is (.) that the
        person who recommends the book goes last (.)
        because we've all read [the book
```

4	M	[yeah yeah
5	R	=we don't need to have a great [exposition
6	M	[yeah yeah
7	R	by the person (0.5) and the third thing is that (.) because some people talk (0.5) less easily than others (0.5) I am on the other end of the spectrum as far as that is concerned (0.5) we make sure that everybody has a chance to speak (0.5) so rather than have a total chaotic discussion everybody has a chance to speak (.) >obviously everybody else can chip in< but we take it in turns to have a little bit of (.) [human talk
8	M	[mmm can I say Ben who came in later (.) as it were
9	R	=yeah
10	M	he is (.) he is very impressed by the way that we (1.0) we communicate
11	R	well it is democratic [isn't it
12	M	[that that's very interesting (.) he said you come (.) and you are subsumed very easily into the group (.) but he said often you go (0.5) because he's been to a lot of things in the city where you feel (0.5) I don't belong here at all (.) he said you are brilliant at actually (0.5) getting people to come in (1.0) I don't know if that is true but that's [what he felt
13	L	[well then xxx hahaha
14	R	=can I (.) can I ask (.) Mark just wait
15	M	((Mark walks away)) I am coming back
16	R	ok (.) can I just [ask
17	C	[I think we followed your rules
18	R	=no no I am not saying we had [but last
19	L	[we normally do
20	R	last time Debbie seemed to give (0.5) >unfortunately she is not here< (.) Debbie seemed to give the impression (.) that we didn't have these rules or she didn't agree with them (.) I just want to ask whether any of you four think it is a good idea to have those (0.5) rudimentary ideas [or not

```
21   L                           [I think Debbie might see it
                 a little bit more free flowing in terms of the
                 conversation
22   R    but it is free flowing (.) Mark was talking (.)
          everybody [else was
23   L                   [yeah
24   R    =I mean it [is not
25   C                   [we have been happily interrupting
          tonight
26   R    yes [yes
27   L        [yes
28   Lu   I don't feel we should feel naughty if we do
          interrupt
29   R    well no no [exactly
30   Lu                   [but sometimes that is what it feels
          like
31   R    nobody
32   Lu   {deeper voice}=what >are you talking about
          there<
33   R    nobody should feel naughty interrupting
          absolutely (.) but everybody should be given a
          chance to have their own time (0.5) even though
          people interrupt (.) when they are talking
34   Lu   do you think that everyone (.) ought to
          recommend a book at some stage
35   R    oh absolutely (1.0) ought is not the right word
          [everybody should be given the chance
36   Lu   [it is the right word because you make it into
          too much of a responsibility though
37   L    =yes
38   Lu   =sometimes you read a book again and think why
          have I suggested this
39   L    =oh I did that yeah
40   Lu   and then you feel like it is (.) almost a
          personal thing (1.0) you are kind of (0.5)
41   C    well no one should feel (0.5) discouraged from
          recommending
42   R    no
43   Lu   =yeah
44   R    =absolutely (.) no I think people should (.)
          [no I agree with you
45   C    [shouldn't feel obliged
```

```
46   R    =no no I think people should recommend books (.)
          but not books that they haven't read (0.5) erm
          (.) I am not blaming [you Colin because you
47   L                         [have we done that recently
48   C    apparently I did
49   L    oh right (.) what did you recommend
50   C    erm [The Lighthouse was mine
51   R        [yes
52   Lu          [sometimes
53   C    which I hadn't read
54   Lu   =sometimes you just want to read a book and you
          wouldn't read it unless you had a
55   R    =yes but then you should read it first (.) and if
          you like it (.) recommend it

          R = Richard; M = Mark; L = Lizzie; C = Colin; Lu
          = Lucia
```

At the start of this extract Richard outlines the group's rules and asks for the others' views on these; following this, the other group members offer their opinions and a debate ensues. Some of the other members criticize the rules, or at least Richard's application of these rules, and Richard attempts to defend his position.

Richard summarizes the rules across Turns 1, 3, 5 and 7 of the extract, describing the rules in turn and providing a rationale for each. Richard seems to be aware of the difficult interactional work he is performing: he is reluctant to describe the rules as such and describes these procedures as 'ad hoc . . . inverted commas rules' (Turn 1), perhaps because the term 'rules' implies that adherence is necessary and that people will be sanctioned for not conforming. These are rules, but the insertion of 'inverted commas' suggests that this is not quite the right term. Richard suggests that these rules have been created by the group through 'our experience', therefore implying that the rules belong to the group and not just him. He is also self-effacing in his attempt to placate the other members, mentioning mistakes that he has personally made in book selection in the past (Turn 3) and suggesting that he has a tendency to talk too much (Turn 7); Richard's mentioning of these things demonstrates that he has as much to gain from upholding the rules as any of the other members. Mark offers support to Richard, citing the example of fellow member Ben (not present at this meeting), who previously commented on the accommodating nature of the group (Turn 12); a quality that seems to result from the group's way of communicating (Turn 10).

The disagreement starts at Turn 15, when Colin interrupts Richard's attempt to formulate a question to the group. Colin addresses Richard, stating that the group had been following 'your rules' this evening, which causes Richard to repair what he has previously said (Turn 18), and forcing him to justify why he has brought up this matter. At Turn 20 Richard identifies Debbie as the source of the problem and as the main dissenting voice against 'these rules' – note the shift back to 'these' rules from Colin's 'your' rules. As Debbie is absent from this meeting, Lizzie offers a reformulation of Debbie's position, stating that she ideally sees the reading group discussion as 'free-flowing' and implying that the rules do not facilitate this (see also Debbie's comment at Turn 17 of Extract 3.21). Richard presents a counterargument, citing that adherence to the rules still allowed for free-flowing talk at the present meeting, with 'everybody' talking (Turn 22). At Turn 25 Colin remarks that members of the group have been 'happily interrupting tonight'; it is difficult to say whether this is offering agreement with Richard's position, but certainly the idea of interrupting (happily or otherwise) is not in spirit of the rules. This seems to be Lucia's understanding of Colin's utterance, as she argues that members of the group should not be made to feel 'naughty' if they do interrupt each other (Turn 28), and that, despite Richard's protestations, that is sometimes what it 'feels like' (Turn 30). Lucia goes further at Turn 32, explicitly identifying Richard as the member who is most fastidious about upholding the rules: she adopts a deeper voice, mimicking Richard chastizing another member of the group for interrupting. This face threat to Richard is left unmitigated and there does not seem to be any attempt from Lucia to hide this comment behind humour; her quoting only serves to demonstrate, and negatively evaluate, what she sees as Richard's normal behaviour in meetings. Richard responds by justifying the rule as it allows every reader to 'have their own time' to talk, although he prefaces this by agreeing with Lucia: 'nobody should feel naughty' (Turn 33).

Having discussed the one-person-speaks rule, Lucia moves on to question the rule concerning book recommendations, asking Richard if he feels that everyone 'ought' to recommend a book at some stage (Turn 34). Richard agrees but disputes whether the word 'ought' is accurate (Turn 35), which causes Lucia to defend her use of the word, stating that Richard makes the act of recommending 'too much of a responsibility' (Turn 36) and that, as a result, she feels personally culpable if she suggests a book that is disliked by the group. Colin offers some conciliatory remarks that suggest agreement with Lucia's position (Turns 41 and 45) and Richard echoes these (Turn 44). However, Richard still wants to uphold the rule, arguing that members should only recommend after they have read a book (Turn 46). For the few remaining turns of the extract Colin's book-recommending faux pas is discussed, with Richard citing this as an example of the value of the rule.

This exchange demonstrates the tensions that arise in the Contemporary Group over the group's rules. There are questions over who the rules belong to (Richard or the group) and how these rules should be applied, if at all. From observing and recording the group it is not surprising that Richard is the main advocate of the rules in this passage of talk. The interview data and Extract 3.21 demonstrate how wedded he is to the 'democratic' nature of the rules, in particular the rule that one person speaks. However, in practice this particular rule is difficult to uphold and in Extract 3.24 Richard has to accept a slightly modified version that allows for some interruption. Richard's defence of the rules may not have been surprising, but the sources of the attacks on the rules were. As shown in the interview data (Extract 3.18), by Richard's reckoning at least, Lucia has the most to gain from the rules as she is more reluctant to speak than others. Although Colin does not present his criticism of the rules as strongly as Lucia, he argues for a more flexible application. As a new member of the group it could be seen as bold for Colin to present dissent to any aspect of the group's status quo, and to make suggestions for how things might be done slightly differently in the future. In CofP terms however, Colin's attempt to 'broker' change within the group is not so surprising given his position. Wenger argues that typical brokers are on 'the boundaries' of a CofP and often attempt to avoid 'being pulled in to become full members and being rejected as intruders' (1998: 109). According to Wenger, the ideal broker is a peripheral participant in a CofP: someone who, unlike a full member of a group, has little or no vested interest in the maintenance of the status quo group practices but, conversely, has 'enough legitimacy to influence the development of a practice' (1998: 109), unlike a marginal member or non-member. If he wants, Colin may well achieve full membership in the future, but at this point he is in a good position to instigate change within the Contemporary Group.

This negotiation over the status of the rules has some important implications for the joint enterprise of the Contemporary Group. There is no dispute that the overarching aim of the group is to meet and discuss literary texts in a focused and serious way, but there are questions over exactly how this aim should be carried out. Some members of the group seem to value 'free-flowing' conversation and a non-judgemental environment above all else, while others place the highest value on the 'democratic' rules that have been developed over time. On occasion, these values are in competition with one another, and the result is dissent from the rules (Extracts 3.22 and 3.23) and the kind of heated exchange seen in Extract 3.24. However, as Mark alluded to in this extract in his paraphrasing of Ben, this group is welcoming and good-natured, and it is testament to this friendly nature that dissent is permitted from full members (i.e. Lucia) and peripheral members (i.e. Colin) and that feelings do not seem to be hurt, even following quite serious face threats.

3.5 Conclusion

This chapter has considered the various ways in which reading groups can organize their discussions of texts. Organization has not referred to how regularly groups meet or where they gather, but rather the focus has been on structural elements within meetings and how talk is managed. For some groups sets of questions positively encourage a structured focus on the text, although these have to be seen as appropriate to the tone and interests of the group. Some groups structure their meetings in more unique ways, such as dedicating a section of their meetings to hearing the views of other, physically absent readers. Other groups organize their meetings in quite elaborate ways, using 'rules' that have developed over time, although these structures can be challenged in quite direct ways. Organization has also been considered on a smaller-scale too, with reader's responses to texts occasionally structured in light of the tastes of absent voices – those of other, non-academic readers (Section 3.3.1) and the voices of professional critics (Section 3.3.2). In their organization reading groups reproduce 'certain values and conventions of both professional and lay readers' (Procter and Benwell, 2014: 22), and the groups in the present study occupy a space somewhere between the highly institutional and the very relaxed, problematizing any clear distinction between professional and non-professional reading.

The ways in which a CofP is organized will reflect the members' concept of their joint enterprise, their task as group. This joint enterprise is clearly to discuss books, but it is also to engage in social relations and to enjoy a relaxed time with friends and acquaintances. Finding a balance between these competing demands of joint enterprise can be tricky and, as we have seen, different members may disagree over the nature of a group's joint enterprise and how this should be carried out. This can lead to the 'amicable disagreement' that is often highly valued by reading groups or can lead to more fractious debates, as seen in later extracts presented in this chapter.

4

Reported Discourse in the Reading Groups

In conversation it is common for us to use reported discourse to quote ourselves or others from another context. In the previous chapter we saw how members of reading groups are constantly in dialogue with the voices of other, physically absent, readers. On some occasions these readers directly quoted other readers, from Amazon customer reviewers to literary critics writing for *The Independent*. This chapter picks up this argument, focusing on how readers systematically invoke speech or thought from outside the here-and-now of the reading group meeting. As an initial example, consider the following from the Forest Group's discussion of *Wolf Hall* (Mantel, 2009):

(A)

```
        [23:46] Forest, Wolf Hall
1   S   it was an everyday occurrence (0.5) nobody turned
        a hair (.) oh yes he has been tortured (0.5) they
        have admitted it oh well (.) burn them like (.)
        you know
```

In this example the bold type-face indicates where Samuel has moved into the voice of characters from the novel.[1] He does not suggest that these are direct quotations from *Wolf Hall*; rather, the direct reported speech serves to give a flavour of the laissez-faire attitude of the characters by producing a rendition of their voice. By contrast, here is an example of indirect speech in which a member of the Forest Group presents the content of another speaker's voice without actually quoting:

(B)

```
        [42:50] Forest, The Shack
1   F    I am glad you brought it to us (1.0) I really
         am you know (2.0) I now know you know how bad
         things could be
2   L    I can't remember how I found it though
3   J    I think you said someone at the library
         recommended it

        F = Frank; L = Lucy; J = Joan
```

At Turn 3, Joan indirectly reports something Lucy has previously said, but maintains her own voice, making no attempt to shift into the voice of Lucy. In this way, Joan's indirect speech 'tells' us what was previously said, while Samuel's direct speech in (A) 'shows' us what was said (Sternberg, 1982). This chapter focuses on reported discourse in its direct form, as in example (A). These direct reports of speech and thought were prevalent in the reading group data, forming a key part of the shared repertoire, or 'shared discourse' (Wenger, 1998: 126) across the four groups.

Examples like (A), where people directly reporting 'the utterances of others' (Myers, 1999a: 376) are referred to as direct reported discourse in the literature, and this chapter describes occasions when readers report their own previous thoughts, address characters and take on the voices of characters or authors. All of the examples presented and analysed in this chapter are quotations of speech or thought and so are instances of 'direct' reported discourse, rather than 'indirect' or narrative reports of thought (for an extensive treatment of different forms of speech and thought representation, see Leech and Short, 1981). As only direct forms are considered, these examples are referred to as 'reported discourse' in this chapter; although other studies may use the term more broadly to cover indirect forms too. Reported speech and reported thought have been shown to have subtly different properties and functions (e.g. Barnes and Moss, 2007; Vásquez and Urzúa, 2009), but in this chapter the two are considered together.

This chapter identifies three distinct *types* of reported discourse in the reading group data and three predominant *functions*. While the types of reported discourse are fairly easily discernible from the data, the functions are determined by the analyst – although evidence from the interactional context is always used in arriving at these conclusions. The three types are listed below and are distinguishable in terms of who is being quoted and who is being addressed in the quotation:

- readers quoting their own previous thoughts (or speech) from private reading
- readers quoting themselves from the past, addressing characters or the author
- readers speaking as a character or characters.

These three types of reported discourse are discussed across Section 4.2, with examples from the reading groups presented and analysed. Following this, the functions of these types of reported discourse are considered in Section 4.3. As mentioned, three functions are discussed: evidential, involving and simulation. It is argued that much of the reported discourse found in reading group talk is found within passages of discourse where readers are offering assessments, which supports previous research that has identified this link between evaluations and reported discourse (e.g. Benwell, 2012; Buttny, 1997; Clift, 2006; Couper-Kuhlen, 2006; Myers, 1999a; Stokoe and Edwards, 2007). A second finding that is more unique to this data-set is that some instances of reported discourse demonstrate readers attempting to engage with the consciousness of a character, imagining their perspective through simulation. For the most part, a discursive approach is taken to the data, with the reported discourse seen as performing interactional work (e.g. involving others in the discussion) or rhetorical work (i.e. strengthening the speaker's argument). By also focusing on the simulative function of reported discourse, however, a partially cognitive approach is taken, one that is less obviously rooted in the discourse and is more based on inferences about how the reader was modelling the mind of the character in his/her reported discourse.

4.1 Previous research into reported discourse

In this chapter reported discourse refers to instances in talk where speakers directly report something that was said or thought on an occasion that is spatially and/or temporally moved from the quoting speech situation. Speakers can quote themselves, in which case the *reporting* speaker and the *reported* are one and the same, or speakers can quote other speakers. Reported discourse has been described as 'one of the most widespread and fundamental topics of human speech' (Bakhtin, 1981: 337) and as 'ubiquitous' to narrative and non-narrative discourse (Myers, 1999b: 573). However, if reported discourse is widespread and ubiquitous, it also creates a fairly unique speech situation; as Sternberg argues, 'quotation markedly differs from all the rest of the patterns by which we communicate and represent the world' because it conflates 'at least two discourse events: that in which things were originally expressed (said, thought, experienced) by one subject (speaker, writer, reflector) and that in which they are cited by another' (1982: 107).

The data presented in this chapter is all in the 'direct' form of reported discourse, and so only occasions when speakers move into a different voice are considered. Sometimes these voices are marked as speech, sometimes thought, while at other times it is not clear whether speech or thought is being quoted. Although it is not the intention of this chapter to make systematic distinctions between reported thought and speech, it is worth noting that reported thought has been rather neglected as an area of research (Barnes and Moss, 2007; Vásquez and Urzúa, 2009). The paucity of research on reported thought compared with reported speech is puzzling, particularly as direct reported thought is highly common in everyday conversation (Rühlemann, 2007: 138).

Much of the research into reported discourse has focused on design and function. In the next section of this chapter, previous research is discussed and reviewed, with a particular focus on the design, the sequential organization, and the functions of these utterances. Following this, research into reported discourse that is most relevant to the present study is discussed, specifically Allington (2012), Benwell (2012) and Whiteley (2011) – all of which consider reported discourse in reading group talk.

4.1.1 Design of reported discourse

Much of the research into reported discourse has focused on turn design, and specifically the form that the reported discourse takes, and how it is distinguished from surrounding talk. When speakers use reported discourse some design features are necessary, while other features are optional. In order to be a direct quotation or thought the speaker must make a deictic shift into the voice of the reported speaker or thinker, with pronouns and address terms, verb tense and aspect, and locative expressions belonging to the other, quoted party rather than the present speaker. For instance, in (C) Molly from the Wanderers Group quotes herself from the past, shifting the tense from past to present continuous

('I thought' – 'I am giving up') and including an adverbial of time ('now') that belongs to the previous quoted time:

(C)

```
        [4:18] - Wanderers, Potter's Hand
1   Mo  I enjoyed bits of it (.) I think it went off
        in the middle (.) about page three hundred I
        thought I am giving up now
```

These various shifts provide an 'insight' into the reported speaker's mind, both for the reporting speaker and for their interlocutors (Holt, 1996: 240). Changes in pitch or prosody are common in distinguishing reported discourse from surrounding talk, but are not necessary. When quoting, the reporting speaker may imitate the reported speaker or thinker in a comic manner or in order to recreate the original source's incredulity (Benwell, 2012: 368). Speakers can also use exaggerated prosody in order to undermine the credibility of the quoted speaker (Buttny, 1997). The quoting speaker may raise or lower the volume of their speech in the reported discourse relative to the surrounding talk, and speed up or slow down their speech in the reported utterance (Barnes and Moss, 2007: 131; Holt, 1996: 223). However, some reported discourse lacks any obvious markers distinguishing the quoting voice from the quoted voice, and in these instances the speaker's interlocutors must use contextual cues to interpret the speech as a direct report (Benwell, 2012; Myers, 1999a).

Reported discourse is rarely longer than one turn construction unit (Couper-Kuhlen, 2006: 91) and reported clauses are often marked off from the framing talk with initial 'response particles' (Heritage, 2005), such as *oh, well, goodness, for God's sake* and so on (Mayes, 1990; Barnes and Moss, 2007: 129) – see example (A) from the start of this chapter for an instance of 'oh' being used in this way. The final design feature to note is the reporting clause, which may come before or after the reported speech or thought, if indeed it is included at all. The quotative marker, such as *I thought*, and the quotation generally form a single turn construction unit with no obvious gap or pause between the two (Couper-Kuhlen, 2006: 91). The reporting clause will be in the voice of the present speaker and will include a pronoun and a verb, usually a verb of speech or cognition: for example *I said, she thought*. As mentioned, however, speaker may choose to use no reporting clause at all (Barnes and Moss, 2007: 128).

Reading group discourse is full of assessments and evaluations from readers. Relevant to the present research, therefore, many studies have noted the co-occurrence of direct reported forms and assessments (e.g. Benwell, 2012; Buttny, 1997; Clift, 2006; Couper-Kuhlen, 2006; Myers, 1999a; Stokoe and Edwards, 2007). When making an assessment or evaluation, whether implicit or explicit, it is likely that a speaker will move into a direct report. Benwell (2012) and Buttny (1997), for instance, have argued that reported discourse is linked to assessments, with Benwell finding that reported discourse can have an '*ironic* and critical function' when used alongside assessments (2012: 368) and Buttny arguing that when people quote conversations or thoughts they do not 'simply report what was said; they also evaluate it' (1997: 485). The evaluation or assessment component can be placed before, after or within the reported discourse (Buttny, 1997: 485–92). Returning to example (C), Molly's assessment – 'I think it went off in the middle' – is prepositioned, occurring before the onset of reported discourse:

(C)

```
       [4:18] - Wanderers, Potter's Hand

1    Mo   I enjoyed bits of it (.) I think it went off
          in the middle (.) about page three hundred I
          thought I am giving up now
```

By contrast, Robert offers his own evaluation of the characters in *Flight Behaviour* at Turn 8, after he has used reported discourse:

(D)

```
       [8:35] - Wanderers, Flight Behaviour

1    L    yes but it could have helped you understand how
          they were growing and the er
2    R    why would you want to understand things (.) you
          could understand everything you possibly could
          from the bible surely from our culture
3    H    =even the two versions
4    R    y- you don't need any of this new-fangled
          science stuff
5    L    no
6    Mo   no
7    L    well
8    R    I mean it was an incredibly narrow minded (.)
          place [wasn't it
9    Mo         [yeah

       L = Laura; R = Robert; H = Hannah; Mo = Molly
```

Lastly, evaluation can co-occur within the reported discourse, embedded within the quotation. In (E), Lizzie and Colin both present their explicit assessments of *Fragrant Harbour* (Lanchester, 2002) within their reported discourse in Turns 6 and 7:

(E)

```
        [37:13] - Contemporary, Fragrant Harbour
1   L   you've got these emails going back
2   M   hahaha
3   L   I know Professor Cobb's work on the yuë-fu
        lyric form which is
4   M   =hahaha
5   L   I would just sit there going
6   C   I just don't [care
7   L              [don't get it (.) I don't know
        who Cobb is (.) I don't know who Wilfred is
        (.) you know what has this got to do with
        anything at this point

        L = Lizzie; M = Mark; C = Colin
```

Assessments often co-occur with reported discourse in ostensibly non-narrative discourse, such as competitive sequences of talk (Clift, 2006) and accounts (Couper-Kuhlen, 2006). Clift (2006: 128) considered the use of reported speech in competitive interactions, finding that the assessment will often be positioned in the turn before a quotation. By contrast, Couper-Kuhlen (2006: 95–6) found more instances in her data of examples like (E) where assessment is embedded within the quotation, arguing that reported discourse rarely forms a conversational turn on its own. Whether these evaluations come before, after or within a quotation, it is generally the case that the audience is provided with 'an interpretative frame' that allows them to identify the reported discourse as separate from the surrounding talk but working alongside any assessment being made (Stokoe and Edwards, 2007: 347).

4.1.2 Functions of reported discourse

The focus of the second half of this chapter is on the functions of reported discourse in the reading group discussions. As previously discussed, reported discourse and assessments are bound up with each other, and all of the examples of reported discourse presented in this chapter involve readers from the groups offering implicit or explicit assessments in the act of quoting. However, other functions have been identified, some of which directly relate to assessing and others that are more distinct from this. In this section evidential, dramatizing or involving, identity management and simulation functions of reported discourse are discussed with reference made to previous research.

Clark and Gerrig (1990) see reported discourse as 'demonstration' rather than 'description' of another voice; by this, they mean that reported speech or thought can demonstrate a personal experience of the quoted voice, while also showing the current speaker's position in relation to it. They argue that direct report has two principal functions: detachment and direct experience (Clark and Gerrig, 1990). When quoting, speakers are detached from the original discourse and 'only take responsibility for presenting the quoted matter' (1990: 792); in doing this, speakers can choose whether or not they are aligned with the original utterance or thought. For recipients of reported discourse, however, it can provide a direct experience of aspects of the original event (1990: 793). Reported discourse serves as a 'frame shift' (Myers, 1999a) that is detached from the current speaking event, yet speakers use reported speech and thought to perform various rhetorical functions in the here-and-now.

As assessments, evaluations and accounts so often co-occur with reported discourse, one of its primary functions is to provide evidence for the speaker's position or stance. This evidential function of reported discourse is very apparent in particular institutional settings such as law-courts and police interviews because in these contexts a high value is placed on exactly what has been said previously by victims and alleged perpetrators of crimes. However, in more mundane contexts where the accuracy of the reported discourse in relation to the original utterance is less important, this evidential function is still clear to see. In his study of reported forms in focus group discourse, Myers (1999a: 387) argues that almost all reported speech seeks to offer evidence and 'factuality'. Holt (1996: 230) argues that reports of speech lend the speaker 'an air of objectivity', demonstrating that the position is one held by more than one person (if the reporting and reported speakers are different people) and that the view being expressed is one formulated over time. Related to this, Couper-Kuhlen (2006: 119) argues that reported discourse supports an assessment by 'adding strategic detail and attesting to its historicity', and Clift (2006, 2007) found that in arguments over epistemic rights to assess reported discourse is 'one of the most powerful evidential displays of having got there first' (2007: 149). Wooffitt (2006: 245) makes a similar point, arguing that the 'authenticity of a claim or the authority of a speaker can be established and defended' through use of reported discourse, while Leudar and Antaki (1996: 24) state that to 'report talk is to offer some kind of guarantee of its authenticity'. This evidential function of reported discourse has been found to be widespread, occurring across various contexts. It is speaker-focused in that it is primarily face-managing for the present speaker doing the quoting. Reported discourse lends credibility, historicity and authenticity to the assessment being offered.

Research has also found that reported discourse has a dramatizing function (Barnes and Moss, 2007; Clark and Gerrig, 1990; Holt, 1996; Myers, 1999a, 1999b; Sams, 2010; Tannen, 2007). In contrast to the evidential function, the dramatizing function is recipient-focused as it encourages 'involvement' (Tannen, 2007) from interlocutors. This function is often linked with narrative speech contexts: Holt (1996: 235) found that direct speech enables a narrating speaker to 'dramatize the events', Clark and Gerrig (1990: 794) argued that direct speech 'reenact or revivify' an event, while Myers (1999a: 383–4) stated that reported discourse can 'intensify an event'. Barnes and Moss's study into the articulation of private thoughts claims that reported thought can 'personalize and dramatize narrative material' (2007: 142), while Sams (2010: 3157) contends that it can be used for 'dramatization of a narrative'. Tannen (2007) sees the dramatization function as important to reported discourse, arguing that direct forms make the represented characters and scenes 'more vivid' (2007: 39) for the recipients of the narrative. Tannen links this dramatizing function with audience-involvement, stating that recipients of reported discourse become involved in the 'drama . . . by actively interpreting the significance of character and action' (2007: 124). Likewise, in a discussion of hypothetical reported discourse, Myers (1999b) found that such forms tended to give rise to highly dynamic and collaborative passages of talk in which participants take up others' reported discourse, adding their own examples.

Thirdly, reported discourse has been shown to do identity work, both for the speaker and for the audience. Identity management and face work are never very far away when we look at instances of reported discourse; for instance, the evidential function reported discourse can perform face work for the speaker, lending credibility to an expressed opinion or stance. However, other research has shown that reported discourse can be community-building and affirming on the positive side, and community-damaging on the negative side. Hamilton (1998) found that reported speech had positive, affirming functions when used by members of an online medical forum. This forum was used by people who had been affected directly or indirectly by bone marrow transplantation, and many of the posts were written by bone marrow recipients and their families. Hamilton was interested in the narratives that people told about their experiences in hospital, and particularly the ways in which conflicts between doctors and patients were narrated. Reported discourse was frequently used by the post-writers to report occasions where the patient or patient's family were shown to know more than the medical professional. In spite of the institutionally sanctioned asymmetry of epistemic rights between the patients and the medical professionals, the patients used the forum to demonstrate the greater knowledge of their condition, relating conversations between themselves and the medical professionals, which showed the doctors' relative lack of knowledge (Hamilton, 1998). The use of reported discourse in these conflict narratives served to produce a sense of community between the various patients and their families, allowing them to 'take pride in their active stance as survivors of life-threatening illnesses and treatments' (Hamilton, 1998: 65). Buttny's (1997) study of conversations about race similarly found an identity managing function of reported speech, although the outcome of this was less positive. When asked about the issue of race at university, interviewees created in-groups and out-groups on ethnic grounds by parodying the talk of an ethnicity different from their own. In the following example an African American speaker is describing his experience of discrimination at university:

> It's like they look at me and go like (*mimic a stereotypical White voice*) Gee them niggers they just must of gotten in on affirmative action or something like that you know.

(Buttny, 1997: 493)

Although relating a far less positive experience than the forum users in Hamilton's (1998) data, Buttny similarly found that the speakers in his corpus used reported discourse to affirm an important aspect of their identity, prompted by the interactional context.

The last function of reported discourse concerns instances where the reported speech or thought is marked as not having been actually said or thought but is rather, imagined. When discussed in relation to the reading group data later in the chapter, this function is referred to as 'simulation'. As mentioned at the start of this chapter, the general approach taken to reported discourse is rhetorical and discursive, but in considering the simulation function this approach also touches on elements of the cognitive. Two pieces of research are discussed in relation to the simulation function (Myers, 1999b; Whiteley, 2011), although it should be noted that neither scholar uses this term to describe the reported discourse in their data.

Myers (1999b) discusses the occurrences of hypothetical reported discourse in his corpus of focus group meetings. Members of focus groups use hypothetical forms of reported speech and thought to create imaginary, possible and impossible situations, with these forms having various functions within the conversations. Reported discourse is imaginary in examples where people propose imaginary ideas, although perhaps involving real places and real people. Myers presents an example in which members of a focus group imagine Niles, a fictional character from TV show *Frasier*, coming to Manchester (1999b: 575–6). At other times hypothetical reported discourse can be marked as conditional; referring to things people might think or say. Myers presents an example of two participants in a focus group discussing the risks of CJD (Creutzfeldt-Jakob disease). While M1 is in favour of a ban on certain beef products, M2 is not:

```
M1    Don't you think there's something wrong they won't
      let you do that, or they wouldn't do that.

M2    Maybe. I mean they come up, possibly. Here again
      the scientists, the scientists are sat in the
      little ivory towers deciding they're on 30, 40,
      50 thousand a year, and they've got to come
      up with something, if they don't come up with
      anything what the bloody hell is he doing all this
      time sat in there. Well maybe we'll have to do
      more tests.
                   (Myers, 1999b: 576, italics in original)
```

Conditional examples, such as the segment of talk in italics, can be distinguished from the imaginary instances because they are marked as situations that might actually happen in reality (Myers, 1999b: 576–7). Lastly, in some of the examples from Myers's data the possibility of some hypothetical reported discourse can be denied entirely. These examples are distinct from the imaginary and conditional instances in being marked as impossible, with speakers explicitly signalling that the reported discourse could not be uttered or thought. For instance, in the following example participants in a focus group are discussing the effectiveness of advertisements used by charities (as before, the reported discourse is in italics):

M3   But I mean if you saw say an advert for like these
      landmines, if you saw the same in a newspaper or
      magazine and you could study it and there's a coupon
      there or something, some people may fill that it and
      send it off, I mean I can't imagine anybody like
      seeing that advert and seeing that name on the top
      and what not and think *oh I'll jot that down and
      send something off.*
M2   Or when the phone number comes up *oh I must ring
      that straight away.*
                              (Myers, 1999b: 578, italics in original)

When analysing his examples of hypothetical reported discourse, Myers focuses on the rhetorical function; that is, the ways in which speakers use reported discourse to persuade others. However, he is also interested in how other members of the group take up others' reported discourse, building on it with their own hypothetical examples (1999b: 573).

   Similar to Myers (1999b), Whiteley (2011) found instances of participants creating hypothetical reported discourse in her reading group data, and specifically enacting utterances or thought that fictional characters might have experienced. These instances are marked as imaginary or conditional (Myers, 1999b) rather than as things that were actually said or thought by characters. For example, here is a reader discussing the title of *Remains of the Day* (Ishiguro, 1989) in relation to the two main characters in the novel:

A   It really is the remains of the day there's
     nothing. . . comforting about that just *this is
     what's left of our relationship* we're having a
     conversation about what might have been at a bus stop
     and you're going back to a person you don't love, who
     you've just told me you don't really love
                              (Whiteley, 2011: 35, italics in original)

Whiteley argues that the reported discourse (in italics) demonstrates the reader psychologically projecting into the narrator's perspective and enacting his role (2011: 35). This is not a direct quotation from the novel but rather what the reader imagines the narrator would have thought about his situation.

Both pieces of research are highly relevant to many of the instances of reported discourse described in this chapter, as Myers (1999b) and Whiteley (2011) are essentially concerned with hypothetical forms of reported speech and thought. Coming from a cognitive perspective, Whiteley (2011) is willing to use spoken discourse to make inferences about the reader's mind and, specifically, to draw conclusions about psychological projection from the reported discourse used by a reader. By contrast, Myers (1999b) is working within the rhetorical tradition and does not make any comments on the minds of his participants, focusing instead on the interactional and interpersonal functions of the reported discourse. Although these two pieces of research do not discuss instances of reported discourse as 'simulation' per se, both Myers (1999b) and Whiteley (2011) allude to this in their respective accounts of reported discourse. In some of the examples of reported discourse analysed later in this chapter, people relate speech or thought that has not happened or could not possibly happen, and where this occurs in the reading group discussions it is argued that these examples perform a simulation function.

4.1.3 Reported discourse in reading groups

In addition to Whiteley (2011), which was discussed at the end of the previous section, a small number of studies have considered the prevalence and functions of reported discourse in reading groups, however none have given this systematic treatment. Benwell (2012; see also Procter and Benwell, 2014) used reading group data to look at how anti-racist discourse is constructed as commonsense, specifically focusing on how this ideology can be packaged in direct and indirect forms of reported speech. Views and opinions that were deemed to be racist were often presented in reported speech, such that the racist view is 'othered' (Benwell, 2012: 362). These quoted racist remarks were generally not marked as being reported by the quoting speaker but were invariably identified as being distinct from the speaker's opinions. The ease with which the racist opinions were identified as being different from the speaker's own views demonstrated the anti-racist commonsense developed within these groups.

Allington and Benwell (2012) and Allington (2012) focused on the functions of reported discourse in analyses of data gathered from reading contexts. Allington and Benwell (2012) considered how readers use reported discourse to authenticate their response to the text on occasions when an assessment was under scrutiny in the group. In one instance, the use of reported discourse served to dramatize the reader's response by emotionally appealing to the other readers, which had the effect of validating her response to the text (Allington and Benwell, 2012: 224–5). Allington (2012) documents the use of reported discourse in university seminar discussions, finding that students in this setting used reported discourse in order to demonstrate how their private reading experience was different from institutionally sanctioned readings and interpretations. One student, for instance, reported that she did not see any homosexual allusions in her private reading of *The Importance of Being Earnest*, and that she was surprised when she heard that this was seen as an important theme within the play: 'I was like "oh okay"' (Allington, 2012: 218). The reported discourse here serves to account for the student's private reading experience, lending evidential support to, and dramatizing, her sense of surprise at literary critical opinion (2012: 219).

4.2 Forms of reported discourse in reading groups

There are three distinct forms of reported discourse used in the reading groups. These forms are discernible from the data, and can be differentiated in terms of whose voice is being reported and who is being addressed. The three forms are as follows:

1. Readers give reports of their own reactions and assessments while reading.
2. Readers give reports of their own (imagined) address to a character or author.
3. Readers give reports of a character's thoughts or voice.

Each of these three forms is described in turn across the following three subsections, with examples of these analysed accordingly.

4.2.1 Thoughts while reading

When offering their views on the text, readers often report their thoughts from the time of reading. This form of reported discourse occurs regularly in the reading group talk and reports of these previous thoughts can be used when offering definitive assessments of the text. This type of reported discourse may also be used when readers are ambivalent about a text and when they have changed their opinion over the course of reading.

In the first example, Molly from the Wanderers Group is describing her experience of reading *The Potter's Hand* (Wilson, 2012):

```
Extract 4.1 'Giving up' on The Potter's Hand
        [04:18] - Wanderers, Potter's Hand
1   Mo  I enjoyed bits of it (.) I think it went off
        in the middle (.) about page three hundred I
        thought I am giving up now
2   L   =mmm
3   Mo  =and then I went back to it (0.5) and actually
        (.) quite enjoyed it

        Mo = Molly; L = Laura
```

Molly begins by offering a fairly ambivalent response, saying that she enjoyed 'bits' of the novel but that it novel 'went off' at the mid-point. She then cites a particular point in the novel ('about page three hundred') and moves into reported thought to demonstrate her thoughts the time of reading: 'I thought I am giving up now' (Turn 1). Following this, Molly describes subsequently going back to the novel and 'actually' quite enjoying it (Turn 3). The use of direct reported thought provides the other readers with an access to her reading experience and, for Molly, evidence of her previously negative opinion of the novel. She presents a contrastive structure (Jefferson, 2004), contextualizing her current opinion on the novel (Turn 3) in terms of her previous view (Turn 1). She has moved from a position of 'giving up' on the novel to one where she 'actually' enjoyed it. Myers found that participants in focus groups use reported discourse to present views they might have had in the past 'without endorsing them in the present' (1999b: 583), and this seems to be what Molly is doing here. Her reported thought is important in providing evidence of her previous view and offering a comparison with her opinion in the here-and-now.

In the next example Connie from the Orchards Group describes changing her opinion of a novel while reading:

Extract 4.2 'I can't put it down'
        [56:00] - Orchards, *The Road*

1   Co   so I was not really looking forward to starting
          it (.) but once I'd started I thought **aaahhh (.)**
          I can't believe it (.) I can't put it down
2   S   mmm mmm
3   Co   and Julia had made the comment (.) because I
          hadn't re- >because she'd read it first< and she
          said to me (.) <u>oh</u> she said I'm really <u>intrigued</u>
          (.) you know I can't wait to find out what
          happens [next
4   S   [well this is it (.) you got to know
          [haven't you
5   Co   [and I kept thinking this and I was reading it
          thinking **oh (.) she's absolutely right (.) I can't**
          wait to know what happens next

        Co = Connie; S = Sue

Connie describes her initial position of 'not looking forward' to reading *The Road*
(McCarthy, 2006) to being totally engrossed in the narrative. She uses reported
discourse in various ways in this extract, reanimating her thoughts while reading
and quoting from a conversation she had with Julia about the novel. At Turn 1,
Connie draws on direct reported thought to convey her highly positive reading
experience. Following the reporting clause, the shift into reported thought is
indicated with the particle 'aaahhh', which seems to indicate satisfaction, and the
move to present tense, both of which provide a visceral sense of her enjoyment
of the novel at the time of reading. Similarly, at Turn 5 the particle 'oh' announces
the start of the direct reported thought and the subsequent present tense confirms
this shift. As in Extract 4.1, a contrastive structure is used here and the examples
of reported thought provide evidence of this change of opinion.

By contrast, in Extract 4.3 there is no such shift in opinion. Instead, Lizzie and
Colin use reported thought to account for their negative reactions to *Fragrant
Harbour* (Lanchester, 2002):

Extract 4.3 'I just don't care'
        [37:13] - Contemporary, *Fragrant Harbour*

1   L   you've got these emails going back
2   M   hahaha
3   L   I know Professor Cobb's work on the yuë-fu
          lyric form which is

```
4    M    =hahaha
5    L    I would just sit there going
6    C    I just don't [care
7    L                 [don't get it (.) I don't know who
          Cobb is (.) I don't know who Wilfred is (.) you
          know what has this got to do with anything at
          this point

          L = Lizzie; M = Mark; C = Colin
```

Lizzie is describing her lack of engagement with the novel and her feeling of distance from the characters. At Turn 5 and Turn 7 she accounts for this by describing her experience of not knowing who characters are or understanding their relevance in terms of reported discourse. Lizzie indicates that she is about to move into reported thought at Turn 5, with 'going' used as a quotative verb. Colin predicts that reported discourse is coming and provides his own completion: 'I just don't care' (Turn 6). Lizzie then overlaps with the end of Colin's turn, almost echoing what Colin has just said: 'don't get it' (Turn 7). This example of joint construction shows the two readers collaboratively building a negative assessment of the novel, and using reported thought to achieve this.

These three examples show readers using reported discourse in the act of describing their reading experience. These reports provide the other members of the group with access to the reader's prior engagement with the novel, which may be private thoughts (Extracts 3.1 and 3.3) or discussions with other readers (Extract 3.2). This form of reported discourse usually documented one reader's experience, an excursion 'into personal life' (Long, 2003: 111), but was also used collaboratively to show a shared reaction to a text (Extract 4.3). In all cases, however, these examples of reported discourse are part of assessment sequences.

4.2.2 Address to character

In this section addresses to fictional characters and authors are considered. While examples of previous private thoughts or speech (described in Section 4.2.1) are often found in other types of talk, particularly where people are offering assessments, the examples presented in this section and the next are more peculiar to the reading group context. When readers address a character or an author using reported discourse they presumably do not believe that this act has any tangible effect; it is not a dyadic conversation, after all. Instead, the purpose of this type of reported discourse seems to be to support the assessment being offered and to dramatize the reading experience, often for comic effect.

In the first example, Laura from the Wanderers Group addresses Ifemelu, the protagonist in *Americanah* (Adichie, 2013):

Extract 4.4 Changing values of a character
              [37:48] – Wanderers, *Americanah*

1   L   the American ideal isn't it the go west thing
          and
2   R   yeah
3   L   this (.) that is still happening (2.0) I
          thought it was interesting when she went (0.5)
          when she first went back to Nigeria and she was
          getting that flat and (.) she made them redo the
          tiling in the bathroom (.) and I thought (.)
          well you probably would have accepted that and
          now you have been to America with the massive
          customer service obsession
4   R   hahaha that's a [bit strange
5   L   [with the shoddy tiling and
          you have demanded that he redoes it (0.5) and
          I thought (.) **I really wonder whether that**
          would have bothered you before you had been to
          America
6   R   = <u>no</u> certainly not

          L = Laura; R = Robert

In this extract Laura is describing Ifemelu's move back to Nigeria from the United States and the changes to her personality and attitude that occur as a result of this move. Laura is attempting to understand the character's beliefs and her shift in values, and finds that the way to account for this is in terms of Ifemelu's internalization of the 'American ideal' (Turn 1). As an example of this, Laura describes the character complaining about the bathroom tiling in her Nigerian flat, and at this point she begins to address the character to tell her that before she lived in the United States 'you probably would have accepted that' (Turn 3). Following agreement from Robert, Laura then returns to addressing the character at Turn 5, summarizing Ifemelu's complaint back at her ('you have demanded that he redoes it') and posing a direct question to the character: 'would that have bothered you before you had been to America?' Reported discourse often comes at the climax of a story (Holt, 2000: 431–2) and here Laura sets the scene from the novel before shifting into direct address to the character. These addresses create an interesting participation framework in the reading group interaction (Goffman, 1981). In linguistic terms Laura is addressing the character by moving into the second-person address 'you', with the other readers in the present here-and-now as an overhearing audience. However, we can assume that Laura does not believe that she is actually addressing the fictional character, and so this reported discourse is of the 'imaginary' kind discussed by Myers (1999b: 575–6). Rhetorically, the addresses seem to be for the benefit of the overhearing audience (i.e. the other members of the group), providing them with a recap of Ifemelu's behaviour and Laura's negative assessment of this. Having said this, these 'participatory responses' (Gerrig, 1993) where Laura directly addresses the character may have more than just a rhetorical purpose, possibly suggesting that Laura has some kind of empathetic relationship with Ifemelu.

In the next example direct address more clearly indexes empathy between the reader and the addressee. In this case Samuel from the Forest Group addresses the author of *Somewhere Close to the End*, Diana Athill:

Extract 4.5 'You're an atheist'

```
        [25:46] - Forest, Somewhere Close to the End
1   S   and that's (.) one thing er er er that warmed
        me to her more than anything else was when I
        discovered she was an atheist (0.5) I thought
        well ah we'll forget haha for all your upper
        class er upbringing because you're an atheist
        ((general laughter))
2   F   =she says she is but er on one page it says erm
        (0.5) the body is merely a vehicle for for life
        to to flow through
3   L   =yeah
4   F   ==now for some people (.) they would say well
        that's not really an atheistic idea

        S = Samuel; F = Frank; L = Lucy
```

Samuel describes 'warming' to Athill after discovering that she is an atheist, and so creates an 'interpretative frame' for the reported discourse that follows (Stokoe and Edwards, 2007: 347). As a staunch atheist himself, Samuel evidently feels an affiliation between himself and Athill, and he uses direct address in Turn 1 to demonstrate this. The direct address takes the form of reported thought, clearly marking the address as not something that was not actually said, either to the author or to anyone else. The address is distinguished from the surrounding utterance by a shift into the present tense and by the particle 'ah', where the latter indicates concession and acceptance of the author's way of life. Samuel's address to the author receives laughter from the group, thus 'involving' the other members of the group (Tannen, 2007) through the dramatization of his reading experience. In the next turn Frank joins in with his own example of reported discourse, but this is in the form of a quotation from the text rather than another direct address (Turn 2). As with Extract 4.4, the direct address here is not to be taken literally, but rather serves to index Samuel's opinion of the author and, by association, his view of the text.

The two examples considered in this section show readers directly addressing textual entities in various ways. In Extract 4.4 a reader seems to 'speak' to a character, while in Extract 4.5 a reader addresses the author of a text. In both instances the address really serves to index the reader's assessment of the character/ author and text for the benefit of the overhearing, reading group audience. Both examples seem to encourage involvement from the other members of the group, thus demonstrating one of the functions of reported discourse identified in the literature (Tannen, 2007; and discussed as a function in Section 4.3.2). This type of reported discourse could be said to indicate empathy between reader and addressee; this relationship is more evident in Extract 4.5, where the content of the address shows affiliation, but may also be seen in Extract 4.4, where the character is taken to be worth addressing directly rather than completely ignored.

4.2.3 Fictional voices

The third and final form of reported discourse identified in the reading group data is the representation of fictional voices. This refers to occasions when readers move into the voices of characters from the texts they are discussing. Within this type of reported discourse readers can represent the fictional voices in a variety of ways: through paraphrases, approximations, negation or through direct quotation. These representations of voice may be marked as being reported or the distinction between this voice and the reader's 'own voice' may be blurred (Myers, 1999a: 396). Lastly, the movement into fictional voices may involve just one speaker and one turn or several speakers and several turns. In the two examples presented below, these fictional voices are not just quotations but rather exist within assessment sequences and function to give a flavour of the character's personality.

The first example is taken from the Wanderers Group's discussion of *Flight Behaviour* (Kingsolver, 2012). At the start of the extract Laura is describing how scientific knowledge could have helped the community in the novel:

Extract 4.6 Narrow-minded voices in *Flight Behaviour*

[8:35] – Wanderers, *Flight Behaviour*

1	L	yes but it could have helped you understand how they were growing and the er
2	R	why would you want to understand things (.) **you could understand everything you possibly could from the <u>bible</u> surely from our culture**
3	H	=even the two versions
4	R	**y- you don't need any of this new-fangled science stuff**
5	L	no
6	Mo	no
7	L	well
8	R	I mean it was an incredibly narrow minded (.) place [wasn't it
9	Mo	[yeah

L = Laura; R = Robert; H = Hannah; Mo = Molly

Laura suggests that possessing scientific knowledge would have helped the rural community to understand how their crops were growing (Turn 1). The 'you' in her turn may function as an address to the characters in this community, although this is not continued across the rest of her utterance. Robert seems to respond to this address, imagining and adopting the voice of the fictional character(s) in an ironic fashion. Speaking as the character(s), he offers a counterargument to Laura's point, questioning why 'you would want to understand things' when the Bible can provide sufficient knowledge (Turn 2). Robert continues in this vein at Turn 4, stating that the 'new-fangled science stuff' that Laura cites is not needed. These are not direct quotations from *Flight Behaviour* (Kingsolver, 2012) and are more like Robert's approximation of the community's voice or what Tannen refers to as the 'inner speech of others' (2007: 115). It is unlikely that any of the other members of the group are going to mistake this irony for Robert's personal opinions, even though his shift into this fictional voice is relatively subtle, with no reporting clause or other linguistic marker to distinguish this from the surrounding discourse. However, he adopts a mock indignant tone while in the voice of the character(s), and closes his reported discourse with an assessment of the community in his own voice, which confirms that the ideas just put forward were not his own: 'it was an incredibly narrow minded place' (Turn 8). The effect of Robert's slip into fictional voice is comic and evaluative, giving a naive and unintelligent voice to the community in the novel. In the reported discourse, he creates 'a portrait of the other' (Buttny, 1997: 480), which is effective in this instance because the Wanderers Group do not share the religious ideology of the community.

The second example comes from the Contemporary Group's discussion of *Americanah* (Adichie, 2013). In this extract Debbie moves into the voice of the protagonist in order to give a sense of her experience:

Extract 4.7 'What's this African American shit?'
          [7:10] – Contemporary, *Americanah*

1	D	I think it was like when the university group got together (0.5) and the people were like (.) **what is this** (.) erm (0.5) and it was the (.) international students (0.5) and it was like **what's this African American shit you know (0.5) you are not African and there is nothing African about [you**
2	R	[yeah
3	D	and so you know (1.0) so (.) I thought that was interesting you know and then like when she said she was sitting in the classroom and she was asked to give (.) <the black perspective> because at that particular time she was the only black student in the class and she was supposed to give the black perspective (.) she was like (0.5) **ok well I am not an American black but I know what they want me to say**
4	M	=yeah [yeah yeah
5	D	**[because I have sat in the class so I can give them what they want to hear** (1.0) that it's so clichéd that she could give them exactly what they wanted to hear

          D = Debbie; R = Richard; M = Mark

As mentioned in relation to Extract 4.4, *Americanah* describes Ifemelu's movement between Nigeria and the United States, focusing on the effect of this migration. In this extract Debbie is describing Ifemelu's experience of attending university in the United States and, specifically, two occasions when her African identity was made salient: first during a university group and second in a seminar. At Turn 1 Debbie describes what happened in the university group, and particularly when the international students questioned the accuracy of the category term 'African-American'. In order to give a sense of what was said in the group, Debbie moves into the voice of the international students: 'what's this African American shit . . . you are not African and there is nothing African about you' (Turn 1). This is not a direct quotation from the novel and is therefore an example of 'imaginary' reported speech (Myers, 1999b), but Debbie's shift into this voice and her use of expletive and aggressive tone serves to represent the voice and the opinions of these fictional characters. Across Turns 3 and 5 Debbie describes a separate narrative event, in which Ifemelu is asked to give 'the black perspective' during a university seminar. There are similarities with Debbie's first shift into character voice at Turn 1: she uses 'like' as the reporting verb to introduce the speech of the character, places emphasis on particular words for effect, and offers a paraphrase of what is said in the novel rather than directly quoting. She indicates that the voice of the character has finished by pausing for one second and then offers her own assessment of the situation: 'it's so clichéd' (Turn 5).

In these two examples the readers adopt the voices of fictional characters or groups of characters in order to carry out certain interactional tasks. Like readers' representations of their own voices (Section 4.2.1) and the addresses to characters (Section 4.2.2), the examples in this section exist within assessment sequences and seem inextricably tied up with evaluations of character and/or the text. In addition, however, the examples in this section serve to dramatize the readers' descriptions of the narrative, bringing a flavour of the original text (i.e. the novel) to the reading group discussion. Representing fictional voices in this way can also serve to simulate the character's mind, perhaps displaying empathy between reader and character. Empathy did not seem to exist between Robert and the characters he was mocking in Extract 4.6, but did seem to be apparent in Debbie's account of Ifemelu's voice in Extract 4.7.

4.3 Functions of reported discourse in the reading groups

In Section 4.2 three different types of reported discourse prevalent in the reading group talk were considered. Accounts of the purposes of the different types of reported discourse was offered on occasion, but this did not constitute a sustained discussion of function. This section focuses on the interactional work that the reported discourse in the reading group discussions performs. Three predominant functions are identified:

- an *evidential* function, lending support to a reader's stance on an element of the text: for example a character, the quality of the writing, or the author;
- an *involving* function, encouraging other members of the group to also engage in reported discourse;
- a *simulation* function, indicating that readers are imagining a character's mind in an attempt to understand his/her actions or beliefs.

These functions are considered over the next three subsections with reference to examples taken from the reading group meetings. The evidential and involving functions of reported discourse have been identified and discussed fairly extensively in previous research (Section 4.1.2), while the simulation function seems less common in other types of talk, and more specific to the reading group context. Although these three functions are conceptually distinct, it is argued that in practice the functions are not exclusive and, theoretically, all three can coexist across a short passage of talk.

4.3.1 Evidential

As discussed in Section 4.1.2, one of the main functions of reported discourse is to provide evidence for a speaker's stance. Whether talk is taking place in a highly institutional context, such as a police interview, or in the everyday context of a chat between parent and child, speakers are likely to invoke what has been said or thought previously in order to support some interactional work being undertaken. Providing evidence and 'factuality' might be the most prevalent function of reported discourse (Myers, 1999a: 387), offering speakers a 'powerful' position (Clift, 2006: 149) and a guarantee of the 'authenticity' of their point (Leudar and Antaki, 1996: 24). As reading groups are places where assessments are offered and debated, the evidential function is highly prevalent. This function is found in all three forms of reported discourse identified in Section 4.2, when thoughts while reading are discussed, when characters or authors are addressed, and when fictional voices are adopted by readers. Most typically, however, this function is associated with occasions when readers are invoking their private reading experience or providing evidence directly from the text, and the two examples presented in this section attest to this.

In the first example of the evidential function Colin from the Contemporary Group is discussing *Fragrant Harbour* (Lanchester, 2002) in terms of the author's other novels:

Extract 4.8 Reassessing a novelist

```
            [14:26] - Contemporary, Fragrant Harbour
1    C      which I remember really enjoying both of those
2    R      =oh
3    C      =and I read this and found it a little bit flat
            (1.0) to me it was kind of like (1.5) he was
            trying to be Graham Greene without the kind of
            (0.5) without the moral complexity
4    R      =interesting
5    C      =or depth of character (.)and I was thinking
            to myself (0.5) I am going to have to go back
            and read those other books which I loved
6    R      mmm
7    C      because maybe they weren't that good after all

            [C = Colin; R = Richard]
```

Colin is arguing that *Fragrant Harbour* does not compare well with Lanchester's other novels, and that as result he feels compelled to return to the other novels to check that he was correct in his original assessments. *Fragrant Harbour* was recommended by Richard (for a discussion of the Contemporary Group's 'rules' over book recommendations, see Section 3.4) and at this stage of the meeting Colin is offering disagreement with Richard's positive appraisal of the novel. In addition to demonstrating that he is well-read (citing Graham Greene) and showing that he has specifically read some of Lanchester's other novels, Colin provides evidence for his opinion by reporting his negative reading experience of *Fragrant Harbour*. As he reaches the climax of his story, Colin moves into reported thought, relating that he will 'have to go back' and check that Lanchester's other books were actually good 'after all' (Turn 5 and Turn 7). In reporting his thoughts at the time of reading Colin shows that he independently reached his negative assessment of the novel prior to the meeting, 'adding strategic detail' to his opinion and 'attesting to its historicity' (Couper-Kuhlen, 2006: 119). He also uses reported discourse to index a change in his epistemic state, a common function of reported thought (Kärkkäinen, 2012: 2203–4). In light of the fact that other readers in the Contemporary Group enjoyed the novel, including Richard – the other speaker in Extract 4.8, it is important that Colin makes his argument as robust as possible and his reported discourse lends evidence to this assessment.

In the next example of the evidential function the Orchards Group is discussing *England, My England* (Lawrence, 1990). This extract comes from near the start of the meeting, at which point the group is discussing reading 'literature' compared with reading 'chick-lit':

Extract 4.9 Literature vs. chick-lit

       [1:15] Orchards, *England, My England*

```
1   A     if you want to read it again you'll get more
          out of it the second time (.) whereas you
          wouldn't with a chick-lit would [you
2   Ja                                     [no
3   Co                                     [no
4   A     =you'd just think oh right
5   S     =mmm
6   Co    =I actually quite enjoyed reading it (.) and I
          was thinking oh I've finished it (.) I was not
          expecting it to be enjoyable

          A = Alex; Ja = Jackie; Co = Connie; S = Sue
```

Members of the group are agreed that *England, My England* is different from 'chick-lit' and that there are benefits to reading such literature more than once because you 'see more depth', especially on a second reading. In this extract Alex describes this difference as something universally experienced by readers, using the second-person 'you' to include readers beyond just herself. At Turn 4 she describes the typical feeling of reading chick-lit, implying that this reading experience is quite shallow. She uses reported discourse to account for this and to provide evidence, claiming that when readers encounter chick-lit they just think 'oh right'. Connie moves the talk onto *England, My England* at Turn 6, reporting that she 'actually' enjoyed the book. Building on Alex's use of reported discourse, Connie employs reported thought to describe her experience of reading and, specifically, her surprise that she enjoyed it and her disappointment that it ended so quickly. Similar to the example on Turn 4, Connie's reported discourse is introduced with the particle 'oh' and a shift in tense from the surrounding talk, showing that this was what she thought at the time of reading: 'oh I've finished it' (Turn 6). This latter reported thought is bracketed by two assessments that praise the 'enjoyable' reading experience; in this way, the reported discourse provides evidence and 'historicity' (Couper-Kuhlen, 2006: 119) for her evaluation of the book.

In the next example we return to the same data from Extract 4.5, although this time focusing on the reported discourse in Turn 2:

```
Extract 4.10 'You're an atheist'
          [25:46] - Forest, Somewhere Close to the End
1    S     and that's (.) one thing er er er that warmed
           me to her more than anything else was when I
           discovered she was an atheist (0.5) I thought
           well ah we'll forget haha for all your upper
           class er upbringing because you're an atheist
           ((general laughter))
2    F     =she says she is but er on one page it says erm
           (0.5) the body is merely a vehicle for for life
           to to flow through
3    L     =yeah
4    F     ==now for some people (.) they would say well
           that's not really an atheistic idea

           S = Samuel; F = Frank; L = Lucy
```

As discussed earlier, in this passage of talk the group is discussing the religious beliefs of the author, Diane Athill. As an atheist himself, Samuel is pleased to read that Athill is an atheist and in the first turn of the extract he jokes that he can forgive her 'upper class upbringing' as a result. In the first part of Turn 2 Frank agrees with this ('she says she is'), but this is only a preface for a disagreement as he provides a counterargument from the text, quoting: 'the body is merely a vehicle for like to flow through'. The quotation serves as evidence in itself, but it also supports Frank's agenda in a less obvious way; as a self-identifying Christian, Frank often comes into conflict with Samuel over religious beliefs and here he is arguing that even seemingly atheistic views can be seen as religious. By claiming that 'some people . . . would say' (Turn 4), Frank 'proposes a stance' (Myers, 1999a: 392) that is held outside of the group, which provides an evidential basis for his opinion. Samuel and Frank both reported enjoying *Somewhere Close to the End*, and both reported experiencing feelings of closeness and affiliation with the author. The use of reported discourse is important in demonstrating this affiliation, especially in Samuel's utterance at Turn 1, but it is also vital in providing evidence, as in Frank's utterance at Turn 2.

In the above examples, reported discourse is seen providing evidence for positions adopted by readers. This evidential function is particularly apparent within sequences of talk where readers are in disagreement (Extracts 4.8 and 4.10), as at these times readers are keen to present their views as factual, historical and/or emanating directly from the text under discussion. In this way, the evidential function of reported discourse is speaker-focused as it primarily serves face managing purposes for the speaker doing the quoting. In the examples analysed above, the reported discourse can lend credibility, historicity and authenticity to the assessment being offered.

4.3.2 Involving

While the evidential function of reported discourse is speaker-focused, the involving function is recipient-oriented. In the examples presented in this section readers share their thoughts through reported discourse, collectively imagining the voices of characters and collaborating to produce shared readings of the texts. The involving function of reported discourse is most associated with Tannen (2007), although it shares similarities with the dramatizing function outlined in Section 4.1.2 (Barnes and Moss, 2007; Clark and Gerrig, 1990; Holt, 1996; Sams, 2010). The key feature of the involving function is that the reported discourse is produced by more than one speaker and is continued across turns. This co-production is possible because reported discourse can create 'vivid' scenes (Tannen, 2007: 39) in which an audience becomes involved and wants to 'actively' interpret (Tannen, 2007: 124). This creates highly dynamic passages of discourse (see also Myers, 1999b), as is evident in the two examples below.

In the first example, the Orchards Group is discussing a character in Lawrence's short story 'England, my England' (Lawrence, 1990):

```
Extract 4.11 Understanding character motivation
            [34:56] - Orchards, England, My England
1   P       he didn't make the decision himself (.) he
            didn't say that's [what I'm going to do
2   R                         [he didn't say I want to join
            up
3   A       =he might he might have seen it as a (.) right
            from this moment onwards my life is going to
            change (.) I'm going to
            [do something constructive
4   P       [mmm no:::
5   Ca      [he didn't see anything anything wrong with
            his life that was the whole thing really (.)
            I think he thought his life was fine (.) that
            there was nothing wrong with his life at all

            P = Peter; R = Roger; A = Alex; Ca = Carol
```

In this passage of talk readers in the group are attempting to understand the motivations of Egbert, the protagonist in the short story. This character is seen by the group as indecisive and inert: 'he didn't make the decision himself' (Turn 1) and 'he thought his life was fine' (Turn 5). Reported discourse is used across the extract as various members of the group speculate about the character's lack of motivation. Roger and Alex develop Peter's initial use of reported discourse in a collective attempt to simulate the character's mind and understand his lack of action. Peter uses reported speech from Egbert at Turn 1 in order to demonstrate the character's lack of decision: 'that's what I'm going to do'. Unlike examples considered so far, Peter's reported discourse is negated in the reporting clause, explicitly marked as something that the character 'didn't say' – an example of an impossible utterance (Myers, 1999b: 577–8). Roger interrupts mid-turn, correctly predicting the end of Peter's utterance and offering his own example of negated reported discourse from the character: 'he didn't say I want to join up' (Turn 2). As is often the case in assessment sequences featuring reported discourse, this interruption is not seen as problematic (Holt, 2000: 445). This sense of what Egbert 'didn't say' is co-constructed by Peter and Roger across the first two turns of the extract. The character is positioned as having different priorities from the group, and the reported discourse is important in this 'othering' process (Buttny, 1997) as the Peter and Roger focus on what he should have said and how he ought to have behaved.

At Turn 3, Alex is more speculative as to what Egbert might have actually thought about his situation, suggesting that his decision to join the army may have served as a catalyst for Egbert: 'from this moment onwards . . . I'm going to do something constructive'. Alex does not explicitly mark the start of her reported discourse through a reporting clause or a particle such as 'oh' (although she does pause briefly before the shift); this is perhaps because the previous two turns at talk have involved readers using reported discourse, and so the talk at this stage is in a reported discourse frame. Peter and Carol both interrupt Alex mid-turn to disagree with Alex's speculation and her more positive assessment of Egbert, with Peter offering unmarked disagreement ('mmm no' – Turn 4) and Carol presenting an alternative view of the character to that of Alex: 'he thought his life was fine' (Turn 5). In her account of Egbert, Carol does not continue with the direct form of reported discourse found in the first three turns of the extract, instead using narrative report of thought.

The reported discourse in Extract 4.11 dramatizes the narrative (Barnes and Moss, 2007; Sams, 2010), making the assessments and speculations about Egbert 'vivid' (Tannen, 2007). The first three turns of the extract focus on things that are not said or thought by the character and so require no special, detailed knowledge of what was actually said in the story; as a result, everyone in the group has access to speculate what Egbert might have said or thought and various readers take up this opportunity through using direct speech or thought or narrative report of thought. This example of reported discourse seems to possess an involving function, and this is demonstrated in the amount of co-construction found in this short passage of talk. For another example of the involving function from this meeting, see Extract 4.9.

In the second example of the involving function of reported discourse we return to the data previously considered in Extract 4.3. In this passage of talk the Contemporary Group is discussing *Fragrant Harbour* (Lanchester, 2002), with Lizzie and Colin relating their experiences of reading the novel.

Extract 4.12 `I just don't care`

```
          [37:13] - Contemporary, Fragrant Harbour
1    L    you've got these emails going back
2    M    hahaha
3    L    I know Professor Cobb's work on the yuë-fu
          lyric form which is
4    M    =hahaha
5    L    I would just sit there going
6    C    I just don't [care
7    L                  [don't get it (.) I don't know who
          Cobb is (.) I don't know who Wilfred is (.) you
          know what has this got to do with anything at
          this point

          L = Lizzie; M = Mark; C = Colin
```

This extract is discussed in detail in Section 4.2.1 and that analysis will not be repeated here. One element of the extract not discussed above is Lizzie's utterance at Turn 3, which seems to quote or paraphrase from the novel. This reported discourse has an evidential function, providing an example of what was contained in the emails mentioned at Turn 1; however, the quote or paraphrase also seems to have an involving function, providing a mutually accessible example from the novel and encouraging other speakers to produce their own reported discourse. This is realized at Turn 6, where Colin joins in and completes Lizzie's utterance. This is quite an unusual example of the involving function, as clearly readers only have access to their own, private reading experience and not those of others; here, however, Lizzie and Colin co-construct the reading experience of not 'caring' or 'getting' what is happening in *Fragrant Harbour* during their own reading experiences.

As stated at the start of this section, one key feature of the involving function is that the reported discourse is produced by more than one speaker and is continued across a number of turns. The examples show this happening in the reading groups as readers create highly dynamic and collaborative acts of shared reading. Reported discourse can be highly involving in reading group talk because the readers have a shared experience of privately reading the book under discussion and crucially, a shared text to discuss; therefore, in theory at least, no one reader has any more privileged access to reading or the text than any other – although see Chapter 5 for some exceptions to this. The involving function rarely stands alone and often exists alongside at least one of the other functions: the reported discourse in Extract 4.12 is also evidential, while Extract 4.11 also shows the readers simulating the character's mind through the reported discourse.

4.3.3 Simulation

Building on Oatley's work (1999), simulation refers to the experience of running a version of another's thoughts and feeling as if they are one's own. Oatley discusses simulation in relation to reading, arguing that fiction 'runs on the minds of the audience or reader as a computer simulation runs on a computer' (1999: 105). Whiteley's comments on reported discourse as psychological projection (2011: 35) clearly makes her research amenable to this idea of reported discourse as simulation, and while Myers is not explicitly interested in the participants' minds, his focus on 'imaginary' reported discourse (1999b: 575–6) must involve the participants simulating the reported speakers' mind on some level. Reported discourse can be used in reading group discussions to simulate the minds of characters, imagining their motivations, desires and beliefs. Some of the examples we have considered so far in this chapter have contained readers attempting to simulate, although in this section this function of reported discourse is considered in more detail. In Extract 4.6 Robert adopted the voice of the rural community from *Flight Behaviour* (Kingsolver, 2012) in order to demonstrate his view that this community was ignorant and 'narrow-minded'. Doing this involved Robert projecting into the mind (or minds) of the fictional community and simulating what he believed to be the community's general outlook on science and religion. In Extract 4.7 Debbie similarly took the voice of a character, this time Ifemelu from *Americanah* (Adichie, 2013), although Debbie's act of simulation was more sympathetic. She shifted into the voice of Ifemelu when describing the character's experience of university life, and although these were based on what was in the novel, Debbie's reported discourse involved a good deal of inference and simulation of character mind. Lastly, in Extract 4.11 the readers in the Orchards Group were attempting to understand a character's motivation through simulating his mind. This was achieved through reported discourse, and the result was a highly involving and collaborative passage of talk.

Reported discourse as simulation is relatively under-researched, but in many respects is the most interesting and unique function within reading group talk. As noted in Section 4.1.2, Myers (1999b) has discussed hypothetical reported discourse, and in his account of 'imaginary' reported forms has touched on the possibility of participants simulating the minds of those being quoted. Similarly, Holt (2006) has argued that people have the ability to 'enact' the voices of others when quoting or imitating. Also working on reading group discourse, and going further than Myers and Holt, Whiteley has argued that readers psychologically project into the perspectives of characters using reported discourse (2011: 35).

In this section instances of the simulation function of reported discourse from one reading group meeting are presented and analysed. In this extended extract readers imagine the mind and motivations of a particular character through using reported discourse. Members of the Orchards Group are discussing David, the central protagonist in *So Many Ways to Begin* (McGregor, 2006). The theme of 'home' was identified by the group as being an important motif in *So Many Ways to Begin*, and the readers discussed the last lines of the novel in which David says to his wife, Eleanor: 'I want to go home' (McGregor, 2006: 373). For some members of the group, this utterance was petulant, signifying David's annoyance at his situation, while for other readers this last line indicated David's acceptance of his situation and his desire to return to normality with his wife. The following two extracts both focus on this theme, but come from different parts of the meeting:

Extract 4.13 'Let's go home'

```
          [33:04] Orchards, So Many Ways to Begin

1    R    but isn't the answer to the question as to
          whether it was (.) worthwhile or whether it
          was a good thing
2    S    mmm
3    R    =linked into the question we were talking
          about earlier on about the ending (0.5) and
          does he get any sort of closure (.) does he
          actually (.) does I'm going home (.) mean I'm
          now going to draw a line under it (.) because
          if it does (.) then that whole experience was
          cathartic [and
```

```
4    A                      [yeah
5    Ja                     [well no XXX
6    Ju                      [I just wondered
7    R                              [I didn't think it did I
          didn't think it meant that but if it
          di[d then it was worthwhile
8    Ja      [an- and if you've got the relationship
9    R      =yes
10   Ja     =back with his wife
11   R      =yes
12   A      =[yeah
13   S      =[yeah
14   Ja     maybe [it was all worth it
15   Ca            [I think the final words I want to go
          home I thought perhaps he felt that
16   Ja     yeah
17   Ca     [ok enough's enough
18   Co     [mmm enough's enough
19   R      =I [think
20   S         [yeah
21   Ca     =I've explained my life to somebody (.) [even
          if it was a shock and
22   R                                              [but I
          want to know how normal he means as in fed up
23   S      mmm
24   R      I want to go home means I'm fed up (.) I just
          want to [er er
25   S             [oh I thought no I thought
26   A      return to secu[rity and warmth and familiarity
27   Ja                   [normality and yea:::::h

          R = Roger; S = Sue; A = Alex; Ja = Jackie; Ju
          = Julia; Ca = Carol; Co = Connie
```

At the start of this extract Roger speculates as to what 'I'm going home' means for David. He uses reported discourse in order to present this speculation to the rest of the group, slipping into the voice of the character: 'I'm now going to draw a line under it' (Turn 3). Roger presents his interpretation at Turn 7 ('I didn't think it meant that'), which goes against that reading he just suggested and recasts his earlier reported discourse on Turn 3 as an impossible utterance (Myers, 1999b: 577–8). At Turn 15 Carol begins to offer her view on the meaning of the final words of the novel, arguing against Roger and presenting a more positive account of David's feelings. She suggests that David might have felt 'enough's enough' (Turn 17), and this shift into the voice of David is simultaneously produced with Connie, demonstrating that the two readers are in agreement and are '*constituting something as consensual*' (Edwards, 1997: 131 – emphasis in original). Carol continues in the character's voice to further describe how David might have felt about the situation: 'I've explained my life to somebody' (Turn 21). In this extract, Roger, Connie and Carol all shift into the character's voice in order to imagine how he might have felt about the situation and what exactly he meant by the line in the novel 'I want to go home' (McGregor, 2006: 373). These readers must make inferences about the character's mind, and the reported discourse that is used simulates his mind and presents different accounts of his voice to the group for evaluation.

This simulation of this character's mind is continued around twenty minutes later in the meeting when Carol returns to the meaning of the line 'I want to go home':

Extract 4.13a `'Let's go home'#2`

```
          [53:03] - Orchards, So Many Ways to Begin
1    Ca    and it was almost like you know th- this
            business with (.) I want to go home
2    R     yeah
3    Ca    and and all the sort of passion at the end
            was like saying right well (.) I've dealt
            with it (.) we've got the funeral done (.)
            I've met up with someone who isn't my mother
            (.) none of it is very satisfactory but at
            the end of the day we've got each other
4    S     =m[mm
5    Ju       [mmm
6    Ca          [let's go home

          Ca = Carol; R = Roger; S = Sue; Ju = Julia
```

As before, Carol is trying to understand David's actions in the novel through simulation of his mind. At Turn 3 she offers her interpretation of 'I want to go home' from the novel by moving into David's voice: 'I've dealt with it . . . but at the end of the day we've got each other.' Similar to the reported discourse in the previous extract, the voice of David here does not come from the text but is hypothetical and the reader's approximation of this voice. As in extracts presented earlier in this chapter (4.6, 4.7 and 4.11), one principal function of the reported discourse for Carol is to imagine the character's voice through hypothetical reported discourse (Myers, 1999b) – taking on David's perspective in order to comprehend his actions and beliefs. Having said this, simulation is not the only function here: Extracts 4.13 and 4.13a involve disagreements between readers over the meaning of a line in the novel, and so the reported discourse can also be seen as supplying evidence for the readers' different interpretations.

Identifying a specific function of an example of reported discourse can be difficult, and many of the extracts presented in this chapter include reported discourse that performs a variety of functions. It was just noted, for instance, that the reported discourse in Extracts 4.13 and 4.13a contained examples of the simulation and the evidential functions, simultaneously. Some examples contain all three functions discussed in Section 4.3, suggesting that reported discourse can perform important and varied interactional work in a conversation. Although only a short stretch of talk, Extract 4.14 contains reported discourse that performs the evidential, involving and simulation functions. In this passage of talk the Contemporary Group is discussing *The Restraint of Beasts* (Mills, 1998), a novel focused on a working-class community in Scotland. At this point in the meeting the readers are talking about the poor working conditions suffered by the characters:

Extract 4.14 Exploited workers
```
            [50:42] - Contemporary, The Restraint of Beasts
1    L      it is completely exploitative
2    D      =of course
3    L      but they just seem (2.0) like they just
            accepted that (0.5) it never occurred to [them
4    M                                                [to
            them that there was nothing better (.) oh why
            should we live in this grot yes
5    L      =yeah (.)or to question it (.) and to go this
            isn't suitable (0.5) we are not going to work
            for you because you are not (1.5) treating us
            properly
6    M      I love I love the bit (1.0) where they get new
            belts to put their tools in (.) and he was a
            foreman he had one anyway
7    C      =yes
8    M      one of them says (1.0) does this come out of
            our wages as well ((laughs))

            L = Lizzie; D = Debbie; M = Mark; C = Colin
```

The readers seem to agree that the working conditions depicted in the novel are 'exploitative' (Turn 1) and in this short passage of talk they try to understand why the characters are so complicit with this. Lizzie argues that the characters 'just accepted' these conditions because it 'never occurred' to them 'to question it' (Turns 3 and 5). At Turn 4 Mark shifts into the voice of the exploited workers, representing what they might have thought or said had they been more aware of their situation: 'oh why should we live in this grot?' This is marked as hypothetical speech or thought by the preceding turn construction unit ('to them there was nothing better'), but this is subtle and has to be understood as hypothetical from the surrounding discourse, and particularly in light of Lizzie's prior turns. Lizzie continues this, also shifting into the voice of the workers and presenting another hypothetical piece of speech or thought: 'this isn't suitable . . . you are not treating us properly' (Turn 5). Given the interactional context, these two examples of reported discourse from Mark and Lizzie are evidently 'impossible' (Myers, 1999b: 577–9) in that these utterances or thoughts could not have been articulated by the characters due to their complicity in their poor working conditions (Turn 3). These examples of reported discourse seem to perform a simulation function for the readers, allowing them to account for why the characters may have behaved as they did. As in Extracts 4.13 and 4.13a, this reported discourse is hypothetical and shows the readers imagining what life would be like from the characters' perspective. The hypothetical status of the reported discourse also means that it can be highly involving, and this is demonstrated in the fact that Lizzie and Mark co-produce the workers' voices. As in Extract 4.11, the reported discourse here is marked as *not* what characters said or thought, and so no special, in-depth knowledge of the text is needed, which theoretically gives all readers in the group the opportunity to add their own versions of the characters' voices. The reported discourse across Turns 4 and 5 also has an evidential function, supporting and supplying evidence for Lizzie and Mark's evaluations of the characters. By presenting what these voices did not say or think, the readers demonstrate the limits of the characters' understanding of their working conditions. While the reported discourse in Turns 4 and 5 seems to display all three functions discussed in this chapter, the example at Turn 8 is more obviously just evidential, with the quotation from the novel supporting the point that the characters are being exploited.

The two passages of talk analysed in this subsection show members of reading groups using reported discourse in order to simulate the minds of fictional characters. This function often occurs when readers take on the voices of characters – the form of reported discourse considered earlier in Section

4.2.3. The extracts discussed in the present section all involve the readers giving a sense of the characters' mind or behaviour through the reported discourse, rather than actually quoting from the literary text. To do this, the readers make inferences about the characters, arriving at approximations of the fictional voices. An argument can be made that these acts of simulation indicate or lead on to an empathetic relationship between reader and character, but based on the examples presented here readers are not necessarily empathizing when they simulate. In Extract 4.6 Robert voices a rural community but presents these characters negatively, and likewise in Extract 4.14 Lizzie and Mark seem to have pity for the characters but not empathy.

4.4 Conclusion

Reported discourse is common across various discourse contexts (Bakhtin, 1981), but seems particularly important in reading group talk. Evaluation of texts, characters and authors are frequently made in the groups, and reported discourse often goes hand-in-hand with these sequences of assessments. Three forms of reported discourse were identified, relating to the speaker and addressee of the reported speech or thought (Section 4.2), and three predominant functions of reported discourse were discussed: evidential, involving and simulation (Section 4.3). For the most part the reported discourse performed rhetorical and interpersonal functions, serving to strengthen a reader's assessment of the text under discussion and create group cohesion through involving others in the reported discourse. At the same time, however, it has been suggested that the reported discourse could demonstrate the kinds of relationships that readers had with characters: in some cases reported discourse was used to index a distance between reader and character (as in Extract 4.6), while on other occasions it was used to show a close, potentially empathetic relationship between reader and character. Whether a particular instance of reported discourse indexed empathetic closeness or distance from a character, its use in certain situations seemed to suggest that readers were treating characters as possible people, as entities that have thoughts, beliefs and feelings beyond those written on the page and constructed synthetically by the author. This idea of readers treating characters as possible people is picked up and given extensive treatment in Chapter 5.

The use of reported discourse across the reading groups was a widespread discursive practice, forming an important part of each of the groups' shared repertoire. Drawing on reported speech and thought served as 'a shared discourse' for approaching texts, and in particular fictional characters. Readers' direct addresses to characters and their simulations of fictional minds may reflect their 'certain perspective on the world' (Wenger, 1998: 83) in which characters are conceived of as possible people. In forming part of the shared repertoire, reported discourse performed an important collaborative function within the groups, becoming a way by which the reading groups in this study constituted themselves as groups (Myers, 1999a: 397).

5

Mimetic Reading in the Groups

Morris Zapp, the brash US literary scholar in David Lodge's novel *Changing* Places, considers 'the root of all critical error' to be a 'naive confusion of literature with life' (Lodge, 1975: 38). For Zapp, life is composed of 'things' whereas literature is composed of 'words' and the failure to keep life and literature distinct from one another leads to 'all kind of heresy and nonsense: to "liking" and "not liking" books' (1975: 38). *Changing Places* is a comic novel and Zapp is an extreme, grotesque version of a certain type of literary critic, but as Guillory notes, professional critics are required to maintain a distinction between themselves and 'lay' readers who merely read for 'pleasure' (2000: 31–3; see also Felski, 2008). At its most extreme, this distinction is enacted in the Zapp-ian views of Bloom (1984), Mudrick (1961) and Weinsheimer (1979), and in less overt ways, through production of highly complex literary theory and the exclusion of any discussion of everyday reading practices in much literary critical discourse. Zapp certainly would not be impressed by the readers in this study, who conflate real life with literature to such an extent that it forms another shared discourse across these groups.[1]

In the previous chapter it was argued that particular forms of reported discourse were prevalent in the reading groups and that these forms became part of the shared repertoire of these groups. This chapter considers mimetic reading as another popular reading practice that becomes part of the groups' shared repertoire, or shared language. Mimetic reading involves readers responding to fictional characters as 'possible people' and to the narrative world as like our own (Phelan, 2005: 20). This practice of reading 'as though it were real life' is occasionally remarked upon in the groups, and so has become a reified and recognized practice (Tusting, 2006: 40), forming an important part of the groups' shared repertoire. Previous studies of reading groups have arrived at similar conclusions, with Long finding that readers moved frequently and easily between real-world and fictional character identities, bringing 'the weight of their lives' to their encounters with books (2003: 29) and readers in Hartley's study reporting that discussions about books can be greatly enhanced if they can relate to texts and can bring in aspects of their own experience to the discussion (2001: 81–2). From the standpoint of literary critics and other professional readers, seeing a continuity between life and art can be regarded as 'naive' and as 'barbarism par excellence' (Bourdieu, 1984: xxviii; 1984: 36), but for the reading groups this conflation of art and reality is not generally seen as problematic and can even lead to greater group cohesion and positive insights. This is not to say that mimetic reading is entirely unchallenged within the groups, however; and as well as considering the prevalence of the form in this chapter, challenges are considered as well.

This chapter will be organized as follows: first, the 'mimetic' model of reading is introduced, with research on this issue surveyed; second, examples of mimetic reading from the book groups are presented and analysed; third, challenges to the mimetic reading norm are considered, with a focus on how these are played out in interaction; and fourth, category entitlements are considered as an interactional resource that is facilitated by the dominance of mimetic reading. Given that mimetic reading and category entitlements involve readers implicating aspects of themselves in the discussions of the texts, the conclusion considers how identity operates within the reading group context.

5.1 Mimetic reading – reading for real life

As noted in Chapter 4, there was a tendency across the reading groups for readers to use reported discourse to address characters, speak as characters and simulate the thoughts and feelings of characters. For the most part the use of reported discourse performed rhetorical and interpersonal functions, serving to strengthen a reader's assessment of the text under discussion and create group cohesion through involving others in the reported discourse. At the same time, however, it was suggested that the reported discourse could demonstrate the kinds of relationships that readers had with characters; in some cases, reported discourse was used to index a distance between reader and character (as in Extracts 4.4 and 4.6), while on other occasions it was used to show a close, potentially empathetic relationship between reader and character. In the present chapter this dual focus on the interpersonal and the cognitive is continued, with mimetic reading discussed in terms of its interpersonal and rhetorical functions in the reading groups and in terms of what it suggests about dominant everyday reading practices. In this section an overview of mimetic reading is offered, with an initial focus on Phelan's research into reader judgement (1996; 2005) and then a more extensive account of other research in this specific area.

In his narratological research Phelan (1996; 2005) argues that readers and audiences are interested in the progression of a narrative and follow the trajectory of instabilities and tensions in a narrative as it progresses. Readers engage in various responses, 'judging characters, developing hopes, desires, and expectations for them, and constructing tentative hypotheses about the overall shape and direction of the narrative' (2005: 20). In accounting for how readers assess fictional characters, Phelan distinguishes between three components that can make up their judgement: mimetic, thematic and synthetic. These three components are not exclusive and readers can move between them in their reading of a character at any one time. Phelan defines the mimetic, thematic and synthetic in the following ways:

- Mimetic responses 'involve an audience's interest in the characters as possible people and in the narrative world as like our own'.
- Thematic responses 'involve an interest in the ideational function of the characters and in the cultural, ideological, philosophical, or ethical issues being addressed by the narrative'.
- Synthetic reactions acknowledge the constructed and artificial nature of literary texts. These reactions are possible 'because any character is constructed and has a specific role to play within the larger construction of the narrative'. (Phelan, 2005: 20; summarized in Peplow et al., 2015: chapter 3)

The focus of this chapter is on the mimetic component. Thematic and synthetic reader responses are discussed at length in Peplow et al. (2015: chapter 3) and specific examples of these forms of reading will only be discussed in the present chapter in relation to challenges to the mimetic norm (Section 5.1.3). Phelan's distinction between these three components of textual interpretation offers a good starting point for considering different types of reader response found in the data, with the mimetic form accounting for much of the dominant reading practices in the reading groups. The practice of treating 'the characters as possible people' (Phelan, 2005: 20) was prevalent in the reading group discussions, and this mimetic reading generally held-up well to criticism within groups. Mimetic reading is part of the shared repertoire of these groups, forming an element of the 'rehearsed character' of the reading groups (Wenger, 1998: 83) and their linguistic routine (Holmes and Meyerhoff, 1999: 176). Such was the pervasiveness of mimetic reading that groups recognized and explicitly commented on it as a method of reading, referring to it as 'reading for real life', or something similar (see Extract 5.6). Tusting argues that when a community gives 'a name' to an element of its repertoire in this way, the language feature becomes 'reified' (2006: 40); that is, the process by which a practice is congealed 'into "thingness"' (Wenger, 1998: 58). Although these three forms of reading are conceptually distinct, it is important to note that these are not mutually exclusive. Readers move between mimetic, thematic and synthetic forms, and can make these subtle shifts across just a few turns (Peplow et al., 2015: chapter 3). While thematic and synthetic forms of reading are present in the data, and shifts between these forms are possible, mimetic reading occurs more frequently in the reading groups and so is the main focus of this chapter.

Although Phelan's terms are used in this analysis, he is not the only scholar to stress the centrality of mimetic reading practices to (non-academic) reading, and in the following section I offer a brief and selective review of research into 'reading for real life' from a range of different academic disciplines.

5.1.1 Research into mimetic reading

Scholars from various fields have argued that readers of fiction often evaluate and interpret texts according to real-life values and expectations. At its strongest, this research argues that readers seek to identify with characters, feeling characters' emotions and engaging with them intellectually. In this section, work from psychology of reading, cognitive poetics and cognitive narratology focusing on the prominence of mimetic reading is considered.

For some working in the psychology of reading, literature is powerful and unique as an art-form because of its capacity to create fictional worlds that readers can relate to their own and characters with whom they can empathize. Research from psychology of reading has found that readers have the ability to 'participate' and 'immerse' themselves in literary texts (Gerrig, 1993; Gerrig and Allbritton, 1990), and some of these studies have argued that, as a default position, readers treat characters and narrative events as replicating the people and the events experienced in everyday life (e.g. Gerrig, 1993). Readers often cross the boundaries between the real-world and the world of the text, and this is most evident in the 'participatory responses' that readers direct towards texts (Gerrig, 1993). Such responses include reader thoughts or verbalizations such as 'watch out!' when a character is in danger, or 'I'm glad that character is happy' following a plot resolution (1993: 65–96). The addresses to character discussed in the previous chapter are particularly good examples of participatory responses. Gerrig suggests that readers often interpret the fictional textual worlds as mimetic of real life, unless the text actively discourages this kind of response (1993: 69) and that readers' memories and experiences are impossible to divorce from their reading because texts 'call forth from memory real-world events and causal possibilities' (1993: 231).

Studies in this area using reading autobiographies have similarly found links between real-life experiences, memories and literary fiction (Andringa, 2004). When reporting on their reading history, readers frequently cited identification with characters as an important part of reading enjoyment (Andringa, 2004: 211). In particular, readers reported experiencing 'similarity identification', seeing similarities between themselves and a character, and deriving pleasure from this (Andringa, 2004: 226; see also Rall and Harris [2000] and Stockwell [2005, 2009]).

Other work in this area has considered reading as a form of simulation (Oatley, 1999, 2002, 2003). As discussed in the previous chapter in relation to reported discourse, this idea of reading as simulation presupposes that readers have a tendency to treat fictional worlds as comparable, and sometimes based on, phenomena in the real world. Oatley argues for similarities between computer simulations and the reading process:

> A play or novel runs on the minds of the audience or reader as a computer simulation runs on a computer. Just as computer simulation has augmented theories of language, perception, problem solving, and connectionist learning, so fiction as simulation illuminates the problem of human action and emotions.
>
> (Oatley, 1999: 105–6)

Oatley (1999) focuses on readers' emotional involvement in narratives, discerning three psychological processes that lead to readers experiencing strong emotions when reading fiction: identification, sympathy and autobiographical memory (1999: 113–14). The process of autobiographical memory is most relevant to the data presented in this chapter. Building on research into how theatre audiences experience emotion (Scheff, 1979), Oatley (1999: 113–14) argues that reading fiction can help us cope with events in our everyday lives that are difficult to understand. He states that when we read of a character's problems, for instance, we run a simulation of this character's predicament, experiencing a version of these emotions as prompted by the text. A reader's feeling of emotion towards a character's predicament will be stronger if the reader has experienced a similar situation to that of the character. There is not an impermeable divide between reading fiction and experiencing reality, and the ways in which readers experience the contents of literary texts are based on the same psychological processes that are run when they experience 'real' emotions and events (Oatley, 1999). Readers' autobiographical memories can be primed by events in the text, and their simulations of the fictional emotions can feedback to their real lives, allowing them to re-evaluate their own, similar experiences (for a similar view on the importance of personal memory in the reading process, see Mar [2004]).

Like Gerrig (1993) and Oatley (1999), Zunshine's work (2006) posits that the act of reading fiction provides 'grist for the mills' of our mind-reading capabilities, even though 'on some level we do remember that literary characters are not real people at all' (2006: 16–17). Zunshine surmises that our default state when reading is to treat characters and events as based (in some way) on reality, judging them according to real-life expectations. Reading fiction allows us to 'try-on' other mental states and identities, which in Zunshine's view helps us to cope with comparable events that may occur to us in the real-world (2006: 17).

The above overview is just a sketch of studies that consider the influence that real-life reader identities, experiences and emotions have on the reading process; for other research in this area, see: cognitive poetics (e.g. Gavins, 2007; Stockwell, 2005, 2009; Whiteley, 2011), literary pragmatics (e.g. MacMahon, 2009a, 2009b) and narratology (e.g. Palmer, 2002, 2004). The research discussed here suggests that the divide between the real world and fictional worlds is not impermeable, and that readers frequently (and perhaps necessarily) move between the two. The emphasis that participants in reading groups place on mimetic reading, or reading for real life, suggests that simulation (Oatley, 1999), participation (Gerrig, 1993) and identification (Andringa, 2004) are at work during the reading process. At the very least, these terms are useful in accounting for the ways in which readers *talk* about texts, even if directly linking these to underlying psychological processes is problematic.

In the following subsection five examples of mimetic reading from the groups are presented and analysed. These examples not only show the prevalence of mimetic reading, but also the ways in which readers orient to this form of reading across multiple turns at talk.

5.1.2 Examples of mimetic reading

As discussed in Chapter 4, the concept of shared repertoire is central to any CofP approach. The analysis in this chapter maintains this focus on the linguistic 'resources' (Meyerhoff, 2002: 528) and 'shared discourse' (Wenger, 1998: 125) drawn on by the reading groups when discussing texts. In addition to particular forms of reported discourse, mimetic reading is seen as comprising part of the groups' shared repertoire, and the examples in this section demonstrate the pervasiveness of this form of reading (for different examples of mimetic reading, see Peplow et al., 2015, chapter 3).

In the first example of mimetic reading, members of the Wanderers Group are discussing two characters from *Flight Behaviour*, Preston and Ovid ('the scientist'):

Extract 5.1 'He was quite bright, wasn't he?'
```
       [21:10] - Wanderers, Flight Behaviour
1   Ma   the little boy (.) Preston (.) he was quite
         bright wasn't he
2   H    =he was [yes
3   Ma           [I loved the way the erm (0.5) the
         scientist encouraged him
4   Mo   =yeah
5   Ma   =he didn't discourage him at all
6   H    =no
7   Ma   =or talk down to him did he (0.5) he sort of
         encouraged him all the way through the book (1.0)
         you could see him almost growing in confidence and
         almost (1.0) forming his ambitions
         [if you like in his life
8   H    [yeah yeah
9   Mo   that was why he was brave enough to go and ask
         about the encyclopaedia wasn't it
10  R    =yes
11  Mo   =if he could buy it all he wouldn't have done
         that before he had met
12  Ma   =yeah
13  H    =mmm
14  Mo   the scientist
15  H    and when they get the book on (1.0) what was it
         erm (0.5) sheep
16  Mo   oh yes (.) learning all about the sheep
17  H    yes ((laughs))
18  R    oh there is the bit about having to swing it
         around your head
19  H    yes (.) yes
20  R    and then they actually try that out later on
         don't they
21  H    yes they do ((laughs))

         Ma = Max; H = Hannah; Mo = Molly; R = Robert
```

The group is discussing the positive effect that Ovid, the scientist, had on Preston and specifically the ways in which Preston developed as a character as a result of their relationship. In discussing this, several readers in the group discuss the characters as if they are real, praising Preston and Ovid and positively assessing their relationship. Max reports that he 'loved' the encouragement that Ovid offered Preston (Turn 3) and that, as a result, 'you could see' Preston 'growing in confidence' and 'forming his ambitions' (Turn 7). Although these consequences are mitigated by 'almost' (Turn 7), Max seems to be presenting the visceral effect that the narrative has had upon him and discussing the development of character in mimetic terms. Molly carries on in the same vein, undertaking inferential work in order to describe the effect of the relationship on Preston: 'that was why he was brave enough to go and ask about the encyclopaedia' (Turn 9). She then speculates that Preston 'wouldn't have done that' before meeting Ovid (Turns 11 and 12). The ways in which Max and Molly emotionally respond to the two characters and the sorts of inferences they make about these characters suggest that these readers are engaging in mimetic reading and interpreting the characters as closely resembling real people.

Similarly, the readers from the Forest Group describe being emotionally affected by characters in *Room* (Donoghue, 2010):

Extract 5.2 'Can you imagine . . . '
    [19:36] – Forest, *Room*

1   Jo   yeah I kept thinking how on earth did he sleep
           in the wardrobe (1.0) can you imagine being
           sorta shoved in a wardrobe and to not make any
           noise (1.0) although he was stunted in growth
           for his age (.) I mean it's not very nice is it
           (3.0)
2   L   no i- i- it felt it felt very oppressive
3   Jo   =mmm
4   L   to me (.) when I was reading it (.) it felt like
           I couldn't breathe (.) sometimes

     Jo = Joan; L = Lucy

The mimetic nature of the response in Extract 5.2 comes from the merging of reader and character, both in terms of voice and through participatory responses. At the start of this extract Joan uses reported discourse, describing her thoughts while reading (as discussed in Section 4.2.1): 'I kept thinking how on earth did he sleep in the wardrobe.' She then encourages the group to take on the role of the child narrator by directing questions to the group: 'can you imagine ...'. Joan then makes the comment, 'it's not very nice' at the end of Turn 1, which, as an evaluation and as a form of participatory response (Gerrig, 1993) only makes sense if we take it that the narrator's experiences are processed by the readers as being 'real' to some degree. What follows justifies this conclusion, as Lucy discusses the palpable effect that the narrative made on her while reading: she says that the narrative 'felt very oppressive' (Turn 2) and reports that it felt like she 'couldn't breathe sometimes' (Turn 4). This extreme physical effect reported by Lucy is a mimetic response, demonstrating an engagement with the narrative and with the experiences the characters undergo as real events. At the very least, these effects are real for the time that Lucy is reading.

Mimetic reading is not just associated with positive experiences with characters. In the next extract Jenny from the Wanderers Group describes her very negative reaction to a character from *The Windsor Faction* (Taylor, 2013):

Extract 5.3 'A warped, twisted man'

```
       [24:52] – Wanderers, The Windsor Faction
1   J   he was a warped (.) twisted man who was leading
        a very warped twisted life and erm (1.0)
2   H   he was only gay
3   Ma  [he was xxxxxxx
4   Mi  [xxxxxxxxxxxxxx
5   R   =that's true
6   J   =it wasn't to do with being gay (.) particularly
        (.) but it was like he was (1.0) I dunno (.) his
        values were so (.) almost (1.0) well to me they
        were just so totally trivial and supercilious
        and yet he had sort of influence didn't he

        J = Jenny; H = Hannah; Ma = Max; Mi = Miriam; R
        = Robert
```

Jenny's reaction to this character is sufficiently strong to indicate that she is engaging in mimetic reading. She initially describes the character as a 'warped, twisted man' (Turn 1) and, following Hannah's criticism of Jenny's position and defence of the character at Turn 2 ('he was only gay'), she then specifies the nature of her dislike: 'his values were so totally trivial and supercilious' (Turn 6). Jenny's strength of feeling against the character seems to result from mimetic reading, even if the effect of this is to produce resentment towards the character. Hannah's criticism of Jenny's position as potentially homophobic (Turn 2) could be interpreted as mimetic reading in itself, as she feels the need to defend the character, and also could be an acknowledgement that Jenny is reading mimetically and bringing in real world prejudices into her interpretation of the character.

The next example of mimetic reading also comes from the Wanderers Group, although the assessment of character is more measured on this occasion. The group is discussing the character of James Bond from *Solo* (Boyd, 2013):

Extract 5.4 'He didn't really have a soul'
          [12:10] – Wanderers, *Solo*

```
1    L    a lot of the army people I went to school with
          that have been married and are divorced again so
          yes you can't help but
2    H    and particularly when you know you are going
          from one air base to another
3    L    =mmm
4    H    =it is bound to be disruptive
5    L    oh yes that must be a difficult (1.0) I mean his
          lifestyle isn't [conducive to commitment is it
6    Mo                   [no no
7    L    but erm
8    Mo   he didn't really have a soul in any way [did he
9    L                                             [no
10   Mo   there was no depth of feeling to him just total
          (.) physical pleasure (1.5) the cars (.) the
          women

          L = Laura; H = Hannah; Mo = Molly
```

This example of mimetic reading is slightly different from the other extracts in this section. The readers are attempting to understand the character of James Bond by comparing his experiences of working for MI6 to their understanding of what it is like to work for the army, bringing in real-world examples and seeing the character as a product of this context. Laura invokes her own experience, observing that 'army people I went to school with' are now divorced (Turn 1), and Hannah adds to this by specifying that 'going from one air base to another' is particularly 'disruptive' for these relationships (Turns 2 and 4). Laura's evaluation at Turn 5 that the situation must be 'difficult' seems to refer to the real-world relationships they have been discussing, but the movement from this discussion back to the fictional character in the second turn construction unit (starting 'I mean . . .') suggests that James Bond's situation is also difficult. Like the people Laura went to school with, the character's lifestyle is not 'conducive to commitment' (Turn 5), and this creates his particular character (Turns 8–10). The fictional character's way of life is seen as a product of his job and in order to comprehend this way of life readers in the Wanderers Group draw on their real-world experiences and their broader understandings of what being employed by the army entails. Using real-world knowledge in this way and applying it to the character of James Bond is not seen as problematic within the group, instead providing the readers with a rich frame of reference.

Similar to the previous two examples, in the next extract the readers in the Orchards Group judged the quality of *The Book Thief* (Zusak, 2005) by invoking the (dis)likeability of the characters. The readers positively evaluated the characters in *The Book Thief*, talking at length about how much they liked the protagonist of the novel, Death:

Extract 5.5 Getting to know Death

```
                [04:32] - Orchards, The Book Thief
1      Ca       I thought he was lovely (.) I'd like to get
                to >know< [hahahahahahahahaha
2      Co                [yes yes almost
3      R        you're calling it a him (.) er er I can't
                remember whether
4      Ca       well I don't know well [er er
5      S                               [I got the impression
                I got the impression it was a him
6      Ca       now that you mention it there was a point
                where (0.5) I think there was there was maybe
                it did allude to the fact that it could be
                (1.0)
7      R        can't remember
8      Co       it was male in my eyes
9      Ca       =[and mine
10     Ja       =[yeah mmm
11     S        =[mmmmmmm no question >you thought it might
                be a female<
12     R        =no no I didn't (.) no I didn't I was just
                questioning (.) I was trying to think
                ((30 seconds of transcript omitted))
13     R        but presumably (.) part of the reason you all
                (.) liked him (.) or her (.) was because of
                this compassion
14     S        mm[m
15     A          [mmm
16     R        =and if you think of it (.) you know (.) can
                you think of a worse job for a compassionate
                person
17     Ca       yeah
```

```
18    R     and that should be exposed to a::ll the
            suffering [so I think that's why
19    Ca                [yeah
20    Co    mmm
21    S     mmm
22    R     er why he's haunted by humans
23    Ca    ye[s
24    R        [because he's a compassionate (.) [entity
25    Ca                                         [yes and
            he's having to pick up all [bad stuff that's
            going
26    R                                          [having to pick up
            all the bad
27    Ca    =ro[und
28    R        [and the good stu[ff
29    Ca                        [an and the good
            st[uff as well
30    R        [and the good stuff (.) but (.) all the bad
            stuff

            Ca = Carol; Co = Connie; R = Roger; S = Sue;
            Ja = Jackie; A = Alex
```

In the first part of this extract (Turns 1–12), the members of Orchards Group attempt to psychologize the character of Death by focusing on an element of the narrator's identity that is not explicitly clarified in the novel: his/her gender. In addition to psychologizing and anthropomorphizing the narrator through this discussion of gender, the readers also make explicit evaluations of character that demonstrate mimetic reading. Carol's description of Death as 'lovely' and her joke that she would 'like to get to know' him (Turn 1) is a good example of this reading preference for mimetic reading.

The group further psychologize and anthropomorphize Death in the second part of this extract, from Turn 13 onwards. On various occasions, Roger describes Death as 'compassionate' (Turns 13, 16 and 24), as he makes a series of claims as to the psychological state of Death; in particular, Roger attempts to infer why Death is 'haunted by humans' (Turn 22) – a direct quotation from the final sentence of the novel (Zusak, 2005). Turn 16 is particularly illustrative of the mimetic, mind-reading practices in evidence in this passage of talk, as Roger discusses Death's 'job' as the Grim Reaper, asking the group 'can you think of a worse job for a compassionate person'. This is accepted by the others as a legitimate question to ask and gives rise to a dynamic and collaborative sequence of turns, as others in the group respond to this. The question Roger poses to the other group members presupposes that the narrative world of *The Book Thief* is similar to the world outside the book, and that characters in the narrative (whether human or superhuman) can be judged by human expectations and real-world values, and their actions and thoughts predicted accordingly.

Although it is mainly Roger who engages in mimetic reading practices in the second part of this extract, other readers in the group offer plenty of positive back-channelling and active listenership to Roger across Turns 13–24. From Turn 25 onwards a highly collaborative floor develops (Coates, 1996; Edelsky, 1981), with Carol and Roger alternately offering turns that build on the other's utterances and jointly constructing comments on Death's character. Building on Roger's earlier point that Death's 'job' must have been difficult for such a 'compassionate' character to undertake (Turn 16), Carol and Roger jointly discuss the way that Death has to 'pick up' all the 'good stuff' and the 'bad stuff' (Turns 25–30). This section of talk is replete with echoic talk: in particular, Roger's near repetition of Carol's prior turn (Turns 25–26), Carol's subsequent echoing of Roger's 'good stuff' (Turns 28–29), and finally Roger's echoic summary of both their points at Turn 30. Although it would be possible to interpret this passage of talk between Carol and Roger as interruptive, as the onset of new speaker turns do not occur at TRPs, in the context this simultaneous talk is better understood as a series of affiliative overlaps (Kitzinger, 2008). Both speakers are engaging in simultaneous talk as much as the other, so there does not appear to be the asymmetry of power that we would associate with hostile interruptions (e.g. Zimmerman and West, 1975) and, indeed, highly institutional talk (Heritage, 2004: 236). Secondly, the simultaneous talk here is not topic-changing as new speakers are repeating what the prior speaker is saying, thus displaying agreement with the other speaker. In addition, the onset of simultaneous talk does not have the effect of silencing the original speaker, which Zimmerman and West (1975) claim is a key feature of interruption.

What is being jointly constructed and collaborated on in Extract 5.5 is mimetic reading from the group members, and specifically, the notion that the narrator of *The Book Thief* resembles a possible person in the world outside the book, displaying human qualities and constrained by most of the same laws. For the Orchards Group, the success of the novel and the character of Death seems to lie in the character's believability, the subsequent opportunities for empathy and identification that this affords, and the fact that his/her actions and emotions can be inferred by the readers' real-world knowledge. This psychologizing practice from the readers is particularly interesting in this case because Death, although being imbued with certain human qualities, is evidently not human in the novel.

The examples discussed in this section demonstrate not just the pervasiveness of mimetic reading in the reading groups but also some of the specific ways in which this form of reading is enacted in discourse. Although the readers in the groups seem to remember that the characters are not real people, the ways that these fictional entities are discussed suggests that readers see continuity between fiction and real life. At various times readers imagine and project onto the mental states of characters (e.g. Extract 5.2), assess characters according to real-life norms and expectations (e.g. Extract 5.5), and bring in aspects of their own experience to understand characters (e.g. Extract 5.4). In spite of its pervasiveness in the groups' discourse, however, mimetic reading is challenged on occasion and in the next section an example of this rebellion from the mimetic norm is presented and analysed.

5.1.3 Deviations from the mimetic norm

Mimetic reading is highly prevalent in all four reading groups considered in this study and in other reading groups beyond (Peplow et al., 2015). The previous examples demonstrate the tendency for readers to engage in this form of reading and the ways in which it is taken up by other members of the groups. Having said this, within each group there is a good deal of diversity in terms of reading practice, and rebellion from mimetic reading was occasionally found in the data. In this section, passages of talk from the Orchards Group are considered, in which the group's focus on mimetic reading is highlighted and questioned by one member, Roger. I focus on two elements: first, what these extracts show about the group's joint enterprise, and second, how these objections are interpreted by the group.

A CofP's joint enterprise 'is defined by the participants in the very process of pursing it' (Wenger, 1998: 77–8); this means that groups often define their joint enterprise, or collective task, through practice rather than through the abstracted rules that precede the practice. Implied by this is the idea that joint enterprise is not often explicitly commented on in CofPs. Peplow et al. (2015: chapter 5) discusses institutional and ordinary talk in reading groups, arguing that one point of difference between these two types of discourse is that whereas institutional talk is likely to contain frequent references to the goals of the interaction, ordinary talk tends to flow without participants frequently alluding to these interactional goals. As alluded to in Chapter 3 when discussing the group's orientation to their sets of questions (see Section 3.2), the Orchard Group's talk lies on the institutional end of the cline. This is further demonstrated below when members of the group draw attention to their task as a reading group. Some of the most overt references to joint enterprise occur when members of the group find a problem with a specific practice of the group.

The following passage of talk provides an example of a reader questioning the way that the group is discussing a book and, specifically, challenging the dependency on mimetic reading in the group. Extract 5.6 is taken from the Orchard Group's meeting on *So Many Ways to Begin* (McGregor, 2006), appearing fifteen minutes into the discussion. Prior to this, the group had been trying to account for some of the characters' actions in the novel and, as Roger's complaint suggests, the readers had been engaged in mimetic reading: treating the novel as real life and the characters as having motivations and beliefs that can be judged according to how people might act in reality. At the start of Extract 5.6 Connie is arguing that the abuse that one of the main characters in *So Many Ways to Begin* (Eleanor) suffered as a child was not particularly unusual because of where the character grew up and when the novel was set:

Extract 5.6 Challenging mimetic reading

```
        [15:15] - Orchards, So Many Ways to Begin
1   Co  they were living in appalling (0.5) depression
        and (.) lack of work and lack of money and don't
        you think that he- that that Eleanor didn't
        probably think she was being particularly badly
        treated (.) because all of her friends were
        being treated in the same way I mean
        [they all had
2   S   [well I don't know that they were though
        [be- because her friends weren't were they
3   P   [no they [weren't
4   Ca           [mmm no
5   S   =the friends weren't being treated like that
6   P   uh no
7   Co  well sh- I know she wanted to spend all the time
        out of the house
8   S   =ye[ah
9   Co     [that she could
```

```
10   S                    [yes yeah
11   R     but there is a problem where I I always find this
           in in these discussions (0.5) there's a problem
           when we're talking like this (.) er because
           we're talking about it as though it were real
           life
12   A     =yes
13   S     =[mmm
14   Ja    =[mmm
15   R     =[and actually [it's a book
16   A                    [yeah
17   S     =yeah I know

           Co = Connie; S = Sue; P = Peter; Ca = Carol; R =
           Roger; Ja = Jackie
```

At the start of the extract, Connie claims that the abuse Eleanor suffered as a child was widespread at the time that the novel was set (Turn 1). Following her negative interrogative ('don't you think that'), others in the group challenge Connie's claim in a variety of ways. At Turn 2 Sue offers fairly categorical disagreement with Connie, although her utterance contains features of dispreferred disagreement: she prefaces her turn with 'well' and initial epistemic uncertainty ('I don't know'), and ends on a tag question ('were they'). Heritage and Raymond argue that negative interrogatives, like the one used by Connie, strongly invite agreement (2005: 22), which may explain the dispreferred features in Sue's turn design. Peter's disagreement is similarly categorical and the construction of his utterance at Turn 3 reflects this definitive disagreement ('no they weren't'), although this is reformulated more hesitantly as 'uh no' at Turn 6. Although there is disagreement here over the conditions under which Eleanor and her friends grew up, there is no suggestion at this stage that the type of reading Connie is engaging in is wrong. She accounts for Eleanor's actions by inferring what the character might have thought about her treatment as a child: for example 'Eleanor probably didn't think . . . ' (Turn 1), and her desires: 'she wanted to spend . . . ' (Turn 7), with the verbs of cognition and desire ('think' and 'wanted') performing this inferential work.

At Turn 11 Roger raises his objection with the mimetic reading that the group is engaged in at this stage. He criticizes the group for 'talking' about the book 'as though it were real life', offering a direct challenge to the mimetic reading practice. At this stage, Roger does not expand on why this is a 'problem', and rather just states that what the group is reading is actually 'a book' (Turn 15). The personal pronouns used at Turn 11 initially present the 'problem' as something that Roger alone experiences, evidenced in the use of the first-person 'I'. At this stage, Roger stresses the extremity and particularity of the problem for him through the extreme case formulation (Edwards, 2000, 2007; Pomerantz, 1986) 'always':

There is a problem where I always find this in these discussions. (Turn 11)

Initially, then, Roger presents his complaint as something personal to him – as *his* reaction to the group's talk. Following a short pause, however, Roger repairs his complaint in the next TCU, making it more categorical and emphatic:

There's a problem when we're talking like this. (Turn 11)

Rather than mitigating the problem as something only he experiences, in this TCU Roger broadens out the problem as more general, switching from 'I' to 'we'. The removal of the first-person singular pronouns in the observation 'there's a problem' indicates that it is an issue that can be observed objectively. Additionally, Roger is at pains to stress that his complaint encompasses the entire group: the personal pronoun 'we' demonstrates that Roger includes himself in his criticism.

In offering this criticism of the group's method of reading, Roger is engaging in synthetic reading, seeing the text under discussion as a 'book' (Turn 15), a constructed entity produced by an author (Phelan, 2005: 20). Roger's complaint pits 'popular' ways of reading against more culturally elite ways of reading, drawing on the latter, 'pure aesthetic' approach in order to criticize what he sees as the reduction of the things of art to the things of life' (Bourdieu, 1984: 36). Although Roger does not explicitly align himself with professional critics, like them he is 'vigilant', standing back 'from the pleasure of reading . . . in order to be wary of it' (Guillory, 2000: 31). As discussed in relation to Extract 5.5, however, Roger actually engages in mimetic reading himself, which suggests that the movement between the synthetic, thematic and mimetic can be fluid.

This passage of talk continues in Extract 5.6a, with Roger elaborating on his criticism of mimetic reading:

Extract 5.6a Challenging mimetic reading #2

[16:32] – Orchards, *So Many Ways to Begin*

1	R	the reason she didn't (.) er er (.) talk to her mother or go back to her mother [er er is then
2	A	[it's a story
3	R	=although it then it then gives us this [real
4	S	[mmm
5	R	=comparison between David [er er who's er
6	Ca	[blind
7	R	you know (.) <u>dying</u> to get this thing (.) and her who echoes [it
8	Ca	[wh- when he already had the living mother
9	S	=it's [it's not enough for him
10	Ca	[xxx can't get that he he needs to learn
11	R	=yes
12	Ca	=like you say he needs to know where he's come [from whereas
13	R	[that's right
14	Ca	she knows where she's come from and she doesn't like it
15	R	but but don't you find that [this has been the problem of our discussions sometimes
16	Ca	[but even contact with xxxxxxxxxxxxxxxxxxxxxx
17	R	=it's you know <u>that's</u> the reason for it it's the author the [all-seeing author had
18	Ju	[yeah but it just means that we really got into the book and identified with it maybe
19	R	=decided to do it like that
20	Co	but who's better off (.) David or Eleanor

R = Roger; A = Alex; S = Sue; Ca = Carol; Ju = Julia; Co = Connnie

In the final section of this passage of talk (Turns 15–20), Roger expands on why he believes that the group's interpretative practice is a problem, arguing that a literary text is a product of an 'all-seeing author' (Turn 17). If the rest of the group is concerned with explaining events in the narrative by way of the motivations of the characters, and therefore treating the characters as 'real people' to some extent, then Roger is claiming that these aspects of narrative are better explained as a product of the author.

In his initial articulation of the 'problem' that he finds in the group's discussions in Extract 5.6, Roger presents it as a declarative: 'but there is a problem where I always find this in these discussions'. A few turns later in Extract 5.6a he invokes the 'problem' again, but this time reformulating the issue as a question to the group. Roger's question is in the negative interrogative form:

But but don't you find that this has been the problem of our discussions sometimes. (Turn 15)

The negative interrogative presents the default, mimetic position of the group as problematic, instead encouraging a problem as the default position, encouraging other group members to explicitly disagree with this position. This form of questioning is not typically understood as a question, either by the speaker or by the recipient (Heritage, 2002). Rather, negative interrogatives are interpreted as a powerful assertion of a position, projecting 'an expected answer' (Heritage, 2002: 1436) and strongly inviting agreement (Heritage and Raymond, 2005: 22). The negative interrogative used by Roger is strong enough to be heard as an assertion and, very likely, as an accusation against the rest of the group. Julia's reply to Roger at Turn 18 suggests that she interprets Roger's turn as an assertion of a position as she disagrees, initially prefacing her counterargument with an agreement token, but then going on to offer disagreement: 'yeah but it just means that we really got into the book and identified with it maybe'. The specific content of Julia's turn following Roger's negative interrogative is discussed in more detail below.

Thinking about both parts of this passage of talk together now, members of the group respond to Roger's complaint in a variety of ways. Alex displays full agreement with Roger, latching onto the ends of his turns with agreement tokens in Extract 5.6a (Turns 12 and 16) and successfully co-constructing the end of Roger's turn at the start of Extract 5.6a with 'it's a story' (Turn 2). This 'cumulative talk' (Mercer, 2000: 31) suggests that Alex agrees with Roger's proposition that there is a problem with mimetic reading group and that it would be better for the group to focus on literary texts as constructed works rather than as directly representative of real life. Alex is the only group member who appears to fully agree with Roger. Although across both extracts Carol and Sue agree with Roger and contribute to his argument that the novel offers a structural comparison between David and Eleanor (Turns 1–14), neither reader articulates any agreement with his overarching point that the group are misdirected in their method of interpretation. Indeed, Carol and Sue continue with the same kind of inferential mind-reading to which Roger is objecting; for example, Carol's comment that Eleanor 'knows where she's come from and she doesn't like it' (Turn 14) with its use of mental state verbs ('know' and 'doesn't like') makes inferences about Eleanor's thoughts. Judging by the fact that Roger then goes on to reiterate his criticism in the turn following this (Turn 15), it would seem that he interprets Carol's point as part of the problematic mimetic reading practice that he criticized in Extract 5.6.

Perhaps, therefore, it is this continuation of the group's mind-reading practice that encourages Roger to persist with his line of attack and explicitly direct a question at the group in Extract 5.6a, asking if the other readers find the same problem with the group's joint enterprise (Turns 15, 17 and 19). As ostensibly the first part of a question/answer adjacency pair, Roger's question strongly encourages a direct answer. As mentioned above, Julia addresses the question, offering a counterargument to Roger in her answer. Like Roger's negative interrogative, Julia's presents her response as a 'natural' position to take. She argues that the group's tendency to read the novel as real life is the natural result of their close engagement with the text: 'it just means that we really got into the book and identified with it maybe' (Turn 18). The minimizer 'just' downplays the significance that Roger seems to want to read into the mimetic reading practice, and the 'maybe' tagged on to the end of Julia's turn has a similar effect. The act of 'really' getting into a book is therefore presented as being a default way to read in the group and not something worth challenging.

First and foremost, Roger's complaint and the group's response confirms that most of the group enjoy reading fictional characters in terms of expectations generated from their real life experience (i.e. mimetically). In criticizing it during a meeting, Roger draws attention to this practice as one of the central facets of the Orchard Group's task (their joint enterprise) and shared repertoire (their way of talking); accordingly, the group's response to this criticism confirms the centrality of this practice. Sue and Carol continue with this practice in spite of Roger's complaint, and while Julia's counterargument accepts that the group indulges in this interpretative practice, she argues that this way of reading is not problematic and that such feelings of empathy and identification constitute a natural way to read. Furthermore, at the end of Extract 5.6a Connie's utterance (Turn 25) redirects the talk back to the set of questions that the group is working through: 'but who's better off (.) David or Eleanor'. This confirms the importance of the preset questions and the mimetic reading practice to the group, moving the discussion back to the consideration of characters as flesh-and-blood people, and effectively ignoring Roger's complaint and his synthetic reading. All this serves as further evidence for the centrality of the interpretative practice of bringing in real-life expectations to which Roger objects. This is not the only occasion that Roger raised this complaint to the group; across the other recorded meetings he offered another three challenges to the group's mimetic reading practice, but none of these seemed to make any lasting change to the Orchard Group's principal way of reading.

From the analysis in this section, it seems that mimetic responses tended to dominate the reading groups' meetings. Other forms of reading response (i.e. synthetic) were occasionally drawn on by particular members, and these could be used for the purpose of challenging the mimetic reading norm. Mimetic reading can take various forms, with readers merging their own voice with that of characters (see also Chapter 4), judging characters according to their real-world beliefs, and reporting 'feeling' the experience of a character. Additionally, characters and narratives were often assessed according to believability, with readers frequently basing their judgements on real-world standards and their experiences of the discourse world. In these judgements, texts that failed to replicate aspects of the readers' experiences or their expectations were often assessed negatively, while texts that the readers could relate to, containing characters that the readers could empathize with, were generally assessed positively.

In all of these examples of mimetic reading participants in the groups moved seamlessly between discussing the real world and the fictional world. In the next section, we consider occasions when readers explicitly invoke aspects of their own lives in their discussions of texts through category entitlements, either drawing on their own direct experience or on the experiences of those whom they know. This was seen explicitly in Extract 5.4, when Laura drew on her knowledge of people in the army who were now divorced in order to understand the character in *Solo* (Boyd, 2013). These invocations of category entitlements were common in the groups and were particularly important in creating and demonstrating the centrality of mimetic reading. In addition to indexing the prevalence of mimetic reading, category entitlements performed rhetorical functions for the speakers who use them, serving to give a basis for an assessment being made. This rhetorical function was particularly in evidence when there is some split of opinion within a group.

5.2 Category entitlement

In this section category entitlement is discussed as an interactional manifestation of mimetic reading. As has been discussed so far in this chapter, any division between the world of the text (the fictional world) and the world beyond the text (the real world) is highly porous in the readers' general approach to texts and in the talk generated by the groups. As a result, the personal backgrounds that readers bring to meetings are interpreted as an important element in leading to a 'good discussion' (Hartley, 2001: 81–2). Reading groups are a site of debate in which different readers' assessments are compared and contested, and readers often invoke their personal background in the form of particular identities and experiences when offering their views on texts. Doing this can strengthen readers' assessments precisely because mimetic reading is such a dominant force. What follows is a brief overview of two discursive features associated with the management of personal background and identity in interaction: stake and category entitlement.

Research within discursive psychology and conversation analysis has considered the ways that people present 'facts' in conversation (e.g. Potter, 1996; Raymond and Heritage, 2006; te Molder and Potter, 2005). Potter's work on how people work up their presentations of opinions such that they appear as facts, or at the very least as highly credible opinions, is particularly relevant. Potter discusses 'stake' and 'category entitlement' as two of the most important concerns for speakers who are giving opinions or assessments. Stake refers to an individual's vested interest in a matter and so can compromise a speaker's neutrality and thus, potentially, the validity of their opinion. Discussing stake, Potter argues that it can be 'used to suggest that the description's speaker, or the institution responsible for the description, has something to gain or lose; that they are not *dis*interested' (Potter, 1996: 122 – emphasis in original). In order to appear to hold a valid opinion, speakers may have to perform stake inoculation (Edwards and Potter, 2005; Potter, 1996), showing that they do not have a particular interest in holding their opinion. In a reading group, for example, a reader may express dislike for *Jane Eyre* by Charlotte Bronte but will probably need to show that the basis for disliking this novel is justified and not based on arbitrary reasons or personal prejudice (i.e. because the reader hates all nineteenth-century novels or because they do not rate female authors). This reader may therefore use stake inoculation in order to show that their view is unbiased: for example 'I love other stuff by Charlotte Bronte but can't stand *Jane Eyre.*'

Similar to stake, category entitlement refers to an individual's interest in the object being assessed. In contrast to stake, however, category entitlement refers to an individual's rights to be an authority due to their experience.

This relies on the idea that certain people are 'knowledgeable . . . simply being a member of some category' (Potter, 1996: 133). In certain contexts membership of a category, for example 'doctor, hockey player, hospital worker' can be seen as justifying an individual's 'knowledge of a specific domain' (Potter, 1996: 133). Category entitlements are highly pervasive in conversation and have been shown to occur across various contexts: for example talk about ethnicity (Phoenix, 2008), in support groups (Horton-Salway, 2004), during football matches (Meân, 2001), and in reading groups (Peplow, 2011; Peplow et al., 2015). Discussing stake and category entitlement together, Potter summarizes how these operate respectively to damage or work-up the validity of a person's position on a matter, at best showing their natural rights for holding a particular viewpoint: '[T]he facticity of an account can be enhanced through working up category entitlements; it can be weakened by emphasizing the personal or institutional stake of the account's author' (Potter, 1996: 122).

The following extract provides an example of category entitlement in action. In this following passage of talk from the Orchards Group, Roger is discussing elements of 'The Dead' (Joyce, 2006) that the group will have 'missed' in their reading:

Extract 5.7 'As a Welsh person'
```
         [11:15] Orchards, The Dead
1   R    of course there are lots of other things that we
         missed
2   S    =yeah
3   R    =or would've missed (0.5) about about the
         culture (0.5) and I feel that as a Welsh person
4   S    =[mmm
5   Ca   =[mmm
6   R    =about should you (0.5) have you got an
         obligation to get to know the culture (0.5) and
         I think this is a lot of what this going west is
         about [and
7   Ca          [mmm
8   R    = and and whether you should [go
9   S                                 [what what do you
         think that going west bit meant (0.5)

         R = Roger; S = Sue; Ca = Carol
```

While discussing the theme of cultural origins in 'The Dead' Roger invokes his Welsh identity, relating his own experience to that of Gabriel, the protagonist in Joyce's short story. Roger states that he and Gabriel are exiles from their country of origin (Wales and Ireland, respectively) and, as Roger sees it, both have experienced pressure to reconnect with their cultural origins. He uses his category entitlement 'as a Welsh person' (Turn 3) in order to suggest closeness to the character and his knowledge of the situation, expanding on this point at Turn 6. The distribution of turns in the extract and the movement towards a more tightly organized, single-voice floor suggests that Roger is taken to hold an 'expert' status by the others in the group on this issue. Roger receives encouraging feedback from others in the group, and Sue asks him a question that seems to nominate him as an expert: 'what do you think that going west bit meant' (Turn 9). Roger's position as an individual with 'epistemic primacy' (Raymond and Heritage, 2006: 694) on this matter results from his working-up of his category entitlement as a 'Welsh person.'

In the remainder of this section extended examples of category entitlements from all four of the reading groups are presented. Owing to the dominance of mimetic reading, the readers in these examples invoke aspects of their own experience and identity, relating these to relevant features of the texts – character, setting, theme and so on. When using category entitlements readers can make various aspects of their identity salient, and the particular element they choose to invoke will be determined by the text under discussion. In Peplow et al. (2015: chapter 3), for instance, a reader's adoptee identity is invoked in response to *So Many Ways to Begin* (McGregor, 2006), while in Peplow (2014) a reader's identity as a Christian is made salient during a discussion of *The Shack* (Young, 2007). In the following analyses various aspects of identity and personal experience are invoked by the readers: geographical (including nationality and experience of living in a village), employment (either the reader's own job or the working experience of a parent), and experience of caring for an elderly relative. These category entitlements are often used rhetorically in order to bolster a reader's interpretation or assessment of a text, especially where there is a split of opinion; however, on occasion readers play down their position of expertise. At all times, the category entitlements that are played up or played down are prompted by, and mediated through, the text under discussion.

In the first example the Contemporary Group is discussing *Harvest* (Crace, 2013), a British novel set in an unspecified rural location at the time of enclosure (circa 1750). Ben relates his reading of the novel to his experience of growing up in a village:

Extract 5.8 Village life

      [21:00] Contemporary, *Harvest*

1	B	having been brought up in a village (.) which to a certain extent (.) was in the early seventies when we moved there (0.5) still stuck in a very old fashioned view where you were a bit like you are a stranger and there was still that culture
2	M	and after twenty-eight years (0.5) despite the fact you have lived in the village more than ninety percent of the villagers (.) you were still a stranger
3	B	yes (1.0) because he starts calling himself a stranger at the end doesn't he
4	R	that's right
5	D	yes
6	M	that is what (1.0) something like twelve years
7	B	that's right but I mean the (0.5) I think all the time back in the village we lived in

      B = Ben; M = Mark; R = Richard; D = Debbie

In this extract Ben draws parallels between his personal experience of being a 'stranger' in a village and the experience of the fictional character. This 'similarity identification' (Andringa, 2004) between reader and character allows Ben to invoke his entitlement to see the novel in a particular way as a result of his experience. His fellow reader Mark, who is also Ben's father, corroborates this story and adds his own details (Turn 2). At Turn 3 Ben moves the talk back to the novel, making the invocation of his personal experience relevant to the wider discussion: like Ben, the narrator of the novel refers to himself as a 'stranger' (Turn 3). Ben's experience of feeling like a stranger in a village seems to provide him with special access to the novel and 'all the time' during reading he was thinking back to the village he lived in.

    In the next extract Molly from the Wanderers Group relates the 'cultural poverty' in *Flight Behaviour* (Kingsolver, 2012) to her experience working as teacher:

Extract 5.9 'Cultural poverty'

    [15:34] Wanderers, *Flight Behaviour*

```
1   Mo    and little details the erm (1.0) there was a
          bit where she had taken Preston he was in the
          laboratory and the scientist erm (1.5) oh it was
          when she had taken the kindergarten class out
          and the scientist had dressed up for the occasion
          and got the tie on (0.5) and erm (1.0) one of
          the little boys said are you the president (0.5)
          and he said why is that because of my dark skin
          (.) he said well no you are wearing a tie and I
          thought that was actually quite moving (2.0) and
          it reminded me when I was (1.0) my last OFSTED
          [place name omitted] was quite (.) I mean you
          know what (1.0) it is quite a poor area and the
          OFSTED inspector went into my role play area
          and read a story to the children and one of the
          little boys was gobsmacked because in his family
          none of the men could read
2   H     ooh
3   Mo    and it just reminded me
4   H     that is awful
5   Mo    yes it was terrible
6   H     that is worse than [place name omitted]
7   Mo    I mean it wasn't (.) I am not saying that was
          the norm (.) but it wasn't that uncommon
8   Ma    but that is what he obviously expected
9   Mo    well yes (.) yes (0.5) and that just reminded
          me and I thought but it is that same cultural
          poverty that you know it's like

          Mo = Molly; H = Hannah; Ma = Max
```

In the first turn of the extract Molly recounts a scene from *Flight Behaviour* in which a scientist who is visiting a school is mistaken by one of the children as the president because he is 'wearing a tie' (Turn 1). Molly offers a participatory response (Gerrig, 1993) in evaluating the scene as 'moving', before moving on to tell her own story from her experience as a teacher in 'quite a poor' urban school. Her personal narrative involves an OFSTED inspector[2] visiting her school and reading a story to a class. One of the boys in the class was 'gobsmacked' because none of the men in his family could read, and Molly reports that the events of the novel reminded her of that real-life event (Turn 3). She argues that she witnessed 'same cultural poverty' in her teaching experience as that found in the novel (Turn 9), and the implication is that this gives her special access and entitlement to interpret this aspect of the novel.

The previous two examples of category entitlement have involved readers invoking rather different experiences and/or identities: growing up in a village and working as a teacher. In both examples, however, the readers see continuity between the narrative worlds and the real world, and similarity between their experiences and those of the characters. This provides these readers with an entitlement to discuss certain aspects of the novels unchallenged. However, category entitlements are more evident in sequences of competitive talk (such as arguments), when this feature can be used to strengthen one perspective over another. The following examples are taken from more competitive interactional contexts and the category entitlements are therefore more obvious.

The next two examples are taken from the same meeting in which the Contemporary Group discussed *Freedom* (2010). There was a split of opinion within the group over the quality of the novel and although most of the group reported mainly enjoying the novel, Debbie was more sceptical. Her behaviour in this meeting was quite unusual and somewhat out of character. She reserved offering her opinion of the novel until over twenty minutes into the meeting, after the others in the group had given their positive assessments of the text – in other words, she adhered to the 'rules' against which she often rebelled (see Chapter 3)! When Debbie did offer her opinion for the first time, however, it was strongly and forcefully articulated:

Extract 5.10 'I know these people'

```
        [23:36] Contemporary, Freedom
1   D   I just think it's patronising (.) it's really
        really patronising (0.5) yes I know these
        people (.) I know these kind of people but I
        just think you can talk about them without
        being so patronising about them a[bout
2   L                                     [but I thought
3   D   =patronising [about
4   L                [it was funny
5   D   =about the mid-west (.) no it's not it's
        patronising

        D = Debbie; L = Lizzie
```

The novel under discussion, *Freedom* (Franzen, 2010), is mainly set in St. Paul, Minnesota: Debbie's home-town. Prior to this extract the readers had agreed that the novel portrays St. Paul quite negatively as the parochial and provincial heartland of America's liberal middle class. While the other readers in the Contemporary Group did not mention any personal connection to the setting of the novel or regard the negative portrayal of Minnesota as particularly significant, Debbie negatively assessed the novel on this basis. As Extract 5.10 demonstrates, the other readers merely found this aspect of the novel 'funny' (Turn 4). This extract is just one example from an ongoing debate from this meeting in which Debbie argues that the novel is 'patronising' (an adjective she uses across all three of her turns in this extract) while other members of the group argue that the representation of the community is just 'funny' (l. 6).

In the first turn of the extract Debbie begins by offering an evaluation of the novel: 'it's patronising', which is then upgraded in the next TCU to the more definitive extreme case formulation 'it's really, really patronising'. She then goes on to elaborate on her basis for holding this opinion, which is her personal experience of growing up near the setting of the novel. In doing this, Debbie acknowledges her stake in holding this negative view of the novel: 'yes I know these people' (Turn 1). The prefacing 'yes' appears to acknowledge that Debbie's close relationship to Minnesota is potentially a biasing factor in her argument against the novel. As discussed, being seen to have a stake in a matter can be rhetorically brittle, especially if it is deemed to be too strong and result in a biased viewpoint (Potter, 1996: 124). One way interlocutors have of dealing with this is to own up to their possible bias by performing 'stake confession' (Potter, 1996: 129–30). If successful, this action will demonstrate that the speaker is aware of their tricky position, presenting them as reasonable and thus strengthening their position. By pre-empting the other readers' claims of stake, interest and bias, Debbie allows herself to put forward her view on the novel and her entitlement to evaluate the novel negatively.

The debate as to whether *Freedom* (Franzen, 2010) is harmlessly 'funny' or crudely 'patronising' extends for roughly one minute following Extract 5.10, after which time Debbie makes the following comment:

Extract 5.10a 'I know these people' #2

       [25:05] – Contemporary, *Freedom*

1   D   my sister also found er Fargo patronising >I
              thought< Fargo was hilarious (.) which again
              (.) is taking (.) completely taking the mickey
              outa Minnesota again (1.0) but here (.) I just
              (0.5) there was (.) I didn't (.) I mean (.)
              it wasn't even like erm (.) an airport novel
              where I could just sit down and read it for the
              enjoyment

Given her close personal connection to the setting of the novel and the potential for her to be biased, Debbie offers stake inoculation. Her discussion of the film *Fargo* and her professed view that the film was 'hilarious' seems intended to play down the sense that she has a partisan view on negative fictional representations of her home state. Although the film *Fargo* is also seen as poking fun at the mid-Western states of Minnesota and North Dakota, Debbie makes clear her enjoyment of the film, even when other members of her family did not agree. Here, we can see Debbie performing the '*dilemma of stake*' (Edwards and Potter, 1992: 158–9 – emphasis in original); the problem of how speakers 'produce accounts which attend to interests without being undermined as interested' (1992: 158). Debbie has a personal connection to the setting of *Freedom* (Franzen, 2010) and she wishes to draw on this when negatively assessing the novel (see Extract 5.10). However, Debbie's dilemma is that she could be accused of having too much of a vested interest in giving her interpretation. Her comments in Extract 5.10a attempt to stave off this potential criticism, playing down the sense that she is predetermined to see the novel in negative terms because of her personal connection to the setting. Debbie found *Fargo* 'hilarious', thus performing stake inoculation and, possibly, demonstrating that her view of *Freedom* is more objective than subjective.

Across these two extracts, Debbie's national and regional identity is made salient in her interpretation of *Freedom* (Franzen, 2010). Debbie's acknowledgement of her personal link to the location of the novel and her subsequent negative evaluation are predicated on the notion that the novel is attempting to replicate and pass comment on the 'real' St. Paul, Minnesota. Debbie's comments, therefore, show her as reading mimetically: she understands the novel to be ridiculing her hometown (not just a fictional version of it) and, as such, she evaluates the novel negatively. Debbie's own comments, however, show the precariousness of her position on the matter, and she is quick to play down any sense that she has any personal vested interest in evaluating the novel in this 'interested' manner.

In another instance of competitive talk from the Contemporary Group, Mark and Richard debate whether a particular character's development is believable. The group is discussing *The Lowland* (Lahiri, 2013) and, specifically, the character of Gori:

Extract 5.11 Personal experience and *The Lowland*

[21:27] Contemporary, *The Lowland*

1	M	I was a bit unconvinced (.) about the philosopher bit (0.5)
2	R	the philosophy
3	M	=not the actual philosophy itself but the idea that she could pick up philosophy (0.5) and move on (0.5) and make a career out of philosophy that (1.0) I didn't quite (0.5) that just didn't quite <u>gel</u> with me
4	R	can I say something here though which is I have direct experience of that (.) my mother was a Jewish German refugee
5	M	=yeah
6	R	=and came to Britain (.) she went to LSE and became an expert in (.) you know (.) in demography
7	M	=yeah
8	R	and so she is a prime example
9	M	=sure
10	R	=of somebody who can be a stranger in a strange land [literally
11	M	[yes yes yes
12	R	that may not speak the language very good to begin with
13	M	=yeah
14	R	=but then becomes you know a highly regarded professional so there is absolutely no reason why Gori shouldn't have done that

M = Mark; R = Richard

In this extract Richard argues that the depiction of Gori was accurate and he appeals to his personal experience in order to make his point. This comes after Mark voices his doubts over the believability of the character and, specifically, whether Gori would have been able to learn philosophy and make 'a career' out of it so easily following her move to a new country. Mark reports that this aspect of the character was 'unconvincing' (Turn 1) and did not 'gel' with him (Turn 3). From Turn 4 onwards Richard disagrees with Mark, using his 'direct experience' of the issue to strengthen his point. He prefaces his story with an announcement that he has 'something' to say in relation to Mark's point, and so secures the floor (Turn 4). He goes on to compare the experience of the character Gori to that of his own mother, reporting that she also became an academic expert in spite of being a refugee. Invoking his mother as a 'prime example' (Turn 8) from his 'direct experience' (Turn 4) of someone who overcame being a 'stranger in a strange land' (Turn 10) and did not 'speak the language' (Turn 12), Richard concludes that there is 'no reason' (Turn 14) why the fictional character would not have been able to achieve the same success. The positive back-channelling from Mark and the absence of any counterargument suggests that he accepts Richard's point. Both readers are approaching the character mimetically, with Mark assessing Gori according to her believability and Richard seeing direct parallels between Gori and the experience of his mother. The category entitlement explicitly invoked by Richard is therefore rhetorically robust partly because the readers are engaged in mimetic reading.

In the examples presented so far, category entitlements have resulted from readers' close engagement with characters (or some other aspect of the text, such as setting), with personal experience worked-up to provide readers with a stronger epistemic position than their group members. The last example is different, as one reader invokes her personal experience of the issues raised in a narrative but on this occasion actively resists using this to bolster her epistemic rights because the content of the text is 'too close to home'. In this extract Lucy from the Forest Group is discussing her response to *Somewhere Towards the End* (Athill, 2008):

Extract 5.12 'A bit too close to home'

```
        [5:31] Forest, Somewhere Towards the End
1    L   I just had mixed feelings about it cos I don't
         think I'm somebody that shies away from (1.0)
         death (2.0) particularly
2    F   =mmm
3    L   cos I y'know did nursing for a couple of years
         (0.5) and y'know (.) I've been (.) around my
         grandparents when they were dying y'know (.)
         they went through all that so I kind of (2.0)
4    F   mmm
5    L   =I've seen it you know what I mean (.) been
         there and (1.0) but
6    F   mmm (2.0)
7    L   it's a difficult subject isn't it >my my dad's<
         (1.0) very old ha (0.5) he's ninety
8    S   =[oh
9    F   =[oh gosh oh
```

```
10    L    cos th- they had they had me and my sister
           late (.)
11    F    mmm
12    L    obviously (0.5) but erm (1.0) so it's kinda
           like (0.5) it's a bit (1.0) I dunno (1.0) a
           bit too close to home in a way
13    F    =real[ly
14    L         [cos m- my [dad thinking
15    F                    [yeah yeah
16    L    =he has y'know (0.5) what does he think (.)
           how is he feeling (0.5) and he doesn't
17    F    =mmm
18    L    =talk about it (1.0) the closest he got to
           talking about it was (1.0) erm (0.5) taking us
           to the bank (0.5) really (.) because that's
           where they keep the wills and everything in
           the safe

           L = Lucy; F = Frank; S = Samuel
```

Lucy reports having 'mixed feelings' about the book because of its focus on death (Turn 1). She discusses her past experience of seeing her grandparents pass away (Turn 3) and her current experience of caring for her elderly father (Turns 7–18); the latter experience especially has resulted in the text being 'too close to home' (Turn 12). At Turn 1 Lucy describes herself as not 'somebody who shies away from death' and goes on to say that she worked as a nurse for a couple of years (Turn 3). This opening statement is an attempt at stake inoculation (Potter, 1996), where Lucy tries to play down any sense that she is predisposed against the book purely because of the death theme. Her description of being around her grandparents 'when they were dying' (Turn 3) seems to perform a similar function, inoculating any sense that she is naturally resistant to discussions of death. While these invocations of her experience seem to manage her identity as a reader who is up to the task of reading about death, Lucy's mention of her father is used to justify why she did not enjoy reading the book. In its focus on the end of life, *Somewhere Towards the End* (Athill, 2008) is 'a bit too close to home' for Lucy (Turn 12), causing her to reflect on what her father thinks and feels about the end of his life (Turn 16).

On the face of it Lucy's discussion of her personal experiences of death from her family and working life provide her with the category entitlement to approach the text from a privileged epistemic position; however, in practice these experiences actually put her off engaging with the text in a positive way. The book has clearly had an effect on Lucy and the events and people described in the text seem to have made an impression on her view of relationships in her life. While she is keen to play down any sense that she is biased against *Somewhere Towards the End* on the basis of it being focused on death, Lucy does not seem to invoke her personal experiences in the form of category entitlement.

5.3 Discussion

The focus in this chapter has been on the shared repertoire that is established by the book groups. If shared repertoire is defined as 'the discourse by which members create meaningful statements about the world' (Wenger, 1998: 83) then a recurring 'discourse' observed across the groups is a preference for evaluating and discussing literary texts as if they are mimetic of real life. In practice, this means that readers frequently talk about fictional worlds in terms of real-life norms and expectations; for instance, seeing fictional characters as reminiscent of, and directly comparable to, real people, and judging them on these terms. Excepting occasional deviations from this mimetic reading norm (see Extracts 5.6 and 5.6a), this way of talking about texts dominates the reading group discussions, shaping the way that the readers regard literary texts. Deviations away from the mimetic norm in the form of synthetic challenges are rare and tend to be marked as deviations, with challengers explicitly labelling the mimetic reading practice in a pejorative way (e.g. Roger criticizing the Orchards Group for discussing the text as though 'it were real life' – Extract 5.6) . Based on the present reading group data and other studies in this area (Hartley, 2001; Long, 2003; Peplow et al., 2015) this 'reading for real life' is a highly popular practice in reading groups and, very likely, in non-academic literary reading contexts more generally. The findings presented in this chapter support a number of other studies that have similarly considered reader self-implication in literary texts (e.g. Andringa, 2004; Rall and Harris, 2000; Stockwell, 2005; Whiteley, 2011) and the simulative nature of literary reading (e.g. Gerrig, 1993; Gerrig and Allbritton, 1990; Oatley, 1999; Palmer, 2002; Zunshine, 2006). The main difference between the present approach and the approaches taken in most other studies is the current focus on the discursive manifestation of mimetic reading. This mimetic form of reading should not be seen as simplistic and it certainly should not be regarded as lacking value. When readers recognize elements of themselves in a literary text the result can be a powerful self-intensification: 'recognizing aspects of ourselves in the description of others, seeing our perceptions and behaviors echoed in a work of fiction, we become aware of our accumulated experiences as distinctive yet far from unique' (Felski, 2008: 39).

One of the most evident interactional manifestations of this mimetic reading practice was found in the category entitlements used by readers across the different groups. The frequent invocations of category entitlements constituted a specific 'shared discourse' for the readers. Owing to the groups' preference to read mimetically, the personal experiences and multilayered identities that the readers brought to the meetings were viewed as important in the process of meaning-making. Thought of another way, category entitlements formed a significant part of the reading groups' shared repertoire because they rely on the readers' conflation of personal experience and elements of the fictional world (e.g. characters, themes, plots) for their effect. Subsequently, category entitlements were generally taken to be a robust way of talking about texts, and the invocation of readers' personal experiences often worked to strengthen textual interpretations. Within meetings, the conversational floor tended to be yielded to those members whose real-life identity and experience closely related to some aspect of the text, and a key way for these readers to talk about these experiences was through category entitlements.

The specific aspects of reader identity and experience that have been discussed in the chapter are, on the one hand, somewhat fixed, existing prior to the group discussions, so Roger would presumably self-define as Welsh across most (if not all) contexts, and the fact that Ben grew up in a village cannot be changed. However, the extent to which these a priori identity categories and personal experiences are oriented to is ultimately dependent on the individual reader, the group, and the specific interactional context. In the reading group context, readers can choose whether or not to present a particular aspect of their identity, and often this decision is dependent on the text under discussion. For instance, Debbie's US national identity was primed by the Contemporary Group's discussion of *Freedom* (Franzen, 2010) but not by *The Lighthouse* (Moore, 2012), and Molly's experience as a teacher was prompted by the Wanderers Group's discussion of *Flight Behaviour* (Kingsolver, 2012) but not by *An Officer and a Spy* (Harris, 2013). The book under discussion, therefore, forms a general frame for what aspects of identity are deemed to be salient. Further to this, although readers tended to nominate themselves as belonging to certain categories and possessing some degree of expert status, in other cases it was other members of the group that make these salient. When assumed expertise is conferred on a reader by another this status can be accepted or resisted by the target reader (for readers resisting other-imposed expert status, see Peplow et al., 2015, chapter 3).

All this suggests that identity is 'emergent' and 'relational' in the reading group context (Bucholtz and Hall, 2005), a product of the talk that is defined in relation to others in the CofP. Category entitlement is not static or unidirectional but needs to be 'worked up by interlocutors' within interaction (Potter, 1996: 137; Antaki and Widdicombe, 1998). Moreover, expert status in the reading group is always partial, 'constantly shifting' (Bucholtz and Hall, 2005) depending on, among other things, the book under discussion.

5.4 Conclusion

In this chapter mimetic reading was identified as a dominant reading strategy within the groups. This 'shared discourse' (Wenger, 1998: 125) involved the groups 'treating characters as possible people and . . . the narrative world as like our own' (Phelan, 2005: 20). This is not to say that the other types of reader response are entirely absent, but where other types of response were articulated by readers these tended to be exceptions to the mimetic norm. In terms of wider significance, these findings lend empirical discursive support for the various cognitive and psychological accounts that argue for much (non-academic) literary reading as self-implication and simulation (e.g. Gerrig, 1993; Gerrig and Allbritton, 1990; Oatley, 1999, 2002, 2003). It also supports the idea that readers experience fictional worlds by drawing heavily on their own real-world knowledge and experiences (e.g. Andringa, 2004; Gavins, 2007; Rall and Harris, 2000; Stockwell, 2009).

In the second half of this chapter the focus was shifted to specific discursive manifestations of this mimetic reading. Category entitlements were discussed as a particularly recurrent shared repertoire and it was argued that this discursive feature offered readers a way of speaking about (and in many cases, validating) their own evaluations and interpretations of the text. Mimetic reading and category entitlements did not just perform rhetorical functions in the sometimes competitive discourse of reading groups, however. CofPs are places of close interpersonal relations and trust, with 'self-disclosure' characteristic of these groups (Fletcher, 2014: 350). Lucy's disclosure of her anxious feelings concerning her father in Extract 5.12, for instance, illustrated the value of talking about books, the close bonds of trust in the reading group and the importance of seeing continuity between art and life for these readers.

6

Conclusion

In the novel *The Universe Versus Alex Woods* (Extence, 2013) the narrator Alex decides to set up a reading group that only reads the works of his favourite author, Kurt Vonnegut. Alex wants to engage in the intellectual, spiritual and moral debate that he supposes happens in churches, but as an atheist who believes that the Bible is not 'exactly a page-turner' (Extence, 2013: 201–2) he feels compelled to establish a reading group, which he calls the Secular Church of Kurt Vonnegut. He realizes that his love for Vonnegut does not have to be only a 'solitary pursuit' but can be shared with others in a 'kind of community' (Extence, 2013: 202). This may be a fictional description of a very unusual reading group, but Alex's account of his reading group as a community is appropriate and his reasons for wanting to belong to such a group are very likely shared by real reading group members around the world.

As natural sites of reading that exist prior to and beyond academic research, reading groups can show us how reading is done outside the academy, while also demonstrating the necessarily social aspects of reading. This study has focused on two aspects of reading groups: the talk produced by groups, and the concept of reading groups as communities. The talk of several reading groups has been analysed using fine-grained interactional analysis, specifically CA, while on a macro-level these reading groups have been approached as CofPs. In practice, these two foci are difficult to separate and this study has shown how talk and community are mutually dependent on one another. The interactions that readers engage in during meetings constantly create and update their sense of group, while extra-linguistic elements of the group (such as rules and procedures) simultaneously produce particular types of interaction. Four reading groups have been studied in detail, with multiple meetings audio-recorded, a selection of meetings observed, and interview data collected from all groups. In addition, documents used by the groups have been considered, such as sets of questions and other readers' reviews.

Seeing the reading groups as CofPs, the preceding chapters have loosely mapped on to the three component parts of a CofP: mutual engagement, joint enterprise and shared repertoire. In detailing the composition of each group and factors such as the regularity of meetings, Chapter 1 addressed the mutual engagement of these groups. All four groups fulfilled this mutual engagement criterion through meeting regularly in familiar settings to discuss books. As these groups were self-constituted and were attended voluntarily by the readers, there was variation from one month to the next in terms of attendance, but generally the reading groups had a core group of full members who attended the vast majority of meetings and peripheral members whose participation in the group was less frequent but still regular. Future research could consider the effects of different levels of engagement on reader orientation to joint enterprise and use of shared repertoire features.

Joint enterprise was the focus of Chapter 3, with the groups' shared tasks indexed by particular organizational practices that had been built up over time. Some of these organizational practices took the form of documents brought to the groups from outside: sets of questions, reading group notes and reviews. In some cases use of these documents served to structure the groups' meetings in a positive way for the readers, helping the groups work towards a 'purpose'. At the same time, the groups did not accept the authority of these resources uncritically. Joint enterprise is rarely reducible to an external mandate; rather it is 'defined by the participants in the very process of pursuing it' and 'belongs to them in a profound sense' (Wenger, 1998: 77). In this spirit, the reading groups often entered into a dialogue with the resources that they used, and contested supposedly culturally prestigious resources, questioning the legitimacy of particular sets of questions and critiquing the views of professional readers. When this was attempted, the critique tended to be accomplished as a group rather than by individuals. On one level, this not only reinforced the cultural capital of these resources but also showed the readers, as collectives, rebelling from any sense of assumed cultural prestige and marking out their tastes as distinct (Bourdieu, 1984).

Chapters 4 and 5 focused on dominant ways of talking about texts that cut across all four reading groups and that subsequently formed elements of shared repertoire. Chapter 4 considered the use of particular forms of reported discourse in the groups and the functions that these served. The use of reported discourse performed rhetorical and interpersonal functions, serving to strengthen a reader's assessment of the text and creating group cohesion. At the same time, it was found that reported discourse was suggestive of the kinds of relationships that readers forged with characters: in some cases reported discourse was used to index distance between reader and character, while on other occasions it seemed to show a close, potentially empathetic relationship. In both cases, this simulation function of reported discourse seemed to show readers treating characters as possible people, as entities that have thoughts, beliefs and feelings beyond those written on the page.

Chapter 5 maintained this focus on shared repertoire, specifically building on the idea developed towards the end of Chapter 4 that readers across the groups have a propensity to discuss the fictional characters and events as though 'it were real life'. These mimetic reading practices were found across the reading groups and invocations of category entitlements formed an important manifestation of this type of reading. Invoking personal experience or an aspect of personal identity in relation to a text often served to lend credibility to a reader's evaluation or interpretation, while also offering the readers an opportunity to compare their own experience of a life event, a feeling, or an aspect of identity with other readers and fictional characters. This mimetic form of reading is at odds with typical literary critical reading practices however (Guillory, 2000), and was not accepted by all members of the reading groups. Roger's challenge to the other members of the Orchards Group detailed in Section 5.1.3 articulated this dissent, demonstrating that CofPs are not always harmonious spaces. In practice, however, Roger's attempt to broker change in the group did not succeed and, if anything, served to strengthen the group's view that reading for real life was legitimate.

Before moving on to discuss some of the wider implications of this study, it is important to acknowledge some of the gaps in this research, in particular the omission of any sustained discussion of gender and online reading groups. Although community of practice research within sociolinguistics has focused heavily on gender practices (see Section 2.2), this has not been a particular concern in this study. Gender has already been discussed extensively in relation to reading, and reading groups (Benwell, 2005; Howie, 1998; Long, 2003; Pearson, 1999; Radway, 1987) and although this amount of coverage does not mean that this aspect of reading groups has been exhausted, gender did not seem highly salient in the groups' discussions in this study. Where aspects of identity are discussed in this study, particularly in Chapter 5, this is in relation to invoked identity categories, such as being American, being Welsh and being a teacher. This is not to say that gender was irrelevant to the groups, but it certainly did not seem to be an issue that was regularly discussed and taking an ethnomethodological perspective requires the researcher to approach data in a 'bottom-up' fashion, considering what is oriented to by the participants (Maynard and Clayman, 2003: 174). The second noticeable absence from this study is discussion of online reading groups. In terms of sheer numbers, participation in online reading groups is almost certainly greater than participation in face-to-face groups, and previous studies have been convincing in demonstrating that, similar to face-to-face groups, online groups create 'a sense of community with books at the center' (Fister, 2005: 309; see also Kiernan, 2011; Lang, 2012; Peplow et al., 2015; Rehberg Sedo, 2011). However, lack of space in the present study meant that online reading groups were not considered. Drawing comparisons between face-to-face reading groups and online reading groups is valid but difficult (Peplow et al., 2015: chapter 6), and as such this study has focused solely on face-to-face collectives.

6.1 Social reading

Five features of reading group talk were identified in Chapter 1, and it is worth revisiting those features in light of the discussion and analysis across Chapters 2–5. These features related to the structure and the content of the reading group talk. As mentioned in Chapter 1, the intention here is not to compile an exhaustive list of all reading group discourse features, but rather to flag up interactional features that appear to be recurrent and important in this talk. The five identified features were:

1. Reading group talk is competitive and argumentative. The judgements of individual readers are often questioned.
2. At the same time, most readers are highly attuned to the face needs of others, packaging their comments to conform to politeness norms and allowing others to talk.
3. Reading group talk contains a lot of co-construction between readers, with collaborative floor generally the norm.
4. Issues of taste are foregrounded in these discussions, which is not surprising given that the fundamental purpose of the groups is to discuss and debate readings and interpretations of a shared object.
5. Related to taste, individual readers' identities are never far away from the discussions. These identities may be constructed by the readers themselves or may be imposed on individual readers by others.

We are now in a position to consider each of these points in a little more detail, based on the analysis in previous chapters. Much of the data presented in this study has confirmed the observation made at (1); indeed, argumentation seems to be a necessary component of reading group discourse, with congruity between readers not always welcomed. The discussions in this setting have the feel of intellectual debate with readers defending their assessments of the text using a variety of rhetorical techniques. However, as (2) suggests, this disagreement and argumentation rarely spills over into something more face-threatening. Readers draw on politeness strategies and other discursive techniques to downplay the significance of disagreements. This sense of 'amicable disagreement' in reading groups was discussed further in Chapter 3. Although (1) suggests that reading groups are predominantly spaces of one-up-manship between readers, groups seem to share a desire that everyone should have their say, which (ironically) leads to the sorts of disagreements witnessed over organization in Chapter 3. Moving on to (3), the vast majority of the extracts presented from reading group meetings show the readers engaged in dynamic multi-party conversation. On plenty of occasions interpretations of a text were co-produced by various participants, so that the readings were no longer the property of one reader but a jointly constructed product across multiple participants (Peplow, 2016; Peplow et al., 2015). The existence of shared repertoires within groups facilitates this, providing some shared ways of discussing texts that all readers can generally agree on. Expanding on (4), it is evident that in debating the merits of literary texts the readers are engaged in heightened acts of classification involving hierarchies of taste. Responding to art is necessarily a 'relation of distinction' (Bourdieu, 1984: 224) and this is even more apparent in the public space of the reading group. We saw this in operation in Chapter 3 particularly, as the readers aligned themselves with, or disassociated themselves from, voices from outside the group. Lastly to elaborate on (5): this point received detail treatment in Chapter 5 as the normative mimetic reading form allows readers to move relatively easily between aspects of their own lives and the lives of fictional characters. Far from being simplistic, this occasionally maligned form of reading allowed readers to self-disclose personal information through discussion of the text: for example, in Extract 5.12 and in examples discussed elsewhere (Peplow et al., 2015: chapter 3).

The five features of reading group discourse described above go some way in producing community in these groups. Of course, there are other important elements that contribute to this, but having shared practices that revolve around these five features seems to be vital to the creation and the maintenance of reading groups. Some of these features of the talk are somewhat contradictory and in many respects reading groups can be seen as hybrid spaces. Reading groups can be highly ritualized and institutional, yet relaxed and friendly. They can be places where a diversity of views is welcomed, but certain readings tend to be prized above others. Readers forge group identities, but their individual, prior identities are never far away. These book clubs are often highly collaborative groups (Donato, 2004), yet argumentation and debate are valued. Lastly, groups appear to have fixed ways of conducting their meetings, but these are constantly under negotiation.

Reading groups are perhaps hybrid spaces because they are a fairly unique context in social life. While there are certainly similarities between reading groups and, say, focus groups and university seminars, the reading group is different from these contexts in fundamental ways. Unlike focus groups, the members of a reading group have mutual access to a shared referent (a text) and meet frequently as a group. Unlike in a seminar or a classroom, in the reading group there is no overt external mandate requiring the readers' attendance and officially assessing the things readers produce. Although other groups meet to watch and discuss films and plays, and listen to and discuss music, these pursuits are not as popular as the reading group – not at least in face-to-face contexts. Readers in this study reported deriving pleasure from sharing responses to texts, collaborating to produce collective interpretations and hearing about other members' experiences in relation to books. However, readers in this context are not merely interacting with other members of the group but are also in dialogue with characters, authors and the voices (imagined or real) of other, absent readers and critics. Literary reading is, perhaps, different from audience engagement with other artistic forms (films, television, drama) because reading offers us greater opportunity for sustained interaction with fictional voices, fictional minds and fictional experiences. For the readers in the four groups, attending meetings provided them with the chance to discuss these fictional encounters with others, negotiating their interpretations and evaluations of texts in an interactionally dynamic community.

Notes

Chapter 1

1 Seven reading groups participated across the two projects, with a further two groups observed but not recorded. The data presented in the current study is from four of these groups: one reading group (Contemporary) was recorded for both projects, while the other three provided data for just one of the projects.
2 Between 2010 and 2011.
3 One reader did not provide this information.
4 It is through this website that I came into contact with the group.

Chapter 2

1 This extract is analysed extensively in Chapter 5.

Chapter 3

1 Thanks to Petros Careswell-Schultz for spotting this.
2 Quotation marks are used in these extracts to signify which parts of the transcripts are quoted.
3 The novel's author D. J. Taylor writes for various newspapers, including *The Independent* and the *Daily Telegraph*, which could explain the positive reviews in these publications; however that is my gloss, not necessarily the interpretation of readers in the Wanderers Group.
4 Northern British English term meaning 'nothing' (informal).

Chapter 4

1 This transcription convention is continued throughout this chapter.

Chapter 5

1 Mimetic reading in reading group discourse is also discussed in Peplow et al.
   (2015: chapter 3), although the focus of that chapter is on the production of reader
   identities. The present chapter is interested in mimetic reading as an element shared
   repertoire and community-building.
2 OFSTED stands for Office for Standards in Education, Children's Service and Skills.
   It is a UK government department and part of its remit includes paying visits to
   state-run schools and 'inspecting' and assessing standards of provision and teaching.

Bibliography

Adichie, C. N. (2013) *Americanah*. New York: A. A. Knopf.

Allington, D. (2012) Private experience, textual analysis, and institutional authority: the discursive practice of critical interpretation and its enactment in literary training. *Language and Literature* 21(2), pp. 211–25.

Allington, D. & Benwell, B. (2012) Reading the reading experience: an ethnomethodological approach to 'booktalk'. In A. Lang (Ed.), *From Codex to Hypertext: Reading at the Turn of the Twenty-First Century*. Boston: University of Massachusetts Press, pp. 217–33.

Allington, D. & Swann, J. (2009) Researching literary reading as social practice. *Language and Literature* 18(3), pp. 219–30.

Andringa, E. (2004) The interface between fiction and life: patterns of identification in reading autobiographies. *Poetics Today* 25(2), pp. 205–40.

Antaki, C. & Widdicombe, S. (Eds.) (1998) *Identities in Talk*. London: SAGE.

Ardichvili, A., Page, V. & Wentling, T. (2003) Motivation and barriers to participation in virtual knowledge communities of practice. *Journal of Knowledge Management* 7(1), pp. 64–77.

Athill, D. (2008) *Somewhere towards an End*. London: Granta.

Atkinson, J. M. & Heritage, J. (Eds.) (1984) *Structures of Social Action: Studies in Conversation Analysis*. Cambridge: Cambridge University Press.

Bakhtin, M. (1935/1981) *The Dialogic Imagination*. Austin: University of Texas Press.

Barnes, R. & Moss, D. (2007) Communicating a feeling: the social organization of 'private thoughts'. *Discourse Studies* 9, pp. 123–48.

Barthes, R. (1977) *Image-Music-Text*. London: Fontana.

Barton, D. & Hamilton, M. (2000) Literacy practices. In D. Barton, M. Hamilton & R. Ivanič (Eds.), *Situated Literacies: Reading and Writing in Context*. Abingdon: Routledge, pp. 7–34.

Benwell, B. (2005) 'Lucky this is anonymous!' Men's magazines and ethnographies of reading: a textual cultural approach. *Discourse and Society* 16(2), pp. 147–72.

Benwell, B. (2009) 'A pathetic and racist and awful character': ethnomethodological approaches to the reception of diasporic fiction. *Language and Literature* 18(3), pp. 300–315.

Benwell, B. (2012) Common-sense anti-racism in book group talk: the role of reported speech. *Discourse & Society* 23(4), pp. 356–76.

Benwell, B., Procter, J. & Robinson, G. (2011) Not reading *Brick Lane*. *New Formations* 73(6), pp. 73–116.

Benwell, B. & Stokoe, E. (2006) *Discourse and Identity*. Edinburgh: Edinburgh University Press.

Blommaert, J. (2005) *Discourse*. Cambridge: Cambridge University Press.

Bloom, A. (1984) *The Closing of the American Mind*. London: Penguin.

Bourdieu, P. (1977) *Outline of a Theory of Practice*. Translated by R. Nice. Cambridge: Cambridge University Press.

Bourdieu, P. (1984/2010) *Distinction: A Social Critique of the Judgement of Taste*. Translated by R. Nice. London: Routledge.

Bourdieu, P. (1993) *The Field of Cultural Production: Essays on Art and Literature*. Edited by R. Johnson. New York: Columbia University Press.

Boyd, W. (2013) *Solo*. London: Jonathan Cape.

Bucholtz, M. & Hall, K. (2005) Identity and interaction: a sociocultural linguistic approach. *Discourse Studies* 7(4–5), pp. 585–614.

Buttny, R. (1997) Reported speech in talking race on campus. *Human Communication Research* 23(4), pp. 477–506.

Cameron, D. (2001) *Working with Spoken Discourse*. London: SAGE.

Chomsky, N. (1965) *Aspects of the Theory of Syntax*. Cambridge, MA: MIT Press.

Clark, H. H. & Gerrig, R. J. (1990) Quotations as demonstrations. *Language* 66, pp. 764–805.

Clark, J. (2013) 'Maybe she just hasn't matured yet': politeness, gate-keeping and the maintenance of status quo in a community of practice. *Journal of Politeness Research* 9(2), pp. 211–37.

Clift, R. (2006) Indexing stance: reported speech as interactional evidential. *Journal of Sociolinguistics* 10(5), pp. 569–95.

Clift, R. (2006) Getting there first: non-narrative reported speech in interaction. In R. Clift & E. Holt (Eds.), *Reporting Talk: Reported Speech in Interaction*. Cambridge: Cambridge University Press, pp. 120–49.

Coates, J. (1996) *Women Talk: Conversation between Women Friends*. Oxford: Blackwell.

Coates, J. (1997) One-at-a-time: the organization of men's talk. In S. Johnson & H. U. Meinhof (Eds.), *Language and Masculinity*. Oxford: Blackwell, pp. 107–29.

Coates, J. (2006) Talk in a play frame: more on laughter and intimacy. *Journal of Pragmatics* 39(1), pp. 28–49.

Coates, J. & Sutton-Spence, R. (2001) Turn-taking pattern in deaf conversation. *Journal of Sociolinguistics* 5(4), pp. 507–29.

Collinson, I. (2009) *Everyday Readers: Reading and Popular Culture*. London: Equinox.

Contu, A. & Willmott, H. (2003) Re-embedding situatedness: the importance of power relations in learning theory. *Organization Science* 14(3), pp. 283–96.

Couper-Kuhlen, E. (2006) Assessing and accounting. In R. Clift & E. Holt (Eds.), *Reporting Talk: Reported Speech in Interaction*. Cambridge: Cambridge University Press, pp. 81–119.

Crace, J. (2013) *Harvest*. London: Macmillan.

Culler, J. (1975/2002) *Structural Poetics: Structuralism, Linguistics and the Study of Literature*. London: Routledge.

Daniels, H. (2002) *Literature Circles: Voice and Choice in Book Clubs and Reading Groups*. 2nd edition. Portland, ME: Stenhouse.

Davies, B. (2005) Communities of practice: legitimacy not choice. *Journal of Sociolinguistics* 9(4), pp. 557–81.

Devlin-Glass, F. (2001) More than a reader and less than a critic: literary authority and women's book-discussion groups. *Women's Studies International Forum* 24(5), pp. 571–85.

Donato, R. (2004) Aspects of collaboration in pedagogical discourse. *Annual Review of Applied Linguistics* 24, pp. 284–302.

Donoghue, E. (2010) *Room*. London: Picador.

Dorfman, M. H. (1996) Evaluating the interpretive community: evidence from expert and novice readers. *Poetics* 23(6), pp. 453–70.

Dowrick, C., Billington, J., Robinson, J., Hamer, A. & Williams, C. (2012) Get into reading as an intervention for common mental health problems: exploring catalysts for change. *Medical Humanities* 38, pp. 15–20.

Drew, P. (2005) Conversation analysis. In K. L. Fitch & R. E. Sanders (Eds.), *Handbook of Language and Social Interaction*. London: Lawrence Erlbaum, pp. 71–102.

Duncan, S. (2012) *Reading Circles, Novels and Adult Development*. London: Continuum.

Duranti, A. (1997) *Linguistic Anthropology*. Cambridge: Cambridge University Press.

Eckert, P. (1989) *Jocks and Burnouts: Social Categories and Identity in the High School*. New York: Teachers College Press.

Eckert, P. (2000) *Linguistic Variation as Social Practice*. Oxford: Blackwell.

Eckert, P. & McConnell-Ginet, S. (1992a) Think practically and look locally: language and gender as community-based practice. *Annual Review of Anthropology* 21, pp. 461–90.

Eckert, P. & McConnell-Ginet, S. (1992b) Communities of practice: where language, gender, and power all live. In K. Hall, M. Bucholtz & B. Moonwomon (Eds.), *Locating Power: Proceedings of the Second Berkeley Women and Language Conference*. Berkeley: Berkeley Women and Language Group, pp. 89–99.

Eckert, P. & McConnell-Ginet, S. (1995) Constructing meaning, constructing selves: snapshots of language, gender and class from Belten High. In K. Hall & M. Bucholtz (Eds.), *Gender Articulated: Language and the Socially Constructed Self*. London: Routledge, pp. 459–507.

Eckert, P. & McConnell-Ginet, S. (1999) New generalisations and explanations in language and gender research. *Language in Society* 28(2), pp. 185–201.

Eckert, P. & McConnell-Ginet (2007) Putting communities of practice in their place. *Language and Gender* 1(1), pp. 27–37.

Edelsky, C. (1981) Who's got the floor? *Language in Society* 10(3), pp. 383–421.

Edwards, D. (1997) *Discourse and Cognition*. London: SAGE.

Edwards, D. (2000) Extreme case formulations: softeners, investment, and doing nonliteral. *Research on Language and Social Interaction* 33(4), pp. 347–73.

Edwards, D. (2007) Managing subjectivity in talk. In A. Hepburn & S. Wiggins (Eds.), *Discursive Research in Practice: New Approaches to Psychology and Interaction*. Cambridge: Cambridge University Press, pp. 31–49.

Edwards, D. & Potter, J. (1992) *Discursive Psychology*. London: SAGE.

Edwards, D. & Potter, J. (2005) Discursive psychology, mental states and descriptions. In H. te Molder & J. Potter (Eds.), *Conversation and Cognition*. Cambridge: Cambridge University Press, pp. 241–59.

Ehrlich, S. (1998) The discursive reconstruction of sexual consent. *Discourse and Society* 9(2), pp. 149–71.

Ehrlich, S. (1999) Communities of practice, gender, and the representation of sexual assault. *Language in Society* 28, pp. 239–56.

Endsley, S., Kirkegaard, M. & Linares, A. (2005) Working together: communities of practice in family medicine. *Family Practice Management* 12(1), pp. 28–32.

Erickson, F. (1982) Money tree, lasagna bush, salt and pepper: social construction of topical cohesion in a conversation among Italian-Americans. In D. Tannen (Ed.), *Analyzing Discourse: Text and Talk*. Washington, DC: Georgetown University Press, pp. 43–70.

Extence, G. (2013) *The Universe versus Alex Woods*. London: Hodder.

Felski, R. (2008) *Uses of Literature*. Oxford: Blackwell.

Fialho, O. (2007) Foregrounding and familiarization: understanding readers' response to literary texts. *Language and Literature* 16(2), pp. 105–23.

Finnis, K. A. (2014) Variation with a Greek-Cypriot community of practice in London: code-switching, gender, and identity. *Language in Society* 43, pp. 287–310.

Fish, S. (1980) *Is There a Text in This Class? The Authority of Interpretive Communities*. Cambridge, MA: Harvard University Press.

Fister, B. (2005) 'Reading as a contact sport': online book groups and the social dimensions of reading. *Reference and User Services Quarterly* 44(4), pp. 303–9.

Fletcher, J. (2014) Social communities in a knowledge setting organizational context: interaction and relational engagement in a community of practice and a micro-community of knowledge. *Discourse & Communication* 8(4), pp. 351–69.

Fought, C. (1999) A majority sound change in a minority community: /u/ fronting in Chicano English. *Journal of Sociolinguistics* 3, pp. 5–23.

Franzen, J. (2010) *Freedom*. London: Fourth Estate.

Freed, A. (1996) Language and gender research in an experimental setting. In V. L. Bergvall, J. M. Bing & A. F. Freed (Eds.), *Rethinking Language and Gender Research: Theory and Practice*. New York: Longman, pp. 54–76.

Garfinkel, H. (1967) *Studies in Ethnomethodology*. Cambridge: Polity Press.

Gavins, J. (2007) *Text World Theory: An Introduction*. Edinburgh: Edinburgh University Press.

Genette, G. (1997) *Paratexts: Thresholds of Interpretation*. Translated by J. E. Lewin. Cambridge: Cambridge University Press.

Gerrig, R. (1993) *Experiencing Narrative Worlds: On the Psychological Activities of Reading.* New Haven, CT: Yale University Press.

Gerrig, R. & Allbritton, D. W. (1990) The construction of literary character: a view from cognitive psychology. *Style* 24, pp. 380–91.

Gertler, M. S. (2001) Best practice? Geography, learning and the institutional limits to strong convergence. *Journal of Economic Geography* 1(1), pp. 5–26

Goffman, E. (1955) On face-work: an analysis of ritual elements in social interaction. *Psychiatry* 18, pp. 213–31.

Goffman, E. (1974) *Frame Analysis: an Essay on the Organization of Experience.* Cambridge, MA: Harvard University Press.

Goffman, E. (1981) *Forms of Talk.* Philadelphia: University of Pennsylvania Press.

Goldberg, J. (1990) Interrupting the discourse on interruptions. *Journal of Pragmatics* 14, pp. 883–903.

Goodwin, C. & Goodwin, M. H. (1992) Assessments and the construction of context. In A. Duranti & C. Goodwin (Eds.), *Rethinking Context: Language as an Interactive Phenomenon.* Cambridge: Cambridge University Press, pp. 146–89.

Graesser, A., Millis, K. & Zwaan, R. (1997) Discourse comprehension. *Annual Review of Psychology* 48, pp. 163–89.

Graesser, A., Kassler, M. A., Kreuz, R. J. & McLain-Allen, B. (1998) Verification of statements about story worlds that deviate from normal conceptions of time: what is true about Einstein's Dreams? *Cognitive Psychology* 35, pp. 246–301.

Green, J. & Bloome, D. (1995) Ethnography and ethnographers of and in education. In F. Flood, S. Heath, D. Alvermann & D. Lapp (Eds.), *A Handbook for Literary Educators.* New York: Macmillan, pp. 181–202.

Guillory, J. (2000) The ethical practice of modernity: the example of reading. In M. Garber, B. Hanssen & R. L. Walkowitz (Eds.), *The Turn to Ethics.* New York: Routledge, pp. 29–46.

Hall, G. (2008) Empirical research into the processing of free indirect discourse and the imperative of ecological validity. In S. Zyngier, M. Bortolussi, A. Chesnokova & J. Auracher (Eds.), *Directions in Empirical Literary Studies.* Amsterdam: John Benjamins, pp. 21–34.

Hamilton, H. E. (1998) Reported speech and survivor identity in on-line bone marrow transplantation narratives. *Journal of Sociolinguistics* 291, pp. 53–67.

Hammersley, M. (2003) Conversation analysis and discourse analysis: methods or paradigms? *Discourse and Society* 14(6), pp. 751–81.

Harding, P. (2009) *Tinkers.* New York: Bellevue Literary Press.

Harris, R. (2013) *An Officer and a Spy.* London: Hutchinson.

Hartley, J. (2001) *Reading Groups.* Oxford: Oxford University Press.

Hazen, K. (2002) The family. In J. K. Chambers, P. Trudgill & N. Schilling-Estes (Eds.), *The Handbook of Language Variation and Change.* Oxford: Blackwell, pp. 500–25.

Heritage, J. (2002) Oh-prefaced responses to assessments: a method of modifying agreement/disagreement. In C. E. Ford, B. A. Fox & S. A. Thompson (Eds.), *The Language of Turn and Sequence*. Oxford: Oxford University Press, pp. 196–224.

Heritage, J. (2004) Conversation analysis and institutional talk: analysing data. In D. Silverman (Ed.), *Qualitative Research: Theory, Method and Practice*. London: SAGE, pp. 222–45.

Heritage, J. (2005) Cognition in discourse. In H. te Molder and J. Potter (Eds.), *Conversation and Cognition*. Cambridge: Cambridge University Press, pp. 184–202.

Heritage, J. & Raymond, G. (2005) The terms of agreement: indexing epistemic authority and subordination in talk-in-interaction. *Social Psychology Quarterly* 68(1), pp. 15–38.

Hodge, S., Robinson, J. & Davis, P. (2007) Reading between the lines: the experiences of taking part in a community reading project. *Medical Humanities* 33, pp. 100–4.

Holmes, J. & Meyerhoff, M. (1999) The community of practice: theories and methodologies in language and gender research. *Language in Society* 28, pp. 173–83.

Holmes, J. & Schnurr, S. (2010) 'Doing femininity' at work: more than just relational practice. In M. Meyerhoff & E. Schleef (Eds.), *The Routledge Sociolinguistics Reader*. Abingdon: Routledge, pp. 448–59.

Holmes, J. & Stubbe, M. (2003) *Power and Politeness in the Workplace*. London: Longman.

Holmes, J., Stubbe, M. & Vine, B. (1999) Constructing professional identity: 'doing power' in policy units. In S. Sarangi & C. Roberts (Eds.), *Talk, Work, and Institutional Power: Discourse in Medical, Mediation and Management Settings*. Berlin: Mouton de Gruyter, pp. 1–35.

Holmes, J. & Woodhams, J. (2013) Building interaction: the role of talk in joining a community of practice. *Discourse & Communication* 7(3), pp. 275–98.

Holt, E. (1996) Reporting on talk: the use of direct reported speech in conversation. *Research on Language and Social Interaction* 29(3), pp. 219–45.

Holt, E. (2000) Reporting and reacting: concurrent responses to reported speech. *Research on Language and Social Interaction* 33(4), pp. 425–54.

Holt, E. (2006) 'I'm eyeing up your chop mind': reporting and enacting. In R. Clift & E. Holt (Eds.), *Reporting Talk: Reported Speech in Interaction*. Cambridge: Cambridge University Press, pp. 47–80.

Horton-Salway, M. (2004). Expertise and experience: the local production of knowledge and identities in ME support group talk. *Health. An Interdisciplinary Journal for the Study of Health, Illness and Medicine* 8(3), pp. 351–71.

Howie, L. (1998) Speaking subjects: a reading of women's book groups. Unpublished PhD thesis. La Trobe University.

Hughes, E. (1970) *The Sociological Eye: Selected Papers*. New York: Aldine.

Hutchby, I. & Wooffitt, R. (2008) *Conversation Analysis*. Cambridge: Polity Press.

Iser, W. (1978) *The Act of Reading: A Theory of Aesthetic Response*. Baltimore, MD: Johns Hopkins University Press.

Ishiguro, K. (1989) *The Remains of the Day*. London: Faber and Faber.

Jefferson, G. (1972) Side sequences. In D. Sudnow (Ed.), *Studies in Social Interaction*. New York: Free Press, pp. 294–338.

Jefferson, G. (1986) Notes on 'latency' in overlap onset. *Human Studies* 9, pp. 153–83.

Jefferson, G. (2004) 'At first I thought'. A normalizing device for extraordinary events. In G. H. Lerner (Ed.), *Conversation Analysis: Studies From the First Generation*. Amsterdam: John Benjamins, pp. 131–67.

Jefferson, G., Sacks, H. & Schegloff, E. A. (1987) Notes on laughter in the pursuit of intimacy. In G. Button & J. R. E. Lee (Eds.), *Talk and Social Organisation*. Clevedon: Multilingual Matters, pp. 152–205.

Johnstone, B. (2000) *Qualitative Methods in Sociolinguistics*. Oxford: Oxford University Press.

Joyce, J. (1914/2006) *Dubliners*. London: W. W. Norton.

Kärkkäinen, E. (2012) *I thought it was very interesting*. Conversational formats for taking a stance. *Journal of Pragmatics* 44, pp. 2194–10.

Kiernan, A. (2011) The growth of reading groups as a feminine leisure pursuit: cultural democracy or dumbing down? In D. N. Rehberg Sedo (Ed.), *Reading Communities: From Salon to Cyberspace*. Basingstoke: Palgrave Macmillan, pp. 123–39.

King, B. (2014) Tracing the emergence of a community of practice: beyond presupposition in sociolinguistic research. *Language in Society* 43, pp. 61–81.

Kingsolver, B. (2012) *Flight Behaviour*. London: Harper Collins.

Kitzinger, C. (2008) Conversation analysis: technical matters for gender research. In K. Harrington, L. Litosseliti, H. Sauntson & J. Sunderland (Eds.), *Gender and Language Research Methodologies*. Basingstoke: Macmillan, pp. 119–39.

Knulst, W. & van der Broek, A. (2003) The readership of books in times of de-reading. *Poetics* 31(3/4), pp. 213–33.

Labov, W. (1972) *Language in the Inner City: Studies in the Black English Vernacular*. Philadelphia: University of Pennsylvania Press.

Lahiri, J. (2013) *The Lowland*. New York: A. A. Knopf.

Lakoff, R. T. (1975) *Language and Woman's Place*. New York: Harper and Row.

Lanchester, J. (2002) *Fragrant Harbour*. London: Faber.

Lang, A. (Ed.) (2012) *From Codex to Hypertext: Reading at the Turn of the Twenty-First Century*. Boston: University of Massachusetts Press.

Laskin, D. & Hughes, H. (1995) *The Reading Group Book*. New York: Plume.

Lave, J. & Wenger, E. (1991) *Situated Learning: Legitimate Peripheral Participation*. Cambridge: Cambridge University Press.

Lawrence, D. H. (1924/1990) *England, My England*. Cambridge: Cambridge University Press.

Leech, J. & Short, M. (1981) *Style in Fiction*. Harlow: Pearson.

Leeds-Hurwitz, W. (2005) Ethnography. In K. L. Fitch & R. E. Sanders (Eds.), *Handbook of Language and Social Interaction*. London: Lawrence Erlbaum, pp. 327–53.

Lerner, G. (2002) Turn-sharing: the choral co-production of talk-in-interaction. In C. A. Ford, B. A. Fox & S. A. Thompson (Eds.), *The Language of Turn and Sequence*. Oxford: Oxford University Press, pp. 225–56.

Leudar, I. and Antaki, C. (1996) Discourse participation, reported speech and research practices in social psychology. *Theory and Psychology* 6(1), pp. 5–29.

Levy, A. (2004) *Small Island*. London: Headline.

Littleton, K. and Mercer, N. (2013) *Interthinking: Putting Talk to Work*. London: Routledge.

Lodge, D. (1975/2011) *Changing Places*. London: Vintage.

Loevy, D. (2006) *The Book Club Companion: A Comprehensive Guide to the Reading Group Experience*. New York: Berkley Books.

Long, E. (1986) Women, reading and cultural authority: some implications of the audience perspective in cultural studies. *American Quarterly* 38, pp. 591–612.

Long, E. (1992) Textual interpretation as collective action. In J. Boyrain (Ed.), *The Ethnography of Reading*. Berkeley: University of California Press, pp. 180–211.

Long, E. (2003) *Book Clubs*. Chicago: University of Chicago Press.

Long, E. (2004) Literature as a spur to collective action: the diverse perspectives of nineteenth and twentieth-century reading groups. *Poetics Today* 25(2), pp. 335–59.

MacMahon, B. (2009a) Metarepresentation and decoupling in Northanger Abbey. *English Studies* 90(5), pp. 518–44.

MacMahon, B. (2009b) Metarepresentation and decoupling in Northanger Abbey. *English Studies* 90(6), pp. 673–94.

Mailloux, S. (1982) Rhetorical hermeneutics. *Critical Inquiry* 11(4), pp. 620–41.

Mantel, H. (2009) *Wolf Hall*. London: Fourth Estate.

Mar, R. A. (2004) The neuropsychology of narrative: story comprehension, story production and their interrelation. *Neuropsychologia* 42, pp. 1414–34.

Martel, Y. (2010) *Beatrice and Virgil*. New York: A. A. Knopf.

Martindale, C. & Dailey, A. (1995) I. A. Richards revisited: do people agree in their interpretations of literature? *Poetics* 23(4), pp. 299–314.

Mayes, P. (1990) Quotation in spoken English. *Studies in Language* 14(2), pp. 325–63.

Maynard, D. W. & Clayman, S. E. (2003) Ethnomethodology and conversation analysis. In L. T. Reynolds & N. J. Herman-Kinney (Eds.), *Handbook of Symbolic Interactionism*. Lanham: Rowman & Littlefield, pp. 173–202.

McCarthy, C. (2006) *The Road*. New York: A. A. Knopf.

McConnell-Ginet, S. (2003) 'What's in a name?' Social labeling and gender practices. In J. Holmes & M. Meyerhoff (Eds.), *The Handbook of Language and Gender*. Oxford: Blackwell, pp. 69–97.

McGregor, J. (2006) *So Many Ways to Begin*. London: Bloomsbury.

McRae, S. (2009) 'It's a blokes' thing': gender, occupational roles and talk in the workplace. In P. Pichler & E. M. Eppler (Eds.), *Gender and Spoken Interaction*. Basingstoke: Palgrave Macmillan, pp. 163–85.

Meân, L. (2001) Identity and discursive practice: doing gender on the football pitch. *Discourse and Society* 12(6), pp. 789–815.

Mendoza-Denton, N. (1997) Chicana/Mexicana identity and linguistic variation: and ethnographic and sociolinguistic study of gang affiliation in an urban high school. Unpublished PhD thesis. Stanford University.

Mercer, N. (2000) *Words and Minds: How We Use Language to Think Together*. London: Routledge.

Meyerhoff, M. (2002) Communities of practice. In J. K. Chambers, P. Trudgill & N. Schilling-Estes (Eds.), *The Handbook of Language Variation and Change*. Oxford: Blackwell, pp. 526–48.

Meyerhoff, M. (2005) Biographies, agency and power. *Journal of Sociolinguistics* 9(4), pp. 595–601.

Miall, D. S. & Kuiken, D. (1994) Foregrounding, defamiliarization, and affect: response to literary stories. *Poetics* 22, pp. 389–407.

Miall, D. S. & Kuiken, D. (2001) Shifting perspectives: readers' feelings and literary response. In W. van Peer & S. Chatman (Eds.), *New Perspectives on Narrative Perspective*. Albany, NY: SUNY Press, pp. 289–301.

Miall, D. S. & Kuiken, D. (2002) A feeling for fiction: becoming what we behold. *Poetics* 30, pp. 221–41.

Mills, M. (1998) *The Restraint of Beasts*. London: Flamingo.

Milroy, J. & Milroy, L. (1993) Mechanisms of change in urban dialects: the role of class, social network and gender. *International Journal of Applied Linguistics* 3(1), pp. 57–78.

Moore, A. (2012) *The Lighthouse*. London: Salt Publishing.

Moore, E. (2006) 'You tell all the stories': using narrative to explore hierarchy within a community of practice. *Journal of Sociolinguistics* 10(5), pp. 611–40.

Morrison, B. (2008) The reading cure. http://www.guardian.co.uk/books/2008/jan/05/fiction.scienceandnature. [Accessed 4 July 2015].

Morrow, D., Bower, G. & Greenspan, S. (1989) Updating situation models from descriptive texts: a test of the situational operator model. *Discourse Processes* 30, pp. 201–36.

Mudrick, M. 1961. Character and event in fiction. *Yale Review* 50, 202–18.

Mullany, L. (2007) *Gendered Discourse in the Professional Workplace*. Basingstoke: Palgrave Macmillan.

Myers, G. (1999a) Functions of reported speech in group discussions. *Applied Linguistics* 20(3), pp. 376–401.

Myers, G. (1999b) Unspoken speech: hypothetical reported discourse and the rhetoric of everyday talk. *Text and Talk* 19(4), pp. 571–90.

Myers, G. (2004) *Matters of Opinion: Talking about Public Issues*. Cambridge: Cambridge University Press.

Myers, G. (2006) Communities of practice, risk and Sellafield. In D. Barton & K. Tusting (Eds.), *Beyond Communities of Practice: Language, Power and Social Context*. Cambridge: Cambridge University Press, pp. 198–213.

Nightingale, V. (1996) *Studying Audiences: The Shock of the Real*. London: Routledge.

Oatley, K. (1999) Meetings of minds: dialogue, sympathy, and identification in reading fiction. *Poetics* 26, pp. 439–54.

Oatley, K. (2002) Emotions and the story worlds of fiction. In M. C. Green, J. J. Strange & T. C. Brock (Eds.), *Narrative Impact: Social and Cognitive Foundations*. Hillside, NJ: Lawrence Erlbaum, pp. 39–69.

Oatley, K. (2003) Writingandreading: the future of cognitive poetics. In G. Steen & J. Gavins (Eds.), *Cognitive Poetics in Practice*. London: Routledge, pp. 161–73.

O'Halloran, K. (2011) Investigating argumentation in reading groups: combining manual qualitative coding and automated corpus analysis tools. *Applied Linguistics* 32(2), pp. 172–96.

O'Hare, M. & Storey, R. (2004) *Recipe for a Book Club*. Hemdon, VA: Capital Books.

Ostermann, A. C. (2003) Communities of practice at work: gender, facework and the power of habitus at an all-female police station and a feminist crisis intervention centre in Brazil. *Discourse and Society* 14(4), pp. 473–505.

Palmer, A. (2002) The construction of fictional minds. *Narrative* 10(1), pp. 28–46.

Palmer, A. (2004) *Fictional Minds*. Lincoln: University of Nebraska Press.

Pearson, J. (1999) *Women's Reading in Britain 1750–1835: A Dangerous Recreation*. Cambridge: Cambridge University Press.

Penguin (2015) Book clubs. http://www.penguin.com/read/book-clubs/ [Accessed 5 July 2015].

Peplow, D. (2011) 'Oh, I've known a lot of Irish people': reading groups and the negotiation of literary interpretation. *Language and Literature* 20(4), pp. 295–315.

Peplow, D. (2012) Negotiating literary interpretations in the reading group. Unpublished PhD thesis: University of Nottingham.

Peplow, D. (2014) 'I've never enjoyed hating a book so much in all my life': The co-construction of identity in the reading group. In S. Chapman & B. Clark (Eds.), *Pragmatics and Literary Stylistics*. Basingstoke: Palgrave, pp. 152–71.

Peplow, D. (2016) Transforming reading: reading and interpretation in book groups. In M. Burke, O. Fiahlo & S. Zyngier (Eds.), *Scientific Approaches to Literature in Learning Environments*. Amsterdam: John Benjamins.

Peplow, D. & Carter, R. (2014) Stylistics and real readers. In M. Burke (Ed.), *The Routledge Handbook of Stylistics*. Abingdon: Routledge, pp. 440–54.

Peplow, D., Swann, J. Trimarco, P. & Whiteley, S. (2015) *The Discourse of Reading Groups: Integrating Cognitive and Sociocultural Perspectives*. New York: Routledge.

Peräkylä, A. (1997/2004) Reliability and validity in research based on naturally occurring social interaction. In D. Silverman (Ed.), *Qualitative Research: Theory, Method and Practice*. London: SAGE, pp. 283–304.

Phelan, J. (1989) *Reading People, Reading Plots: Character, Progression, and the Interpretation of Narrative*. Chicago: University of Chicago Press.

Phelan, J. (1996) *Narrative as Rhetoric: Technique, Audiences, Ethics, Ideology*. Athens, OH: Ohio University Press.

Phelan, J. (2005) *Living to Tell about It: A Rhetoric and Ethics of Character Narration.* Ithaca, NY: Cornell University Press.

Phoenix, A. (2008) Analyzing narrative contexts. In M. Andrews, C. Squire & M. Tamboukou (Eds.), *Doing Narrative Research.* London: SAGE, pp. 64–77.

Pomerantz, A. (1984a) Agreeing and disagreeing with assessments: some features of preferred/dispreferred turn shapes. In J. M. Atkinson & J. Heritage (Eds.), *Structures of Social Action: Studies in Conversation Analysis.* Cambridge: Cambridge University Press, pp. 57–101.

Pomerantz, A. (1984b) Giving a source or basis: the practice in conversation of telling 'how I know'. *Journal of Pragmatics* 8, pp. 607–25.

Pomerantz, A. (1986) Extreme case formulations: a way of legitimizing claims. *Human Studies* 9, pp. 219–29.

Potter, J. (1996) *Representing Reality: Discourse, Rhetoric and Social Construction.* London: SAGE.

Pratt, M. L. (1982) Interpretive strategies/strategic interpretations: on Anglo-American reader-response criticism. *Boundary 2* 11(1/2), pp. 201–31.

Pratt, N. & Back, J. (2009) Spaces to discuss mathematics: communities of practice on an online discussion board. *Research in Mathematics Education* 11(2), pp. 115–30.

Procter, J. & Benwell, B. (2014) *Reading Across Worlds: Transnational Book Groups and the Reception of Difference.* Basingstoke: Palgrave Macmillan.

Psathas, G. (1995) *Conversation Analysis: The Study of Talk-In-Interaction.* Thousand Oaks: Sage.

Radway, J. A. (1987) *Reading the Romance: Women, Patriarchy, and Popular Culture.* London: Verso.

Radway, J. A. (1997) *A Feeling For Books: The Book-of-the-Month Club, Literary Taste, and Middle-Class Desire.* Chapel Hill: University of North Carolina Press.

Rall, J. & Harris, P. L. (2000) In Cinderella's slippers? Story comprehension from the protagonist's point of view. *Developmental Psychology* 36(2), pp. 202–8.

Raymond, G. & Heritage, J. (2006) The epistemics of social relations: owning grandchildren. *Language in Society* 35, pp. 677–705.

ReadingGroupGuides.com (2015) ReadingGroupGuides.com Blog. http://www.readinggroupguides.com/ [Accessed 5 July 2015].

Rehberg Sedo, D. (2002) Predictions of life after Oprah: a glimpse of the power of book club readers. *Publishing Research Quarterly* 18(3), pp. 11–22.

Rehberg Sedo, D. (2011) 'I used to read anything that caught my eye, but . . ': cultural authority and intermediaries in a virtual young adult book club. In D. Rehberg Sedo (Ed.), *Reading Communities from Salons to Cyberspace.* Basingstoke: Palgrave Macmillan, pp. 101–22.

Richards, K. (2006) *Language and Professional Identity: Aspects of Collaborative Interaction.* Basingstoke: Palgrave Macmillan.

Rühlemann, C. (2007) *Conversation in Context: A Corpus-Driven Approach.* London: Continuum.

Sacks, H. (1984) Notes on methodology. In J. M. Atkinson & J. Heritage (Eds.), *Structures of Social Action: Studies in Conversation Analysis.* Cambridge: Cambridge University Press, pp. 21–7.

Sacks, H. (1987) On the preferences for agreement and contiguity in sequences in conversation. In G. Button & J. R. E. Lee (Eds.), *Talk and Social Organisation.* Clevedon, PA: Multilingual Matters, pp. 54–69.

Sacks, H. (1992) *Lectures on Conversation.* 2 volumes. Oxford: Blackwell.

Sacks, H., Schegloff, E. A. & Jefferson, G. (1974) A simplest systematics for the organization of turn-taking for conversation. *Language* 50(4), pp. 696–735.

Sams, J. (2010) Quoting the unspoken: an analysis of quotations in spoken discourse. *Journal of Pragmatics* 42, pp. 3147–60.

Scheff, T. J. (1979) *Catharsis in Healing, Ritual, and Drama.* Berkeley: University of California Press.

Schegloff, E. A. (1968) Sequencing in conversational openings. *American Anthropologist* 70, pp. 1075–95.

Schegloff, E. A. (1997) Whose text? Whose context? *Discourse and Society* 8, pp. 165–87.

Schegloff, E. A. (2007) *Sequence Organization in Interaction: A Primer in Conversation Analysis.* Volume 1. Cambridge: Cambridge University Press.

Scollon, R. (2001) *Mediated Discourse: The Nexus of Practice.* London: Routledge.

Semino, E. & Culpeper, J. (Eds.) (2002) *Cognitive Stylistics: Language and Cognition in Text Analysis.* Amsterdam: John Benjamins.

Shriver, L. (2008) *The Book Club Bible: The Definitive Guide that Every Book Club Member Needs.* London: Michael O'Mara.

Slezak, E. (2000) *The Book Group Book: A Thoughtful Guide to Forming and Enjoying a Stimulating Book Group Discussion.* Chicago: Chicago Review Press.

Smith, Z. (2000) *White Teeth.* London: Penguin.

Sotirova, V. (2006) Readers' responses to narrative point of view. *Poetics* 34(2), pp. 108–33.

Steen, G. (1994) *Understanding Metaphor in Literature: An Empirical Approach.* London: Longman.

Sternberg, M. (1982) Proteus in quotation-land: mimesis and the forms of reported discourse. *Poetics Today* 3(2), pp. 107–56.

Stockwell, P. (2002) *Cognitive Poetics: An Introduction.* London: Routledge.

Stockwell, P. (2005) Texture and identification. *European Journal of English Studies* 9(2), pp. 143–54.

Stockwell, P. (2009) *Texture: A Cognitive Aesthetics of Reading.* Edinburgh: Edinburgh University Press.

Stokoe, E. & Edwards, D. (2007) 'Black this, black that': racial insults and reported speech in neighbour complaints and police interrogations. *Discourse & Society* 18, pp. 337–72.

Swann, J. & Allington, D. (2009) Reading groups and the language of literary texts: a case study in social reading. *Language and Literature* 18(3), pp. 247–64.

Swann, J. & Maybin, J. (2008) Sociolinguistic and ethnographic approaches to language and gender. In K. Harrington, L. Litosseliti, H. Sauntson & J. Sunderland (Eds.), *Gender and Language Research Methodologies*. New York: Palgrave Macmillan, pp. 21–8.

Tannen, D. (1984) *Conversational Style*. Norwood, NJ: Ablex.

Tannen, D. (1987) *That's Not What I Meant! How Conversational Style Makes or Breaks Your Relations with Others*. London: Virago.

Tannen, D. (1991) *You Just Don't Understand: Women and Men in Conversation*. London: Virago.

Tannen, D. (1989/2007) *Talking Voices: Repetition, Dialogue, and Imagery in Conversational Discourse*. Cambridge: Cambridge University Press.

Taylor, D. J. (2013) *The Windsor Faction*. London: Chatto & Windus.

te Molder, H. & Potter, J. (Eds.) (2005) *Conversation and Cognition*. Cambridge: Cambridge University Press.

ten Have, P. (1999) *Doing Conversation Analysis: A Practical Guide*. London: Sage.

Tusting, K. (2006) Language and power in communities of practice. In D. Barton & K. Tusting (Eds.), *Beyond Communities of Practice: Language, Power and Social Context*. Cambridge: Cambridge University Press, pp. 36–54.

Van Peer, W. (1986) *Stylistics and Psychology. Investigations of Foregrounding*. London: Croom Helm.

Vásquez, C. & Urzúa, A. (2009) Reported speech and reported mental states in mentoring meetings: exploring novice teacher identities. *Research on Language and Social Interaction* 42(1), pp. 1–19.

Vickers, C. H., Deckert, S. K., Smith, W. B. & Morones, J. R. (2012) Who's the expert here? Shifts in the powerful identity in a sewing cooperative community of practice. *Sociolinguistic Studies* 6(3), pp. 421–44.

Weinsheimer, J. (1979) Theory of character: 'Emma'. *Poetics Today* 1, pp. 185–211.

Wenger, E. (1998) *Communities of Practice: Learning, Meaning, and Identity*. Cambridge: Cambridge University Press.

Wesley, P. W. & Buysse, V. (2001) Communities of practice: expanding professional roles to promote reflection and shared inquiry. *Topics in Early Childhood Special Education* 21(2), pp. 114–23.

West, C. & Zimmerman, D. H. (1977) Women's place in everyday talk. *Social Problems* 24, pp. 521–9.

Whiteley, S. (2011) Text world theory, real readers and emotional responses to The Remains of the Day. *Language and Literature* 20(1), pp. 23–42.

Whyte, W. F. (1943) *Street Corner Society*. Chicago: University of Chicago Press.

Wilson, A. N. (2012) *The Potter's Hand*. London: Atlantic Books.

Wimsatt, W. K. & Beardsley, M. C. (1946) The intentional fallacy. *The Sewanee Review* 54, pp. 468–88.

Wooffitt, R. (2006) The dead in the service of the living. In R. Clift & E. Holt (Eds.), *Reporting Talk: Reported Speech in Interaction*. Cambridge: Cambridge University Press, pp. 244–69.

Young, W. P. (2007) *The Shack*. New York: Windblown Media.

Zimmerman, D. H. & West, C. (1975) Sex roles, interruptions and silences in conversation. In B. Thorne & N. Henley (Eds.), *Language and Sex: Difference and Dominance*. Rowley, MA: Newbury House, pp. 105–29.

Zunshine, L. (2006) *Why We Read Fiction: Theory of the Mind and the Novel*. Columbus: Ohio State University Press.

Zusak, M. (2005) *The Book Thief*. London: Random House.

Zwaan, R. (1994) Effects of genre expectations on text comprehension. *Journal of Experimental Psychology: Learning, Memory, and Cognition* 20, pp. 920–33.

Zwaan, R. (2004) The immersed experiencer: toward an embodied theory of language comprehension. *The Psychology of Learning and Motivation* 44, pp. 35–62.

Index

4/18/18

CPSIA information can be obtained
at www.ICGtesting.com
Printed in the USA
LVOW13s1729230318

570973LV00008B/80/P

9 781350 045538